Nora Ephron

"Nora Ephron can write about anything better than anybody else can write about anything."
—*The New York Times*

"Stylish, opinionated, with a kind of take-no-prisoners fearlessness rooted in both the women's movement and the equally complex terrain of her own emotions." —*Los Angeles Times*

"As tart and refreshing as the first gin and tonic of summer." —*The New York Times Book Review*

"A brilliant, restless mind." —*Ms.*

"Funny, shrewd, devastating." —*Newsweek*

"Nora Ephron is, in essence, one of the original bloggers—and if everyone could write like her, what a lovely place the Internet would be. . . . Telling stories that were, more often than not, ultimately about herself, and doing so with such warmth, wit and skill that they became universal."
—*The Seattle Times*

"Always funny." —*Mademoiselle*

"Pure delight." —*Playboy*

Praise for

Nora Ephron

Crazy Salad & Scribble Scribble

Nora Ephron is also the author of the best-sellers *I Feel Bad About My Neck*, *I Remember Nothing*, and *Heartburn*. She received Academy Award nominations for Best Original Screenplay for *When Harry Met Sally . . .*, *Silkwood*, and *Sleepless in Seattle*, which she also directed. Her other credits include the plays *Imaginary Friends* and *Love, Loss, and What I Wore*, and the films *You've Got Mail* and *Julie & Julia*, both of which she wrote and directed. She died in 2012.

BOOKS BY NORA EPHRON

FICTION
Heartburn

ESSAYS
I Remember Nothing

I Feel Bad About My Neck

Nora Ephron Collected

Scribble Scribble

Crazy Salad

Wallflower at the Orgy

DRAMA
Love, Loss, and What I Wore (with Delia Ephron)

Imaginary Friends

SCREENPLAYS

Julie & Julia

Bewitched (with Delia Ephron)

Hanging Up (with Delia Ephron)

You've Got Mail
(with Delia Ephron)

Michael (with Jim Quinlan, Pete Dexter, and Delia Ephron)

Mixed Nuts (with Delia Ephron)

Sleepless in Seattle (with David S. Ward and Jeff Arch)

This Is My Life
(with Delia Ephron)

My Blue Heaven

When Harry Met Sally . . .

Cookie (with Alice Arlen)

Heartburn

Silkwood (with Alice Arlen)

Crazy Salad
&
Scribble Scribble

SOME THINGS ABOUT WOMEN & NOTES ON THE MEDIA

Nora Ephron

Vintage Books

A DIVISION OF RANDOM HOUSE, INC.

NEW YORK

FIRST VINTAGE BOOKS EDITION, OCTOBER 2012

Portions of Crazy Salad have appeared in Esquire magazine,
New York magazine, and Rolling Stone.

The articles in Scribble Scribble have been previously published
in Esquire magazine, except "Gentleman's Agreement" which
appeared in MORE magazine.

Grateful acknowledgment is made to Viking Press, Inc.,
for permission to reprint ten lines of poetry from
The Portable Dorothy Parker. Copyright © 1926, renewed
1954 by Dorothy Parker.

The stories in Scribble Scribble have been previously
published in Esquire magazine.

The Cataloging-in-Publication data is available at the
Library of Congress.

Vintage ISBN: 978-0-345-80474-7

Printed in the United States of America
10 9 8 7 6 5 4 3 2 1

Contents

Crazy Salad

For my sisters:
Delia, Hallie, and Amy

It's certain that fine women eat
A crazy salad with their meat

—WILLIAM BUTLER YEATS

2

Crazy Salad

Preface to *Crazy Salad*

I began writing a column about women in *Esquire* magazine in 1972. The column was my idea, and I wanted
to do it for a couple of specific, self-indulgent reasons
and one general reason. Self-indulgent specifics first: I
needed an excuse to go to my tenth reunion at Wellesley
College, and I was looking for someone to pay my way to
the Pillsbury Bake-Off. Beyond that, and in general, it
seemed clear that American women were going through
some changes; I wanted to write about them and about
myself. When I began the column, the women's movement was in a period of great activity, growth, and anger;
it is now in a period of consolidation. The same is true for
me, and it has something to do with why it has become
more and more difficult for me to write about women.
Also, I'm afraid, I have run out of things to say.

There are twenty-five articles in this book that
glance off and onto the subject of women, and as I go
through them, I can think of dozens of others I could
have done instead. I don't deal with lesbianism here
and, except peripherally, I don't deal with motherhood.
Month by month, I took what interested me most, and
so I never wrote about a number of things that inter-

ested me somewhat: panty hose, tampons, comediennes, the Equal Rights Amendment, Fascinating Womanhood, Bella Abzug, *The Story of O*, the integration of the Little League—I could go on and on. The point here is simply to say that this book is not intended to be any sort of definitive history of women in the early 1970s; it's just some things I wanted to write about.

A Few Words About Breasts

I have to begin with a few words about androgyny. In grammar school, in the fifth and sixth grades, we were all tyrannized by a rigid set of rules that supposedly determined whether we were boys or girls. The episode in *Huckleberry Finn* where Huck is disguised as a girl and gives himself away by the way he threads a needle and catches a ball—that kind of thing. We learned that the way you sat, crossed your legs, held a cigarette, and looked at your nails—the way you did these things instinctively was absolute proof of your sex. Now obviously most children did not take this literally, but I did. I thought that just one slip, just one incorrect cross of my legs or flick of an imaginary cigarette ash would turn me from whatever I was into the other thing; that would be all it took, really. Even though I was outwardly a girl and had many of the trappings generally associated with girldom—a girl's name, for example, and dresses, my own telephone, an autograph book—I spent the early years of my adolescence absolutely certain that I might at any point gum it up. I did not feel at all like a girl. I was boyish. I was athletic, ambitious, outspoken, competitive, noisy, rambunctious. I had scabs on my knees and my socks slid into my loafers and I could throw a football. I wanted desperately not to be that way, not to be a mixture of both things, but instead just one, a girl, a definite indisputable girl. As soft and as pink as a nursery. And nothing would do that for me, I felt, but breasts.

I was about six months younger than everyone else in my class, and so for about six months after it began, for six months after my friends had begun to develop (that was the word we used, develop), I was not particularly worried. I would sit in the bathtub and look down at my breasts and know that any day now, any second now, they would start growing like everyone else's. They didn't. "I want to buy a bra," I said to my mother one night. "What for?" she said. My mother was really hateful about bras, and by the time my third sister had gotten to the point where she was ready to want one, my mother had worked the whole business into a comedy routine. "Why not use a Band-Aid instead?" she would say. It was a source of great pride to my mother that she had never even had to wear a brassiere until she had her fourth child, and then only because her gynecologist made her. It was incomprehensible to me that anyone could ever be proud of something like that. It was the 1950s, for God's sake. Jane Russell. Cashmere sweaters. Couldn't my mother see that? *I am too old to wear an undershirt.* Screaming. Weeping. Shouting. "Then don't wear an undershirt," said my mother. "But I want to buy a bra." "What for?"

I suppose that for most girls, breasts, brassieres, that entire thing, has more trauma, more to do with the coming of adolescence, with becoming a woman, than anything else. Certainly more than getting your period, although that, too, was traumatic, symbolic. But you could see breasts; they were there; they were visible. Whereas a girl could claim to have her period for months before she actually got it and nobody would ever know the difference. Which is exactly what I did. All you had to do was make a great fuss over having enough nickels for the Kotex machine and walk around clutching your stomach and moaning for three to five days a month about The Curse and you could convince anybody. There is a school of thought somewhere in the women's lib/women's mag/gynecology establishment that claims that menstrual cramps are purely psychological, and I lean toward it. Not that I didn't have them finally. Agonizing cramps, heating-pad cramps, go-down-to-the-school-nurse-and-lie-on-the-cot cramps. But, unlike any pain I had ever suffered, I adored the pain of cramps, welcomed it, wallowed in it, bragged about it. "I can't go. I have cramps." "I can't do that. I have cramps." And most of all, gigglingly, blushingly: "I can't swim. I have cramps." Nobody ever used the hard-core word. Menstruation. God, what an awful word. Never that. "I have cramps."

The morning I first got my period, I went into my mother's bedroom to tell her. And my mother, my utterly-hateful-about-bras mother, burst into tears. It was really a lovely moment, and I remember it so clearly not just because it was one of the two times I ever saw my mother cry on my account (the other was when I was caught being a six-year-old kleptomaniac), but also because the incident did not mean to me what it meant to her. Her little girl, her firstborn, had finally become a woman. That was what she was crying about. My reaction to the event, however, was that I might well be a woman in some scientific, textbook sense (and could at least stop faking every month and stop wasting all those nickels). But in another sense—in a visible sense—I was as androgynous and as liable to tip over into boyhood as ever.

I started with a 28 AA bra. I don't think they made them any smaller in those days, although I gather that now you can buy bras for five-year-olds that don't have any cups whatsoever in them; trainer bras they are called. My first brassiere came from Robinson's Department Store in Beverly Hills. I went there alone, shaking, positive they would look me over and smile and tell me to come back next year. An actual fitter took me into the dressing room and stood over me while I took off my blouse and tried the first one on. The little puffs stood out on my chest. "Lean over," said the fitter. (To this day, I am not sure what fitters in bra departments do except to tell you to lean over.) I leaned over, with the fleeting hope that my breasts would miraculously fall out of my body and into the puffs. Nothing.

"Don't worry about it," said my friend Libby some months later, when things had not improved. "You'll get them after you're married."

"What are you talking about?" I said.

"When you get married," Libby explained, "your husband will touch your breasts and rub them and kiss them and they'll grow."

That was the killer. Necking I could deal with. Intercourse I could deal with. But it had never crossed my mind that a man was going to touch my breasts, that breasts had something to do with all that, petting, my God, they never mentioned petting in my little sex manual about the fertilization of the ovum. I became dizzy. For I knew instantly—as naïve as I had been only a moment before—that only part of what she was saying was true: the touching, rubbing, kissing part, not the growing part. And I knew that no one would ever want to marry me. I had no breasts. I would never have breasts.

My best friend in school was Diana Raskob. She lived a block from me in a house full of wonders. English muffins, for instance. The Raskobs were the first people in Beverly Hills to have English muffins for breakfast. They also had an apricot tree in the back, and a badminton court, and a subscription to *Seventeen* magazine, and hundreds of games, like Sorry and Parcheesi and Treasure Hunt and Anagrams. Diana and I spent three or four afternoons a week in their den reading and playing and eating. Diana's mother's kitchen was full of the most colossal assortment of junk food I have ever been exposed to. My house was full of apples and peaches and milk and homemade chocolate-chip cookies—which were nice, and good for you, but-not-right-before-dinner-or-you'll-spoil-your-appetite. Diana's house had nothing in it that was good for you, and what's more, you could stuff it in right up until dinner and nobody cared. Bar-B-Q potato chips (they were the first in them, too), giant bottles of ginger ale, fresh popcorn with melted butter, hot fudge sauce on Baskin-Robbins jamoca ice cream, powdered-sugar doughnuts from Van de Kamp's. Diana and I had been best friends since we were seven; we were about equally popular in school (which is to say, not particularly), we had about the same success with boys (extremely intermittent), and we looked much the same. Dark. Tall. Gangly.

It is September, just before school begins. I am eleven

years old, about to enter the seventh grade, and Diana and I have not seen each other all summer. I have been to camp and she has been somewhere like Banff with her parents. We are meeting, as we often do, on the street midway between our two houses, and we will walk back to Diana's and eat junk and talk about what has happened to each of us that summer. I am walking down Walden Drive in my jeans and my father's shirt hanging out and my old red loafers with the socks falling into them and coming toward me is . . . I take a deep breath . . . a young woman. Diana. Her hair is curled and she has a waist and hips and a bust and she is wearing a straight skirt, an article of clothing I have been repeatedly told I will be unable to wear until I have the hips to hold it up. My jaw drops, and suddenly I am crying, crying hysterically, can't catch my breath sobbing. My best friend has betrayed me. She has gone ahead without me and done it. She has shaped up.

Here are some things I did to help:

Bought a Mark Eden Bust Developer.

Slept on my back for four years.

Splashed cold water on them every night because some French actress said in *Life* magazine that that was what *she* did for her perfect bustline.

Ultimately, I resigned myself to a bad toss and began to wear padded bras. I think about them now, think about all those years in high school I went around in them, my three padded bras, every single one of them with different-sized breasts. Each time I changed bras I changed sizes: one week nice perky but not too obtrusive breasts, the next medium-sized slightly pointy ones, the next week knockers, true knockers; all the time, what-

ever size I was, carrying around this rubberized appendage on my chest that occasionally crashed into a wall
and was poked inward and had to be poked outward—
I think about all that and wonder how anyone kept a
straight face through it. My parents, who normally had
no restraints about needling me—why did they say
nothing as they watched my chest go up and down? My
friends, who would periodically inspect my breasts for
signs of growth and reassure me—why didn't they at
least counsel consistency?

And the bathing suits. I die when I think about the
bathing suits. That was the era when you could lay an
uninhabited bathing suit on the beach and someone
would make a pass at it. I would put one on, an absurd
swimsuit with its enormous bust built into it, the bones
from the suit stabbing me in the rib cage and leaving little red welts on my body, and there I would be, my chest
plunging straight downward absolutely vertically from
my collarbone to the top of my suit and then suddenly,
wham, out came all that padding and material and wir-
ing absolutely horizontally.

Buster Klepper was the first boy who ever touched them.
He was my boyfriend my senior year of high school.
There is a picture of him in my high-school yearbook
that makes him look quite attractive in a Jewish, horn-
rimmed-glasses sort of way, but the picture does not
show the pimples, which were air-brushed out, or the
dumbness. Well, that isn't really fair. He wasn't dumb.
He just wasn't terribly bright. His mother refused to
accept it, refused to accept the relentlessly average
report cards, refused to deal with her son's inevitable
destiny in some junior college or other. "He was tested,"

she would say to me, apropos of nothing, "and it came
out a hundred and forty-five. That's near-genius." Had
the word "underachiever" been coined, she probably
would have lobbed that one at me, too. Anyway, Buster
was really very sweet—which is, I know, damning with
faint praise, but there it is. I was the editor of the front
page of the high-school newspaper and he was editor of
the back page; we had to work together, side by side, in
the print shop, and that was how it started. On our first
date, we went to see *April Love*, starring Pat Boone. Then
we started going together. Buster had a green coupe, a
1950 Ford with an engine he had hand-chromed until it
shone, dazzled, reflected the image of anyone who looked
into it, anyone usually being Buster polishing it or the
gas-station attendants he constantly asked to check the
oil in order for them to be overwhelmed by the sparkle
on the valves. The car also had a boot stretched over the
back seat for reasons I never understood; hanging from
the rearview mirror, as was the custom, was a pair of
angora dice. A previous girl friend named Solange, who
was famous throughout Beverly Hills High School for
having no pigment in her right eyebrow, had knitted
them for him. Buster and I would ride around town, the
two of us seated to the left of the steering wheel. I would
shift gears. It was nice.

There was necking. Terrific necking. First in the car,
overlooking Los Angeles from what is now the Trous-
dale Estates. Then on the bed of his parents' cabana at
Ocean House. Incredibly wonderful, frustrating necking, I loved it, really, but no further than necking, please
don't, please, because there I was absolutely terrified of
the general implications of going-a-step-further with a
near-dummy and also terrified of his finding out there

was next to nothing there (which he knew, of course; he wasn't that dumb).

I broke up with him at one point. I think we were apart for about two weeks. At the end of that time, I drove down to see a friend at a boarding school in Palos Verdes Estates and a disc jockey played "April Love" on the radio four times during the trip. I took it as a sign. I drove straight back to Griffith Park to a golf tournament Buster was playing in (he was the sixth-seeded teen-age golf player in southern California) and presented myself back to him on the green of the 18th hole. It was all very dramatic. That night we went to a drive-in and I let him get his hand under my protuberances and onto my breasts. He really didn't seem to mind at all.

"Do you want to marry my son?" the woman asked me.

"Yes," I said.

I was nineteen years old, a virgin, going with this woman's son, this big strange woman who was married to a Lutheran minister in New Hampshire and pretended she was gentile and had this son, by her first husband, this total fool of a son who ran the hero-sandwich concession at Harvard Business School and whom for one moment one December in New Hampshire I said—as much out of politeness as anything else—that I wanted to marry.

"Fine," she said. "Now, here's what you do. Always make sure you're on top of him so you won't seem so small. My bust is very large, you see, so I always lie on my back to make it look smaller, but you'll have to be on top most of the time."

I nodded. "Thank you," I said.

"I have a book for you to read," she went on. "Take it

with you when you leave. Keep it." She went to the book-
shelf, found it, and gave it to me. It was a book on frigid-
ity.
   "Thank you," I said.

That is a true story. Everything in this article is a true
story, but I feel I have to point out that that story in
particular is true. It happened on December 30, 1960.
I think about it often. When it first happened, I naturally assumed that the woman's son, my boyfriend, was
responsible. I invented a scenario where he had had a
little heart-to-heart with his mother and had confessed
that his only objection to me was that my breasts were
small; his mother then took it upon herself to help out.
Now I think I was wrong about the incident. The mother
was acting on her own, I think: that was her way of being
cruel and competitive under the guise of being helpful
and maternal. You have small breasts, she was saying;
therefore you will never make him as happy as I have.
Or you have small breasts; therefore you will doubtless have sexual problems. Or you have small breasts;
therefore you are less woman than I am. She was, as
it happens, only the first of what seems to me to be a
never-ending string of women who have made competitive remarks to me about breast size. "I would love to
wear a dress like that," my friend Emily says to me,
"but my bust is too big." Like that. Why do women say
these things to me? Do I attract these remarks the way
other women attract married men or alcoholics or homosexuals? This summer, for example. I am at a party in
East Hampton and I am introduced to a woman from
Washington. She is a minor celebrity, very pretty and
Southern and blond and outspoken, and I am flattered

because she has read something I have written. We are talking animatedly, we have been talking no more than five minutes, when a man comes up to join us. "Look at the two of us," the woman says to the man, indicating me and her. "The two of us together couldn't fill an A cup." Why does she say that? It isn't even true, dammit, so why? Is she even more addled than I am on this subject? Does she honestly believe there is something wrong with her size breasts, which, it seems to me, now that I look hard at them, are just right? Do I unconsciously bring out competitiveness in women? In that form? What did I do to deserve it?

As for men.

There were men who minded and let me know that they minded. There were men who did not mind. In any case, *I* always minded.

And even now, now that I have been countlessly reassured that my figure is a good one, now that I am grown-up enough to understand that most of my feelings have very little to do with the reality of my shape, I am nonetheless obsessed by breasts. I cannot help it. I grew up in the terrible fifties—with rigid stereotypical sex roles, the insistence that men be men and dress like men and women be women and dress like women, the intolerance of androgyny—and I cannot shake it, cannot shake my feelings of inadequacy. Well, that time is gone, right? All those exaggerated examples of breast worship are gone, right? Those women were freaks, right? I know all that. And yet here I am, stuck with the psychological remains of it all, stuck with my own peculiar version of breast worship. You probably think I am crazy to go on like this: here I have set out to write a confession that is meant to hit you with the shock of recognition, and instead you are sitting there thinking I am thoroughly warped. Well, what can I tell you? If I had had them, I would have been a completely different person. I honestly believe that.

After I went into therapy, a process that made it possible for me to tell total strangers at cocktail parties that breasts were the hang-up of my life, I was often told that I was insane to have been bothered by my condition. I was also frequently told, by close friends, that I was extremely boring on the subject. And my girl friends, the ones with nice big breasts, would go on endlessly about how their lives had been far more miserable than mine. Their bra straps were snapped in class. They couldn't sleep on their stomachs. They were stared at whenever the word "mountain" cropped up in geography. And *Evangeline*, good God what they went through every time someone had to stand up and recite the Prologue to Longfellow's *Evangeline*: " . . . stand like druids of eld . . . / With beards that rest on their bosoms." It was much worse for them, they tell me. They had a terrible time of it, they assure me. I don't know how lucky I was, they say.

I have thought about their remarks, tried to put myself in their place, considered their point of view. I think they are full of shit.

May, 1972

Fantasies

One of the trump cards that men who are threatened by women's liberation are always dredging up is the question of whether there is sex after liberation. I have heard at least five or six experts or writers or spokesmen or some such stand up at various meetings and wonder aloud what happens to sex between men and women when the revolution comes. These men are always hooted down by the women present; in fact, I am usually one of the women present hooting them down, sniggering snide remarks to whoever is next to me like well-we-certainly-know-how-sure-of-himself-*he*-is. This fall, at the *Playboy* Writers' Convocation, an author named Morton Hunt uttered the magic words at a panel on The Future of Sex, and even in that room, full of male chauvinism and *Playboy* philosophers, the animosity against him was audible.

I spend a great deal of my energy these days trying to fit feminism into marriage, or vice versa—I'm never sure which way the priorities lie; it depends on my mood—but as truly committed as I am to the movement and as violent as I have become toward people who knock it, I think it is unfair to dismiss these men. They deserve some kind of answer. Okay. The answer is, nobody knows what happens to sex after liberation. It's a big mystery. And now that I have gotten that out of the way, I can go on to what really interests and puzzles me about sex and liberation—which is that it is difficult for me to see how sexual behavior and relations between the sexes can change at all unless our sexual fantasies change. So many of the conscious and unconscious ways men and women treat each other have to do with romantic and sexual fantasies that are deeply ingrained, not just in society but in literature. The movement may manage to clean up the mess in society, but I don't know whether it can ever clean up the mess in our minds.

I am somewhat liberated by current standards, but I have in my head this dreadful unliberated sex fantasy. One of the women in my consciousness-raising group is always referring to her "rich fantasy life," by which I suppose she means that in her fantasies she makes it in costume, or in exotic places, or with luminaries like Mao Tse-tung in a large bowl of warm Wheatena. My fantasy life is unfortunately nowhere near that interesting.

Several years ago, I went to interview photographer Philippe Halsman, whose notable achievements include a charming book containing photographs of celebrities jumping. The jumps are quite revealing in a predictable sort of way—Richard Nixon with his rigid, constricted jump, the Duke and Duchess of Windsor in a deeply dependent jump. And so forth. In the course of the interview, Halsman asked me if I wanted to jump for him; seeing it as a way to avoid possibly years of psychoanalysis, I agreed. I did what I thought was my quintessential jump. "Do it again," said Halsman. I did, attempting to duplicate exactly what I had done before. "Again," he said, and I did. "Well," said Halsman, "I can see from your jump that you are a very determined, ambitious, directed person, but you will never write a novel." "Why is that?" I asked. "Because you have only one jump in you," he said.

At the time, I thought that was really unfair—I had, after all, thought he wanted to see the *same* jump, not a different one every time; but I see now that he was exactly right. I have only one jump in me. I see this more and more every day. I am no longer interested in thirty-one flavors; I stick with English toffee. More to the point, I have had the same sex fantasy, with truly minor variations, since I was about eleven years old. It is really a little weird to be stuck with something so crucially important for so long; I have managed to rid myself of all the other accouterments of being eleven—I have pimples more or less under control, I can walk fairly capably in high heels—but I find myself with this appalling fantasy that has burrowed in and has absolutely nothing to do with my life.

I have never told anyone the exact details of my particular sex fantasy: it is my only secret and I am not going to divulge it here. I once told *almost* all of it to my former therapist; he died last year, and when I saw his obituary I felt a great sense of relief: the only person in the world who almost knew how crazy I am was gone and I was safe. Anyway, without giving away any of the juicy parts, I can tell you that in its broad outlines it has largely to do with being dominated by faceless males who rip my clothes off. That's just about all they have to do. Stare at me in this faceless way, go mad with desire, and rip my clothes off. It's terrific. In my sex fantasy, nobody ever loves me for my mind.

The fantasy of rape—of which mine is in a kind of prepubescent sub-category—is common enough among women and (in mirror image) among men. And what I don't understand is that with so many of us stuck with these clichéd feminine/masculine, submissive/dominant, masochistic/sadistic fantasies, how are we ever going to adjust fully to the less thrilling but more desirable reality of equality? A few months ago, someone named B. Lyman Stewart, a urologist at Cedars of Lebanon Hospital in Los Angeles, attributed the rising frequency of impotence among his male patients to the women's movement, which he called an effort to dominate men. The movement is nothing of the kind; but it and a variety of other events in society have certainly brought about a change in the way women behave in bed. A young man who grows up expecting to dominate sexually is bound to be somewhat startled by a young woman who wants sex as much as he does, and multi-orgasmic sex at that. By the same token, I suspect that a great deal of the difficulty women report in achieving orgasm is traceable— sadly—to the possibility that a man who is a tender fellow with implicit capabilities for impotence hardly fits into classic fantasies of big brutes with implicit capabilities for violence. A close friend who has the worst marriage I know—her husband beats her up regularly— reports that her sex life is wonderful. I am hardly suggesting that women ask their men to beat them—nor am I advocating the course apparently preferred by one of the most prominent members of the women's movement, who makes it mainly with blue-collar workers and semi-literates. But I wonder how we will ever break free from all the nonsense we grew up with; I wonder if our fantasies can ever catch up to what we all want for our lives.

It is possible, through sheer willpower, to stop having unhealthy sex fantasies. I have several friends who did just that. "What do you have instead?" I asked. "Nothing," they replied. Well, I don't know. I'm not at all sure I wouldn't rather have an unhealthy sex fantasy than no sex fantasy at all. But my real question is whether it is possible, having discarded the fantasy, to discard the thinking and expectations it represents. In my case, I'm afraid it wouldn't be. I have no desire to be dominated. Honestly I don't. And yet I find myself becoming angry when I'm not. My husband has trouble hailing a cab or flagging a waiter, and suddenly I feel a kind of rage; ball-breaking anger rises to my T-zone. I wish he were better at hailing taxis than I am; on the other hand, I realize that expectation is culturally conditioned, utterly foolish, has nothing to do with anything, is exactly the kind of thinking that ought to be got rid of in our society; on still another hand, having that insight into my reaction does not seem to calm my irritation.

My husband is fond of reminding me of the story of Moses, who kept the Israelites in the desert for forty years because he knew a slave generation could not found a new free society. The comparison with the women's movement is extremely apt, I think; I doubt that it will ever be possible for the women of my generation to escape from our own particular slave mentality. For the next generation, life may indeed be freer. After all, if society changes, the fantasies will change; where women are truly equal, where their status has nothing to do with whom they marry, when the issues of masculine/feminine cease to exist, some of this absurd reliance on role playing will be eliminated. But not all of it. Because even after the revolution, we will be left

with all the literature. "What will happen to the literature?" Helen Dudar of the *New York Post* once asked Ti-
Grace Atkinson. "What does it matter what happens?"
Ms. Atkinson replied. But it does. You are what you eat.
After liberation, we will still have to reckon with the
Sleeping Beauty and Cinderella. Granted there will also
be a new batch of fairy tales about princesses who refuse
to have ladies-in-waiting because it is exploitative of the
lower classes—but that sounds awfully tedious, doesn't
it? Short of a mass book burning, which no one wants,
things may well go on as they are now: women pulled
between the intellectual attraction of liberation and the
emotional, psychological, and cultural mishmash it's
hard to escape growing up with; men trying to cope with
these two extremes, and with their own ambivalence
besides. It's not much fun this way, but at least it's not
boring.

July, 1972

On Never Having Been
a Prom Queen

The other night, a friend of mine sat down at the table and informed me that if I was going to write a column about women, I ought to deal straight off with the subject most important to women in all the world. "What is that?" I asked. "Beauty," she said. I must have looked somewhat puzzled—as indeed I was—because she then went into a long and painful opening monologue about how she was losing her looks and I had no idea how terrible it was and that just recently an insensitive gentleman friend had said to her, "Michelle, you used to be such a beauty." I have no idea if this woman is really losing her looks—I have known her only a couple of years, and she looks pretty much the same to me—but she is certainly right in saying that I have no idea of what it is like. One of the few advantages to not being beautiful is that one usually gets better-looking as one gets older; I am, in fact, at this very moment gaining my looks. But what interested me about my response to my friend was that rather than feeling empathy for her—and I like to think I am fairly good at feeling empathy—I felt nothing. I like her very much, respect her, even believe she believes she is losing her looks, recognize her pain, but I just couldn't get into it.

Only a few days later, a book called *Memoirs of an Ex-Prom Queen*, by Alix Kates Shulman (Knopf), arrived in the mail. Shulman, according to the jacket flap, had written a "bitterly funny" book about "being female in America." I would like to read such a book. I would like to write such a book. As it turns out, however, Alix Shulman hasn't. What she has written is a book about the anguish and difficulty of being beautiful. And I realized, midway through the novel, that if there is anything more boring to me than the problems of big-busted women, it is the problems of beautiful women.

"They say it's worse to be ugly," Shulman writes. "I think it must only be different. If you're pretty, you are subject to one set of assaults; if you're plain you are subject to another. Pretty, you may have more men to choose from, but you have more anxiety too, knowing your looks, which really have nothing to do with you, will disappear. Pretty girls have few friends. Kicked out of mankind in elementary school, and then kicked out of womankind in junior high, pretty girls have a lower birthrate and a higher mortality. It is the beauties like Marilyn Monroe who swallow twenty-five Nembutals on a Saturday night and kill themselves in their thirties."

Now I could take that paragraph one sentence at a time and pick nits (What about the pretty girls who *have* friends? What has Marilyn Monroe's death to do with all this? What does it mean to say that pretty girls have a lower birthrate—that they have fewer children or that there are less of them than there are of us?), but I prefer to say simply that it won't wash. There isn't an ugly girl in America who wouldn't exchange her problems for the problems of being beautiful; I don't believe there's a beautiful girl anywhere who would honestly prefer not to be. "They say it's worse to be ugly," Alix Shulman writes. Yes, they do say that. And they're right. It's also worse to be poor, worse to be orphaned, worse to be fat. Not just *different* from rich, familied, and thin—actually worse. (I am a little puzzled as to why Ms. Shulman uses the words "plain" and "ugly" interchangeably; the difference between plain and ugly is as vast as the one between plain and pretty. As William Raspberry pointed out in a recent *Washington Post* column, ugly women are the most overlooked victims of discrimination in America.)

The point of all this is not about beauty—I hope I have made it clear that I don't know enough about beauty to make a point—but about divisions. I am separated from Alix Shulman and am in fact almost unable to judge her work because she is obsessed with being beautiful and I am obsessed with not being beautiful. We might as well be on separate sides altogether. And what makes me sad about the women's movement in general is my own inability, and that of so many other women, to get across such gulfs, to join hands, to unite on anything.

The women's liberation movement at this point in history makes the American Communist Party of the 1930s look like a monolith. I have been to meetings where the animosity between the gay and straight women was so strong and so unpleasant that I could not bear to be in the room. That is the most dramatic division in the movement, and one that has considerably slowed its forward momentum; but there are so many others. There is acrimony between the single and married women, working women and housewives, childless women and mothers. I have even heard a woman defend her affection for cooking to an incredulous group who believed that to cook at all—much less to like it—was to swallow the worst sort of cultural conditioning. Once I tried to explain to a fellow feminist why I liked wearing makeup; she replied by explaining why she does not. Neither of us understood a word the other said.

Every so often, I turn on the television and see one of the movement leaders being asked some idiot question like, "Isn't the women's movement in favor of all women abandoning their children and going off to work?" (I can hear David Susskind asking it now.) The leader usually replies that the movement isn't in favor of all women doing anything; what the movement is about, she says, is options. She is right, of course. At its best, that is exactly what the movement is about. But it just doesn't work out that way. Because the hardest thing for us to accept is the right to those options. I hear myself saying those words: *What this movement is about is options.* I say it to friends who are frustrated, or housebound, or guilty, or child-laden, and what I am really thinking is, If you really got it together, the option you would choose is mine.

I would like to be able to leap across the gulf that divides me from Alix Shulman. After all, her experience is not totally foreign to me: once I had a date with someone who thought I was beautiful. He talked all night, while I—who spent years developing my conversational ability to compensate for my looks (my life has been spent in compensation)—said nothing. At the end of the evening, he made a pass at me, and I was insulted. So I understand. I recognize that people who are beautiful have problems. But so do people who get upset stomachs from raw onions, and men with blue-orange color blindness, and left-handed persons everywhere. I just can't get into it; what interests me these days tends to have more to do with the problems of women who were not prom queens in high school. I'm sorry about this—my point of view is not fair to Alix Shulman, or to my friend who thinks she is losing her looks, or to me, or to the movement. But that's where it is. I'm working on it. Like all things about liberation, sisterhood is difficult.

August, 1972

The Girls in the Office

I have not looked at *The Best of Everything* since I first bought it—in paperback—ten years ago, but I have a perverse fondness for it. In case you somehow missed it, *The Best of Everything* was a novel by Rona Jaffe about the lives of four, or was it five, single women in New York; it was pretty good trash, as trash goes, which is not why I am fond of it. I liked it because it seemed to me that it caught perfectly the awful essence of being a single woman in a big city. False pregnancies. Real pregnancies. Abortions. Cads. Dark bars with married men. Rampant masochism. I remember particularly a sequence in the book where one of the girls, rejected by a lover, goes completely bonkers and begins spending all her time spying on him, poking through his garbage for discarded love letters and old potato peelings; ultimately, as I recall, she falls from his fire escape to her death. The story seemed to me only barely exaggerated from what I was seeing around me, and, I am sorry to say, doing myself.

I was, naturally, single when I read the novel, unhappily single, mired in the Dorothy Parker telephone-call syndrome ("Please, God, let him telephone me now. . . .

I'll count five hundred by fives, and if he hasn't called me then, I will know God isn't going to help me, ever again. That will be the sign. Five, ten, fifteen . . .") and well aware of its hopeless banality. It occurred to me as I read *The Best of Everything* that it would be practically impossible to write an accurate novel about the quality of life for single women in New York without writing a B novel, for the simple reason that life for single women in New York *is* a B novel. Even Dorothy Parker's short story about the phone call, horribly accurate—a classic, even—belongs in the pages of *Cosmopolitan* magazine.

I like to think that things have changed since my early years in New York. A lot has happened in the world, clearly. The women's movement, birth-control pills, legalized abortions in New York—life ought to have changed in some way. I want very much to believe this; like many married women, I have managed to romanticize my single years beyond recognition and I spend a lot of time daydreaming about what it would have been like to be single knowing then what I know now—or simply what it would be like to be single again.

In any event, I have just read a book that is enough to make me stop daydreaming for at least a week or two. Actually it's not a good book, or even a book in any real sense, but a series of tape-recorded interviews with fifteen single women who all work in the same New York office (Time-Life, thinly disguised). It is called *The Girls in the Office* (Simon & Schuster) and it has an incredibly old-fashioned, *Best of Everything*, trash epic quality: it is full of dreadful cartoon people who seem straight out of every junky fifties novel—the difference being, of course, that *The Girls in the Office* is nonfiction, real, an honest-to-God case of life imitating trash. Its author,

Jack Olsen, has not really written anything; he has instead been content merely to edit the tapes, neaten up the interviews, give them snappy endings, reconstruct them to the point where they seem too pat, too slick, too much, maybe not even true. But they are true, I'm afraid. Bizarre and weird, but true. And because they are, the book, in its sleazy, slapdash, pseudo-sociological way, is fascinating—both for what it says about the women as for the men in their lives.

The women in *The Girls in the Office* range from twenty-four to fifty years old and all of them live alone in Manhattan, surrounded and—as they testify— tormented by exhibitionists, flashers, rapists, muggers, goosers, breathers, feelers, and Peeping Toms. Almost none of them has an executive-level job, and none seems to have ambitions toward anything higher. Their competitiveness is directed solely toward other women; their energies are spent scrambling for little favors and petty advances within the lower realm of the company reserved for women only. That men are responsible for keeping them down does not seem to have occurred to them; in any case, they are not interested in getting up from under. What they are looking for is a husband. In the meantime, they want not a better slot but a comfortable niche, the warm feeling of working in a nice, big, airconditioned, wall-to-wall carpeted office full of friendly faces and office parties. The office becomes their world, the employees their surrogate family. As one of the women explains: "[We're] producing a product in close conjunction with brilliant men, just as married couples produce children." The men—most of them married— dominate it all, flirt with them, date them, seduce them, string them along, and manage to convince them that all of it is worth it to spend time with such extraordinary creatures. "You have to learn quickly that the super-talented, super-creative geniuses in our company are different from other men," says one of the women in the book. Says another: "The hotshots at The Company [are] so glamorous. How could I get interested in a fifth assistant teller at a bank in the Bronx, when the man in the next cubicle at the office has just got back from Hong Kong?"

The parade of married men who traipse through these women's apartments turns their lives into parodies of *Back Street*. The women wait, year after year, for the men to leave their wives. They never do. Year after year of one or two nights a week, furtive lunches, nooners at midtown hotels, tacky confrontations with their wives. Even the girls who manage to avoid the married men make a mess of their lives. A few become tough in a way that is simply inhumane: "I learned how to turn the men's lust against them. I'd pretend to be interested in one of them and I'd get him to talk to me for three hours and let him think he was making a great successful pass, and then I'd turn around and leave!" The rest manage to come up with relationships with single men that are quite as demeaning and unhealthy as those with married men. One woman Olsen calls Jayne Gouldtharpe has an affair for a year with an insurance man whose idea of rebellion is to throw egg yolks at the wall. After a year or so of what Nichols and May used to call proximity but no relating, he comes over for dinner one night. "We were taking a shower together," Jayne recalls, "and he said, 'You know, all we ever talk about is you. I have problems too. . . .'

"'What do you mean?'

" 'Well, I'm going to Italy tomorrow for a long visit, and my big problem is how to tell you that this is the last time we'll ever be together.' "

After two days of misery, Jayne takes a week off from work, flies to Rome with no idea of where her lover is staying, and spends seven days looking for him. She returns to New York, only to find that he had never intended to go to Italy in the first place. "He was a sadist dealing with a masochist," she concludes, "and the ultimate bit of sadism was to stand in my shower naked and tell me that we were through."

There is another woman in the book Olsen calls Gloria Rolstin, who falls in love with an executive named Tom Lantini. (Names are not Olsen's strong point.) Lantini is divorced and lives with his invalid mother in a town house downtown. Within a few months, he has moved Gloria in as an ersatz nurse's aide: she changes his mother's clothes, takes her to the bathroom, cleans up after her, feeds her medicine, plays honeymoon bridge—"And the old lady barely able to tell what was trump!" All the while, she sleeps alone on a couch downstairs while Tom and his mother sleep in adjoining bedrooms above.

The affair between Gloria and Tom, such as it is, lasts seven years, the last three or four punctuated by a long series of physical brawls—"He cut my nose. I sprained his wrist. He blackened my eye. I pulled out about five square inches of his curls. . . . He smashed me so hard on the side of my head that he knocked me down, and my ear was ripped open from his ring. . . ." And so forth. The acts of violence become so commonplace in this book that at one point, when one Vanessa Van Durant is locked in her apartment by her boyfriend

and beaten and buggered for two weeks, I found myself
shrugging and thinking, Ah, yes, the old lock-her-in-the-
apartment-and-beat-her-and-bugger-her routine. What
is most frightening about all these fights is not just their
frequency but that the women accept it as a matter of
course, and even blame themselves for it. "I'll get a little
pushy or a little whiny," one explains, "and a man will
haul off and smack me. It's usually my own fault." I'm a
masochist, he's a sadist; I drove him to it; it's as simple
as that. It is, of course nowhere near as simple as that. I
don't pretend to be able to provide an answer as to why
these women put up with what they do, but some of it
has to do with a society structured in such a way as to
make women believe that to be with a man—any man,
on whatever terms—is better than being alone. Only one
of the women sees the women's movement as providing
any relevance to her situation. The rest want nothing
to do with it. Says one: "I endorse the economic side of
Women's Lib completely, but I don't go around marching or burning my bra, because I think things like that
only tend to emasculate men, and the New York male
has already been emasculated beyond recognition."

The men in this book are in every way as pathetic
as the women they victimize. I could give example after
example. There is a chronically impotent married man
who attempts to seduce several of the women in this book
and always insists the problem has merely to do with too
much liquor. ("Foreplay is fine for about an hour," says
one of the women who becomes involved with him, "but
when it goes on for a month, that's a pretty good sign
something's very wrong.") There is an executive, Peter-
principled into a job he cannot handle, who hangs on
and spends his time whacking off while dictating letters

to his secretary. There is another man who becomes so disturbed when his girl breaks off their affair that he sends her a hot-pepper explosive in the mail, telephones her all night and hangs up, substitutes Drano for salt in her salt shakers, and slips a vial of acid into her loafers which burns her toes.

One of the themes the women return to frequently in *The Girls in the Office* is their belief that men are just little boys, infants with "hang-ups in their brains like spider webs." I have heard this theme song so many times from so many women; and every time I hear it, I recoil. It is, quite obviously, a profoundly anti-male remark; it is also, I'm afraid, partly true. Saying it's so gets us nowhere, though. The unhappy corollary to the fact that a lot of men are just little boys is the fact that so many women put up with it—cater to it, in fact, mother them, bolster their egos by subjugating their own—and feed right into the real problem, which is not that men are little boys but that men don't like women very much, can't deal with their demands, their sexuality, their equality. The role of a corporation like Time-Life in this—which underlines the pattern by delivering to each male employee a secretary or researcher he can dominate—would make an interesting book. The lives of fifteen single women in New York would also make an interesting book someday. This one isn't it.

September, 1972

Reunion

A boy and a girl are taking a shower together in the bathroom. How to explain the significance of it? It is a Friday night in June, the first night of the tenth reunion of the Class of 1962 of Wellesley College, and a member of my class has just returned from the bathroom with the news. A boy and a girl are taking a shower together. No one can believe it. Ten years and look at the changes. Ten years ago, we were allowed men in the rooms on Sunday afternoons only, on the condition the door be left fourteen inches ajar. One Sunday during my freshman year, a girl in my dormitory went into her room with a date and not only closed the door but put a sock on it. (The sock—I feel silly remembering nonsense like this, but I do—was a Wellesley signal meaning "Do Not Disturb.") Three hours later, she and the boy emerged and she was wearing a different outfit. No one could believe it. We were that young. Today boys on exchange programs from MIT and Dartmouth live alongside the girls, the dormitory doors lock, and some of the women in my class—as you can see from the following excerpt from one letter to our tenth-reunion record book—have been through some changes themselves:

"In the past five years I have (1) had two children and two abortions, (2) moved seriously into politics, working up to more responsible positions on bigger campaigns, (3) surrendered myself to what I finally acknowledged was my lifework—the women's revolution, (4) left my husband and children to seek my fortune and on the way (5) fallen desperately, madly, totally in love with a beautiful man and am sharing a life with him in Cambridge near Harvard Square where we're completely incredibly happy doing the work we love and having amazing life adventures."

I went back to my reunion at Wellesley to write about it. I'm doing a column, that's why I'm going, I said to New York friends who were amazed that I would want anything to do with such an event. I want to see what happened, I said—to my class, to the college. (I didn't say that I wanted my class and the college to see what had happened to me, but that of course was part of it, too.) A few years ago, Wellesley went through a long reappraisal before rejecting coeducation and reaffirming its commitment to educating women; that interested me. Also, I wondered how my class, almost half of which has two or more children, was dealing with what was happening to women today. On Friday evening, when my classmate and I arrived at the dormitory that was our class headquarters, we bumped into two Wellesley juniors. One of them asked straight off if we wanted to see their women's liberation bulletin board. They took us down the corridor to a cork board full of clippings, told us of their battle to have a full-time gynecologist on campus, and suddenly it became important for us to let them know we were not what they thought. We were not those alumnae who came back to Wellesley because it was the best time of their lives; we were not those cardigan-sweatered, Lilly Pulitzered matrons or Junior League members or League of Women Voters volunteers; we were not about to be baited by their bulletin board. We're not Them. I didn't come to reunion because I wanted to. I'm here to write about it. Understand?

Wellesley College has probably the most beautiful campus in the country, more lush and gorgeous than any place I have ever seen. In June, the dogwood and azalea are in bloom around Lake Waban, the ivy spurts new growth onto the collegiate Gothic buildings, the huge maples are obscenely loaded with shade. So idyllic, in the literal sense—an idyll before a rude awakening. There was Wellesley, we were told, and then, later, there would be the real world. The real world was different. "Where, oh where are the staid alumnae?" goes a song Wellesley girls sing, and they answer, "They've gone out from their dreams and theories. Lost, lost in the wide, wide world." At Wellesley we would be allowed to dream and theorize. We would be taken seriously. It would not always be so.

Probably the most insidious influence on the students ten years ago was the one exerted by the class deans. They were a group of elderly spinsters who believed that the only valuable role for Wellesley graduates was to go on to the only life the deans knew anything about—graduate school, scholarship, teaching. There was no value at all placed on achievement in the so-called real world. Success of that sort was suspect; worse than that, it was unserious. Better to be a housewife, my dear, and to take one's place in the community. *Keep a hand in.* This policy was not just implicit but was actually articulated. During my junior year, in a romantic episode that still embarrasses me, I became engaged to a humorless young man whose primary attraction was that he was fourth in his class at Harvard Law School. I went to see my class dean about transferring to Barnard senior year before being married. "Let me give you some advice," she told me. "You have worked so hard at Wellesley. When you marry, take a year off. Devote yourself to your husband and your marriage." I was incredulous. To begin with, I had not worked hard at Wellesley—anyone with my transcript in front of her ought to have been able to see that. But far more important, I had always intended to work after college; my mother was a career woman who had successfully indoctrinated me and my sisters that to be a housewife was to be nothing. Take a year off being a wife? Doing what? I carried the incident around with me for years, repeating it from time to time as positive proof that Wellesley wanted its graduates to be merely housewives. Then, one day, I met a woman who had graduated ten years before me. She had never wanted anything but to be married and have children; she, too, had gone to see this dean before leaving Wellesley and marrying. "Let me give you some advice," the dean told her. "Don't have children right away. Take a year to work." And so I saw. What Wellesley wanted was for us to avoid the extremes, to be instead that thing in the middle. Neither a rabid careerist nor a frantic mamma. That thing in the middle: a trustee. "Life is not all dirty diapers and runny noses," writes Susan Connard Chenoweth in the class record. "I do make it into the real world every week to present a puppet show on ecology called *Give A Hoot, Don't Pollute.*" The deans would be proud of Susan. She is on her way. A doer of good works. An example to the community. Above all, a Samaritan.

I never went near the Wellesley College chapel in my four years there, but I am still amazed at the amount of Christian charity that school stuck us all with, a kind of glazed politeness in the face of boredom and stupidity. Tolerance, in the worst sense of the word. Wellesley was not alone in encouraging this for its students, but it always seemed so sad that a school that could have done so much for women put so much energy into the one area women should be educated out of. How marvelous it would have been to go to a women's college that encouraged impoliteness, that rewarded aggression, that encouraged argument. Women by the time they are eighteen are so damaged, so beaten down, so tyrannized out of behaving in all the wonderful outspoken ways unfortunately characterized as masculine; a college committed to them has to take on the burden of repair—of remedial education, really. I'm not just talking about vocational guidance and placement bureaus (which are far more important than anyone at these schools believes) but also about the need to force young women to define themselves before they abdicate the task and become defined by their husbands. *What do you think? What is your opinion?* No one ever asked. We all graduated from Wellesley able to describe everything we had studied—Baroque painting, Hindemith, Jacksonian democracy, Yeats—yet we were never asked what we thought of any of it. *Do you like it? Do you think it is good? Do you know that even if it is good you do not have to like it?* During reunion weekend, at the Saturday-night class supper, we were subjected to an hour of dance by a fourth-rate Boston theatre ensemble which specializes in eighth-rate Grotowski crossed with the worst of *Marat/Sade*. Grunts. Moans. Jumping about imitating lambs. It was absolutely awful. The next day, a classmate with the improbable name of Muffy Kleinfeld asked me what I thought of it. "What did *you* think of it?" I replied. "Well," she said, "I thought their movements were quite expressive and forceful, but I'm not exactly sure what they were trying to do dramatically." *But what did you think of it?*

I am probably babbling a bit here, but I feel a real anger toward Wellesley for blowing it, for being so damned irrelevant. Like many women involved with the movement, I have come full circle in recent years: I used to think that anything exclusively for women (women's pages, women's colleges, women's novels) was a bad idea. Now I am all in favor of it. But when Wellesley decided to remain a women's college, it seemed so pointless to me. Why remain a school for women unless you are prepared to deal with the problems women have in today's society? Why bother? If you are simply going to run a classy liberal-arts college in New England, an ivory tower for $3,900 a year, why not let the men in?

Wellesley *has* changed. Some of the changes are superficial: sex in the dorms, juicy as it is, probably has more to do with the fact that it is 1972 than with real change. On the other hand, there are changes that are almost fundamental. The spinster deans are mostly gone. There is a new president, and she has actually been married. Twice. Many of the hangovers from an earlier era—when Wellesley was totally a school for the rich as opposed to now, when it is only partially so—have been eliminated: sit-down dinners with maids and students waiting on tables; Tree Day, a spring rite complete with tree maidens and tree plantings; the freshman-class banner hunt. Hoop rolling goes on, but this year a feminist senior won and promptly denounced the rite as trivial and sexist. Bible is no longer required. More seniors are applying to law school. "They are not as polite as you were," says history professor Edward Gulick, which sounds promising. Yet another teacher tells me that the students today are more like us than like the class of 1970. The graduation procession is an endless troupe of look-alikes, cookie-cutter perfect faces with long straight hair parted in the middle. Still, there are at least three times as many black faces among them as there were in my time.

And there is the graduation speaker, Eleanor Holmes Norton, a black who is New York City Commissioner of Human Rights. Ten years ago, our speaker was Santha Rama Rau, who bored us mightily with a low-keyed speech on the need to put friendship above love of country. The contrast is quite extraordinary: Norton, an outspoken feminist and mesmerizing public speaker, raises her fist to the class as she speaks. "The question has been asked," she says, " 'What is a woman?' A woman is a person who makes choices. A woman is a dreamer. A woman is a planner. A woman is a maker, and a molder. A woman is a person who makes choices. A woman builds bridges. A woman makes children and makes cars. A woman writes poetry and songs. A woman is a person who makes choices. You cannot even simply become a mother anymore. You must *choose* motherhood. Will you choose change? Can you become its vanguard?" It is a moving speech, full of comparisons between women today and the young blacks of the 1960s; midway through, a Madras-jacketed father, absolutely furious, storms down the aisle, collars his graduating daughter, and drags her off to tell her what he thinks of it. She returns a few minutes later to join her class in a standing ovation.

As for my class, two things are immediately apparent. The housewives, who are openly elated at being sprung from the responsibility of children for a weekend, are nonetheless very defensive about women's liberation and wary of those of us who have made other choices. In the class record book, the most common expression is "women's lib notwithstanding," as in this from Janet Barton Mostafa: "I'm thrilled to find, women's lib to the contrary notwithstanding, that motherhood is a pretty joyful experience. Shakespeare will have to wait in the wings a year or two." *You cannot even simply become a mother anymore. You must* choose *motherhood.* "I steeled myself against coming," one of the housewives said at reunion. "I was sure I was going to have to defend myself." Neither she nor any other housewife will have to defend herself this trip; we are all far too polite. Still, it is interesting that the housewives—not the working mothers or the single or divorced women—are self-conscious. Which brings me to the second trend: the number of women at reunion who are not just divorced but proudly divorced, wearing their new independence as a kind of badge. I cannot imagine that previous Wellesley reunions attracted any divorced women at all.

On Saturday afternoon, our class meets formally. The meeting is conducted by the outgoing class president, B. J. Diener, the developer of Breck One Dandruff Shampoo. She has brought each of us a bottle of the stuff, a gesture some of the class think is in poor taste. I think it is sweet. B. J. is saying that the college ought to do more

for its alumnae—hold symposia around the country, provide reading lists on selected subjects, run correspondence
courses for graduate-school credits. I find myself involved
in a debate about the wisdom of all this—I hadn't meant
to get involved, but here I am, with my hand up, about to
say that it sounds suspiciously like suburban clubwomen.
As it happens, I am sitting in the back with a small group
of fellow troublemakers, and we all end up waving our
hands and speaking out. "It seems to me," says one, "that
all this is in the same spirit of elitism we've tried to get
away from since leaving Wellesley." Says another: "Where
is the leadership of Wellesley when it comes to graduate-
school quotas for women? If Wellesley is going to stand
out and be a special place for women, it should be standing up and making a loud noise about it." One thing leads
to another, and the Class of 1962 ends up passing a unan-
imous resolution urging the college to take a position of
leadership in the women's movement. It seems a stunning and miraculous victory, and so, giddy, we push on to
yet another controversial topic. That morning, graduation
exercises had been leafleted by a campus group urging
Wellesley to sell its stocks in companies manufacturing
products for war; we think the class should support them.
President Diener thinks this is a terrible idea, and she
musters all her Harvard Business School expertise to
suggest instead that we ask the college to vote its shares
against company management. Hands are up all over the
room. "The whole purpose of Wellesley's investment is to
make money," says one woman, "and I for one don't care
if they want to invest it in whorehouses." The motion to
urge the college to sell its war stocks is defeated 30–8. The
eight of us leave together, flushed with the partial success of our troublemaking, and suddenly I feel depressed

and silly. We had come back to make a little trouble but, like the senior who won hoop rolling and denounced it, we all tend toward tiny little rebellions, harmless nips at the system. We will never make any real trouble. Wellesley helped see to that.

And the nonsense. My God, the nonsense. At reunion, most of the students are gone and classes are over for the year. All that remains is a huge pile of tradition. Singing on the chapel steps. Fruit punch and tea in the afternoon. Class cheers and class songs. On Sunday morning, the last day of a hopelessly over-scheduled weekend, the reunion classes parade down to the alumnae meeting. Each class carries a felt banner and each woman wears a white dress decorated with some kind of costume insignia, also in class colors. My class is holding plastic umbrellas trimmed with huge bouquets of plastic violets and purple ribbons. The Class of 1957 is waving green feather dusters. Nineteen thirty-two is wearing what look like strawberry shortcakes but turn out to be huge red crowns; 1937 is in chefs' hats and aprons with signs reading, " '37 is alive and cooking!" I am standing on the side, defiant in my non-umbrellaness, as the Class of 1952 comes down the path with red backpacks strapped on; in the midst of them I see a woman I know, a book editor, who is marching with her class but is not wearing a backpack. I start to laugh, because it seems clear to me that we both think we are somehow set apart from all this—she because she is not wearing anything on her back, I because I am taking notes. We are both wrong, of course.

I can pretend that I have come back to Wellesley only because I want to write about it, but I am really here because I still care, I still care about this Mickey Mouse institution; I am foolish enough to think that someday it will do something important for women. That I care at all, that I am here at all, makes me one of Them. I am not exactly like them—I may be a better class of dumb— but we are all dumb. This college is about as meaningful to the educational process in America as a perfume factory is to the national economy. And all of us care, which makes us all idiots for wasting a minute thinking about the place.

October, 1972

Miami

It's about this mother-of-us-all business.

It is Sunday morning in Miami Beach, the day before the Democratic Convention is to begin, and the National Women's Political Caucus is holding a press conference. The cameras are clicking at Gloria, and Bella has swept in trailed by a vortex of television crews, and there is Betty, off to the side, just slightly out of frame. The cameras will occasionally catch a shoulder of her flowered granny dress or a stray wisp of her chaotic graying hair or one of her hands churning up the air; but it will be accidental, background in a photograph of Gloria, or a photograph of Bella, or a photograph of Gloria and Bella. Betty's eyes are darting back and forth trying to catch someone's attention, anyone's attention. No use. Gloria is speaking, and then Bella, and then Sissy Farenthold from Texas. And finally . . . Betty's lips tighten as she hears the inevitable introduction coming: "Betty Friedan, the mother of us all." That does it. "I'm getting sick and tired of this mother-of-us-all thing," she says. She is absolutely right, of course: in the women's movement, to be called the mother of anything is rarely a compliment. And what it means in this context, make no

mistake, is that Betty, having in fact given birth, ought
to cut the cord. Bug off. Shut up. At the very least, retire
gracefully to the role of senior citizen, professor emeritus. Betty Friedan has no intention of doing anything of
the kind. It's her baby, damn it. Her movement. Is she
supposed to sit still and let a beautiful thin lady run off
with it?

The National Women's Political Caucus (N.W.P.C.) was
organized in July, 1971, by a shaky coalition of women's
movement leaders. Its purpose was to help women in and
into political life, particularly above the envelope-licking
level. Just how well the caucus will do in its first national
election remains to be seen, but in terms of the Democratic Convention it was wildly successful—so much so,
in fact, that by the time the convention was to begin, the
N.W.P.C. leaders were undergoing a profound sense of
anticlimax. There were 1,121 women delegates, up from
13 percent four years ago to nearly 40 percent. There
was a comprehensive and stunning women's plank in
the platform; four years ago there was none. There were
battles still to be fought at the convention—the South
Carolina challenge and the abortion plank—but the first
was small potatoes (or so it seemed beforehand) and the
second was a guaranteed loser. And so, in a sense, the
major function for the N.W.P.C. was to be ornamental—
that is, it was simply to be *there*. Making its presence
felt. Putting forth the best possible face. Pretending to
a unity that did not exist. Above all, putting on a good
show: the abortion plank would never carry, a woman
would not be nominated as Vice-President this year,
but the N.W.P.C. would put on a good show. Nineteen
seventy-six, and all that. Punctuating all this would be

what at times seemed an absurd emphasis on semantics: committees were run by "spokespersons" and "chairpersons"; phones were never manned but "womanned" and "personned." All this was public relations, not politics. They are two different approaches: the first is genteel, dignified, orderly, goes by the rules, and that was the one the women planned to play. They got an inadvertent baptism in the second primarily because George McGovern crossed them, but also because politics, after all, is the name of the game.

In 1963, Betty Friedan wrote *The Feminine Mystique* and became a national celebrity. She moved from the suburbs to Manhattan, separated from her husband, and began to devote much of her time to public speaking. She was a founder of the N.W.P.C. and of the National Organization for Women (N.O.W.), from whose national board she resigned voluntarily last year. This year she ran and lost as a Chisholm delegate to the convention. Among the high points of her campaign was a press release announcing she would appear in Harlem with a "Traveling Watermelon Feast" to distribute to the natives. In recent months, her influence within the movement has waned to the point that even when she is right (which she is occasionally, though usually for the wrong reasons), no one pays any attention to her. Two weeks before the convention, the N.W.P.C. council met to elect a spokesperson in Miami and chose Gloria Steinem over Friedan. The election was yet another chapter in Friedan's ongoing feud with Steinem—the two barely speak—and by the time Betty arrived in Miami she was furious. "I'm so disgusted with Gloria," she would mutter on her way to an N.W.P.C. meeting. Gloria was selling

out the women. Gloria was ripping off the movement.
Gloria was a tool of George McGovern. Gloria and Bella
were bossing the delegates around. Gloria was part of a
racist clique that would not support Shirley Chisholm
for Vice-President. And so it went. Every day, Friedan
would call N.W.P.C. headquarters at the dingy Betsy
Ross Hotel downtown and threaten to call a press conference to expose the caucus; every day, at the meetings
the N.W.P.C. held for press and female delegates, movement leaders would watch with a kind of horrified fasci-
nation to see what Betty Friedan would do next.

And Gloria. *Sic transit*, etc. Gloria Steinem has in
the past year undergone a total metamorphosis, one
that makes her critics extremely uncomfortable. Like
Jane Fonda, she has become dedicated in a way that
is a little frightening and almost awe-inspiring; she
is demanding to be taken seriously—and it is the one
demand her detractors, who prefer to lump her in with
all the other radical-chic beautiful people, cannot bear
to grant her. Once the glamour girl, all legs and short
skirts and long painted nails, David Webb rings, Pucci,
Gucci, you-name-it-she-had-it, once a fixture in gossip
columns which linked her to one attractive man after
another, she has managed to transform herself almost
totally. She now wears Levi's and simple T-shirts—and
often the same outfit two days running. The nails are as
long as ever, but they are unpolished, and her fingers
bare. She has managed to keep whatever private life she
still has out of the papers. Most important, she projects
a calm, peaceful, subdued quality; her humor is gentle,
understated. Every so often, someone suggests that Gloria Steinem is only into the women's movement because
it is currently the chic place to be; it always makes me

smile, because she is about the only remotely chic thing connected with the movement.

It is probably too easy to go on about the two of them this way: Betty as Wicked Witch of the West, Gloria as Ozma, Glinda, Dorothy—take your pick. To talk this way ignores the subtleties, right? Gloria is not, after all, uninterested in power. And yes, she manages to remain above the feud, but that is partly because, unlike Betty, she has friends who will fight dirty for her. Still, it is hard to come out anywhere but squarely on her side. Betty Friedan, in her thoroughly irrational hatred of Steinem, has ceased caring whether or not the effects of that hatred are good or bad for the women's movement. Her attack on Steinem in the August *McCall's*, which followed the convention by barely a week, quoted Steinem out of context (Steinem's remark, "Marriage is prostitution," was made in the course of a speech on the effects of discrimination in marriage laws) and implied that Gloria was defiantly anti-male, a charge that is, of course, preposterous. I am not criticizing Friedan for discussing the divisions in the movement; nor do I object to her concern about man-haters; if she wants to air all that, it's okay with me. What I do not understand is why—for any but personal reasons—she chooses to discredit Steinem (and Bella Abzug) by tying them in with philosophies they have absolutely nothing to do with.

At a certain point in the convention, every N.W.P.C. meeting began to look and sound the same. Airless, windowless rooms decked with taffeta valances and Miami Beach plaster statuary. Gloria in her jeans and aviator glasses, quoting a female delegate on the gains women have made in political life this year: "It's like pushing marbles through a sieve. It means the sieve will never be the same again." Bella Abzug in her straw hat, bifocals cocked down on her nose, explaining that abortion is too a Constitutional right and belongs in a national platform. "I would like an attorney to advise us on this," says a New York delegate who believes it is a local matter. "One just did," Bella replies. Clancy and Sullivan, two women delegates from Illinois whose credentials are being challenged by the Daley machine, stand and are cheered. Germaine Greer, in overalls, takes notes quietly into a tiny tape recorder. Betty looks unhappy. The South Carolina challenge is discussed: the women want to add seven more delegates to the nine women already serving on the thirty-two-member delegation. "Are these new delegates going to be women or wives?" asks one woman. "Because I'm from Missouri and we filed a challenge and now we have twelve new delegates who turned out to be sisters of, wives, daughters of. . . . What is the point of having a woman on a delegation who will simply say, 'Honey, how do we vote?'" The microphone breaks down. "Until women control technology," says Gloria, "we will have to be dependent in a situation like this." The days pass, and "Make Policy Not Coffee" buttons are replaced by "Boycott Lettuce" buttons are replaced by "Sissy for Vice-President" buttons. The days pass, and Betty is still somewhat under control.

The task Friedan ultimately busied herself with was a drive to make Shirley Chisholm Vice-President, something Shirley Chisholm had no interest whatsoever in becoming. Friedan began lobbying for this the Friday before the convention began, when she asked the N.W.P.C. to endorse Chisholm for Vice-President; the

council decided to hold back from endorsing anyone
until it was clear who wanted to run. And meanwhile
it would be ready with other women's names; among
those that came up were Farenthold, Abzug, Steinem,
and Representative Martha Griffiths. Jane Galvin
Lewis, a black who was representing Dorothy Height
of the National Council of Negro Women at the convention, had suggested Steinem at the meeting. The night
Shirley Chisholm was to arrive in Miami, Lewis went up
to the Deauville Hotel to welcome her and bumped into
Betty Friedan in the lobby.

"What are you doing here?" Friedan asked.

"I'm here to meet Shirley," said Lewis.

"You really play both ends, don't you?" said Friedan.

"Explain that," said Lewis.

"What kind of black are you anyway?"

"What are you talking about?"

"You didn't even want to support Shirley Chisholm,"
Friedan said, her voice rising. "I heard you. I heard you
put up somebody else's name."

"That was after we decided to have a list ready," said
Lewis. "Stop screaming at me."

"I'm going to do an exposé," shouted Friedan. "I'm
going to expose everyone. If it's the last thing I do, I'm
going to do it. I'm going to do it." She turned, walked off
to a group of women, and left Jane Lewis standing alone.

"It's like pushing marbles through a sieve," Gloria is
saying. Monday, opening day, and the N.W.P.C. is holding a caucus for women delegates to hear the Presidential candidates. Betty has publicly announced her drive
to run Chisholm for Vice-President. The ballroom of the

Carillon Hotel, packed full of boisterous, exuberant delegates, activists, and press, gives her suggestion a standing ovation; minutes later, it is hissing Chisholm with equal gusto for waffling on the California challenge. I am sitting next to Shirley MacLaine, McGovern's chief adviser on women's issues, and she is explaining to fellow delegate Marlo Thomas that McGovern will abandon the South Carolina challenge if there is any danger of its bringing up the procedural question of what constitutes a majority. McGovern, she is saying, plans to soft-pedal the challenge in his speech here—and here he is now, pushing through another standing ovation, beaming while he is graciously introduced by Liz Carpenter. "We know we wouldn't have been here if it hadn't been for you," she says. "George McGovern didn't talk about reform—he did something about it." The audience is McGovern's. "I am grateful for the introduction that all of you are here because of me," says the candidate rumored to be most in touch with women's issues. "But I really think the credit for that has to go to Adam instead. . . ." He pauses for the laugh and looks genuinely astonished when what he gets instead is a resounding hiss. "Can I recover if I say Adam and Eve?" he asks. Then he goes on to discuss the challenges, beginning with South Carolina. "On that challenge," he says, "you have my full and unequivocal support." Twelve hours later, the women find out that full and unequivocal support from George McGovern is considerably less than that.

"We were screwed," Debbie Leff is saying. Leff is press liaison for the N.W.P.C., and she is putting mildly what the McGovern forces did to the women. Monday night,

the caucus, under floor leader Bella Abzug, delivered
over 200 non-McGovern delegate votes on South Carolina—100 more than they had been told were necessary—
and then watched, incredulous, as the McGovern staff
panicked and pulled back its support. Tuesday night,
the fight over the abortion plank—which was referred
to as the "human-reproduction plank" because it never
once mentioned the word "abortion"—produced the most
emotional floor fight of the convention. The McGovern
people had been opposed to the plank because they
thought it would hurt his candidacy; at the last minute,
they produced a right-to-lifer to give a seconding speech,
a move they had promised the women they would not
make. "Because of that pledge," said Steinem, "we didn't
mention butchering women on kitchen tables in our
speeches, and then they have a speaker who's saying,
'Next thing you know, they'll be murdering old people.'"
Female members of the press lobbied for the plank. Male
delegates left their seats to allow women alternates to
vote. The movement split over whether to have a roll
call or simply a voice vote. At four in the morning, Bella
Abzug was screaming at Shirley MacLaine, and Steinem,
in tears, was confronting McGovern campaign manager
Gary Hart: "You promised us you would not take the low
road, you bastards." The roll call on the plank was held
largely at Betty Friedan's insistence. She and Martha
McKay of North Carolina were the only N.W.P.C. leaders
who were willing to take the risk; the rest thought the
roll call would be so badly defeated that it would be best
to avoid the humiliation. Friedan was in this case right
for the wrong reasons: "We have to find out who our enemies are," she said. Incredibly, the plank went down to a

thoroughly respectable defeat, 1572.80 against, 1101.37 for.

Thursday. A rumor is circulating that Gloria Steinem is at the Doral Hotel to speak with McGovern. I find her in the lobby. "I didn't see him," she says. "I don't want to see him." She is walking over to the Fontainebleau for a meeting; and on the way out of the Doral, Bob Anson, a former *Time* reporter, who interviewed her for a McGovern profile, says hello.

"At some point I'd like to talk to you about the socks," Gloria says.

"What do you mean?" asks Anson.

"You said in that article that I give him advice about socks and shirts. I don't talk to him about things like that. He listens to men about clothes."

Anson apologizes, claims he had nothing to do with the error, and as we leave the hotel, I suggest to Gloria that such incorrect facts stem from a kind of newsmagazine tidbit madness.

"That's not it," says Gloria. "It's just that if you're a woman, all they can think about your relationship with a politician is that you're either sleeping with him or advising him about clothes." We start walking up Collins Avenue, past lettuce-boycott petitioners and welfare-rights pamphleteers. "It's just so difficult," she says, crying now. I begin babbling—all the pressures on you, no private life, no sleep, no wonder you're upset. "It's not that," says Gloria. "It's just that they won't take us seriously." She wipes at her cheeks with her hand, and begins crying again. "And I'm just tired of being screwed, and being screwed by my friends. By George McGovern, whom I raised half the money for in his first campaign, wrote his speeches. I can see him. I can get in to see him. That's easy. But what would be the point? He just doesn't understand. We went to see him at one point about abortion, and the question of welfare came up. 'Why are you concerned about welfare?' he said. He didn't understand it was a women's issue." She paused. "They won't take us seriously. We're just walking wombs. And the television coverage. Teddy White and Eric Sevareid saying that now that the women are here, next thing there'll be a caucus of left-handed Lithuanians." She is still crying, and I try to offer some reassuring words, something, but everything I say is wrong; I have never cried over anything remotely political in my life, and I honestly have no idea of what to say.

And so Friday, at last, and it is over. Sissy Farenthold has made a triumphant, albeit symbolic, run for the Vice-Presidency and come in second; as a final irony, she was endorsed by Shirley Chisholm. Jean Westwood is the new chairperson of the Democratic National Committee, although she prefers to be called chairman. I am talking to Martha McKay. "I'm fifty-two years old," she is saying. "I've gotten to the point where I choose what I spend time on. Look at the situation in North Carolina. Forty-four percent of the black women who work are domestics. In the eastern part of the state, some are making fifteen dollars a week and totin'. You know what that is? That's taking home roast beef, and that's supposed to make up for the wages. We're talking about bread on the table. We're talking about women who are heads of households who can't get credit. They hook up with a man, he signs the credit agreement, they make the payments, and in the end he owns the house. When things like this are going on in the country, who's got time to get caught in the rock-crushing at the national level? I'm just so amazed that these gals fight like they do. It's so enervating."

November, 1972

Vaginal Politics

We have lived through the era when happiness was a warm puppy, and the era when happiness was a dry martini, and now we have come to the era when happiness is "knowing what your uterus looks like." For this slogan, and for what is perhaps the apotheosis of the do-it-yourself movement in America, we have the Los Angeles Self-Help Clinic to thank: this group of women has been sending its emissaries around the country with a large supply of plastic specula for sale and detailed instructions on how women can perform their own gynecological examinations and abortions. Some time ago, two of its representatives were in New York, and Ellen Frankfort, who covers health matters for the *Village Voice*, attended a session. What she saw makes the rest of the women's movement look like a bunch of old biddies at an American Legion Auxiliary cake sale:

"Carol, a woman from the . . . Clinic, slipped off her dungarees and underpants, borrowed somebody's coat and stretched it out on a long table, placed herself on top, and, with her legs bent at the knees, inserted a speculum into herself. Once the speculum was in place, her cervix was completely visible and each of the fifty women present took a flashlight and looked inside.

" 'Which part is the cervix? The tiny slit in the middle?'

" 'No, that's the os. The cervix is the round, doughnut-shaped part.' "

Following the eyewitness internal examination, Carol and her colleague spoke at length about medical ritual and how depersonalizing it is, right down to the drape women are given to cover their bodies; they suggested that women should instead take the drape and fling it to the ground. If the doctor replaces it, they suggest throwing it off again. And if he questions this behavior (and one can only wonder at a doctor who would not), they recommend telling him that California doctors have stopped draping. "And if you're in California, tell him that doctors in New York have stopped this strange custom." The evening ended with a description of the most radical self-help device of all: the period extractor, a syringe-and-tube contraption that allows a woman to remove her menstrual flow, all by herself, in five minutes; if she is pregnant, the embryo is sucked out instead. Color slides were shown: a woman at home, in street clothes, gave herself an early abortion using the device. "I hesitate to use the word 'revolutionary,' " Frankfort wrote of the event, "but no other word seems accurate. . . ."

Ellen Frankfort's report on this session is now reprinted as the opening of her new book, *Vaginal Politics* (Quadrangle Books). When I first read it in the *Voice*, I was shocked and incredulous. At the same time, it seemed obvious that at the rate things were going in the women's movement, within a few months the material

would not be surprising at all. Well, it has been over a
year since the Los Angeles Self-Help Clinic brought the
word to the East, and what they advocate is as shocking
and incredible as ever. I mean, it's awfully perplexing
that anyone would suggest throwing linens all over an
examination room when a simple verbal request would
probably do the trick. And when Frankfort informs us,
as she does at the end of her book, that "there are several groups of women who get together in New York City
and on their dining room tables or couches look at the
changes in the cervix," it is hard not to long for the days
when an evening with the girls meant bridge.

On the other hand . . .

On the other hand, the self-help movement and
the concern with health issues among women's groups
spring from a very real and not at all laughable dissatisfaction with the American medical establishment, and
most particularly with gynecologists. In New York, the
women's movement has turned this dissatisfaction to
concrete achievement in placing paid women counselors
in major abortion clinics and in working to lower rates
and change procedures at these clinics; in Boston, the
Women's Health Collective has produced a landmark
book, *Our Bodies, Our Selves*, a comprehensive compila-
tion of information about how the female body works.
But the animosity against doctors has also reached
the point where irresponsibility, not to mention hard-
core raunchiness, has replaced reason. When Frankfort asked Carol about the possible negative effects of
period extraction, her question was taken as a broad-
scale attack on feminism. The fact is that if doctors were
prescribing equipment as untested as these devices are,
equipment which clearly violates natural body func-

tions, the women's health movement would be outraged. It has been justifiably incensed that birth-control pills were mass-marketed after only three years' observation on a mere 132 women. The Los Angeles women are advocating a device that has not been tested at all for at-home use; in hospitals, it has been used safely, but by doctors, and primarily for early abortion. There is a horrifying fanaticism to all this, and it springs not just from the zeal to avoid doctors entirely, but from something far more serious. For some time, various scientists have been attacking women's liberation by insisting that because of menstruation, women are unfit for just about everything several days a month. In a way, the Los Angeles women are supporting this assertion in their use of period extraction for non-abortion purposes; what they are saying, in effect, is, yes, it *is* awful, it is truly a curse, and here is a way to be done with it in five minutes. I am not one of those women who are into "blood and birth and death," to quote Joan Didion's rather extraordinary and puzzling definition of what it means to be female, but I do think that the desire to eliminate the first of these functions springs from a self-hate that is precisely parallel to the male fear of blood that underlies so many primitive taboos toward women.

In any event, the extremist fringe of the self-help movement in no way invalidates the legitimate case women have against gynecologists. These doctors are undoubtedly blamed for a great deal that is not their fault; they are, after all, dealing in reproductive and sexual areas, two of the most sensitive and emotionally charged for women. Still, I have dozens of friends who have been mis-diagnosed, mis-medicated, mistreated and misinformed by them, and every week, it seems,

I hear a new gynecological atrocity tale. A friend who asks specifically not to be sedated during childbirth is sedated. Another friend who has a simple infection is treated instead for gonorrhea, and develops a serious infection as a side effect of the penicillin. Another woman tells of going to see her doctor one month after he has delivered her first child, a deformed baby, born dead. His first question: "Why haven't you been to see me in two years?" Beyond all this, there are the tales of pure insensitivity to psychological problems, impatience with questions, preachy puritanism particularly toward single women, and, for married women, little speeches on the need to reproduce. My usual reaction to these stories is to take a feminist line, blame it all on complicated sexism or simple misogyny. But what Ellen Frankfort has managed to do in *Vaginal Politics*—and what makes her book quite remarkable—is to broaden women's health issues far beyond such narrow analyses. "The mystique of the doctor, profound as it is, is not the only negative feature of the present health system," she writes. "Unfortunately, the women from the Los Angeles Self-Help Clinic . . . seemed to be focusing mainly on this aspect of the problem while ignoring the need for institutional change. Feminist politics cannot be divorced from other political realities, such as health care and safety."

The problems women face with doctors stem not just from their own abysmal lack of knowledge about their bodies, and not just from female conditioning toward male authority figures. (The classic female dependency on the obstetrician, Frankfort notes, transfers at childbirth to dependency on the pediatrician, all this "in perfect mimicry of the dependency relationship of marital roles.") They stem also from inequities in the health system and from the way doctors are educated. The brutalizing, impersonal training medical students receive prepares them perfectly to turn around and treat their patients in exactly the same way: as infants. Writes Frankfort: "We feel hesitant to question their procedures, their fees or their hours, and often we're simply grateful that we're able to see them at all, particularly if they're well recommended." My sister-in-law, who is pregnant, told me the other day that she was afraid to bother her gynecologist with questions for fear of "getting on his wrong side." As Frankfort points out: "The fear that a patient will be punished unless he or she is totally submissive reveals a profound distrust of the people in control of our bodies." (I have, I should point out, exactly the same fears about my lawyer, my accountant, and my maid. Generally speaking, none of us is terribly good at being an employer.)

Vaginal Politics covers a wide range of health subjects: the New York abortion scene, drugs, psychoanalysis, breast cancer, venereal disease, the law, the growth of the consumer health movement in America. At times, the tone is indignant to the point of heavy-handedness. Also, I caught several factual errors. But Frankfort has written with contagious energy and extraordinary vitality; without exaggeration, her book is among the most basic and important written about women's issues, and I hope it will not be overlooked now that the more faddish women's books have had their day.

The tendency in reviewing this book, of course, is to stress the more outlandish and radical aspects of the health movement, but Frankfort's real strength lies in her painstaking accumulation of political incidents.

There is the case of Shirley Wheeler, who had an abortion and was convicted for manslaughter under an 1868
Florida law. The condition of her probation: marry the
man she lives with, or return to her parents in North
Carolina. If she refused, if she, for example, lived instead
with a woman, her parole would be rescinded and she
would be sent to jail. There are the guidelines for sterilization proposed by the American College of Obstetri-
cians and Gynecologists: no woman can be sterilized
unless her age multiplied by the number of children she
has borne is 120 or more. Writes Frankfort: "The logic
behind this sliding scale of reproductive output has it
that in order to earn her right to not have children, a
woman must first produce some." For men, under the
same guidelines, voluntary sterilization is available to
anyone over twenty-one. Period. Another incident in
the book, and one that is particularly compelling, is the
case of Dr. Joseph Goldzieher, who is at the Southwest
Foundation for Research and Education in San Antonio,
Texas. Some years ago, Dr. Goldzieher got to wondering
whether one reason birth-control pills prevent concep-
tion might simply be psychological, and he decided to
run a test to see. There were 398 women, most of them
Chicanos, coming to the clinic, and one fifth of them were
given placebos instead of contraceptives. Within a year,
six of the women, all mothers of at least three other
children, had given birth. Writes Frankfort: "The ethics of a researcher who considers an unwanted child an
unfortunate 'side effect' of an experimenter's curiosity
needs no further commentary. However, what should be
pointed out . . . is that not only does Dr. Goldzieher work
at a research institute where poor nonwhite women are
selected for experimentation, but he is also a consultant

to several drug companies. In fact, the experiment was sponsored by Syntex, a leading pill manufacturer. . . ."

And so the doctors work for the drug companies and prescribe accordingly, the hospitals take advantage of the poor, the laws are antiquated, it goes on and on. Knowing what your uterus looks like can't hurt, I suppose, and knowing more about your body can only help, but it seems a shame that so much more energy is being directed into this sort of contemplation and so little into changing the political structure. There is a tendency throughout the movement to overindulge in confession, to elevate The Rap to a religious end in itself, to reach a point where self-knowledge dissolves into high-grade narcissism. I know that the pendulum often has to swing a few degrees in the wrong direction before righting itself, but it does get wearing sometimes waiting for the center to catch hold.

December, 1972

Bernice Gera, First Lady Umpire

Somewhere in the back of Bernice Gera's closet, along with her face mask and chest protector and simple spiked shoes, is a plain blue man's suit hanging in a plastic bag. The suit cost $29 off the rack, plus a few dollars for shortening the sleeves and pants legs, but if you ask Bernice Gera a question about that suit—where she bought it, for example, or whether she ever takes it out and looks it over—her eyes widen and then blink, hard, and she explains, very slowly so that you will not fail to understand, that she prefers not to think about the suit, or the shoes, or the shirt and tie she wore with it one summer night last year, when she umpired what was her first and last professional baseball game, a seven-inning event in Geneva, New York, in the New York–Pennsylvania Class A League.

It took four years for Bernice Gera to walk onto that ball field, four years of legal battles for the right to stand in the shadow of an "Enjoy Silver Floss Sauerkraut" sign while the crowd cheered and young girls waved sheets reading "Right On, Bernice!" and the manager of the Geneva Phillies welcomed her to the game. "On behalf of professional baseball," he said, "we say good luck and

God bless you in your chosen profession." And the band played and the spotlights shone and all three networks recorded the event. Bernice Gera had become the first woman in the 133-year history of the sport to umpire a professional baseball game.

I should say, at this point, that I am utterly baffled as to why any woman would want to get into professional baseball, much less work as an umpire in it. Once I read an article in *Fact* magazine that claimed that men who were umpires secretly wanted to be mother figures; that level of idiotic analysis is, as far as I am concerned, about what the game and the profession deserve. But beyond that, I cannot understand any woman's wanting to be the first woman to do anything. I read about those who do—there is one in today's newspaper, a woman who is suing the State of Colorado for the right to work on a team digging a tunnel through the Rocky Mountains—and after I get through puzzling at the strange desires people have, awe sets in. I think of the ridicule and abuse that woman will undergo, of the loneliness she will suffer if she gets the job, of the role she will assume as a freak, of the smarmy and inevitable questions that will be raised about her heterosexuality, of the derision and smug satisfaction that will follow if she makes a mistake, or breaks down under pressure, or quits. It is a devastating burden and I could not take it, could not be a pioneer, a Symbol of Something Greater. Once I was the first woman to deposit $500 in a bank that was giving out toasters that day, and I found even that an uncomfortable responsibility. The point of all this, though, is Bernice Gera, and the point of Bernice Gera is that Bernice Gera failed to play out the role. In her first game, she made a mistake. And broke down under pressure.

And couldn't take it. And quit. Which was not the way
it was supposed to happen: instead, she was supposed
to have been tougher and stronger and better than any
umpire in baseball and end up a grim stone bust in the
Cooperstown Hall of Fame. Bernice Gera turned out to
be only human, after all, which is not a luxury pioneers
are allowed. At the time, I thought it was all hideously
ironic and even a little funny; a few months later, I got
to wondering what had really happened and what was
happening to Mrs. Gera now, now that she had blown
her modest deferred dream.

Bernice Gera lives in a three-room walk-up apartment in Queens. In it there is a candle shaped like a
softball, an ashtray shaped like a mitt, a lighter shaped
like a bat, a crocheted toaster cover shaped like a doll
wearing a baseball cap, an arrangement of dried flowers containing a baseball, powder puffs, and a small
statue of Mickey Mouse holding a bat. On the wall is
a very large color photograph of Mrs. Gera in uniform
holding a face mask, and a few feet away hangs a poem
that reads: "Dear God, Last night I did pray/That You
would let me in the game today./And if the guys yell
and scream,/Please, God, tell them You're the captain
of the team." All the available shelf space is crammed
with trophies and plaques; there must be forty or fifty
of them, some for bowling (she averages 165) but most
for baseball, for her career on a women's softball team in
Detroit, and for her charity batting exhibitions against
people like Roger Maris and Sid Gordon. "I can hit the
long ball," she says, and she can, some 350 feet. There
is also a framed clipping of an old Ripley's Believe It Or
Not, a syndicated feature that has come a long way since
the days when it printed items that were remotely unbe-

lievable. "Believe It Or Not," it reads, "a New York City housewife has won 300 large dolls for needy youngsters living at the children's shelter of the Queensboro Society for the Prevention of Cruelty to Children by her skill at throwing a baseball at amusement parks."

Mrs. Gera is a short, slightly chunky woman who wears white socks and loafers; her short blondish-brown hair is curled and lacquered. Around her neck is a gold charm decorated with a bat, mitt, and pearl baseball which she designed and had made up by a local jeweler. Her voice is flat and unanimated, unless, of course, she is talking about baseball: she can describe, exultantly, one of the happiest days of her life, when she had a tooth extracted and was able to stay home from work to see the Pirates win the World Series in 1960. Bernice Gera is, more than anything, a fan, an unabashed, adoring fan, and her obsession with baseball dates back to her childhood, when she played with her older brothers on a sandlot in the Pennsylvania mining town where she was raised. "I have loved, eaten, and lived baseball since I was eight years old," she says. "Put yourself in my shoes. Say you loved baseball. If you love horses, you can be a jockey. If you love golf or swimming, look at Babe Didrikson and Gertrude Ederle. These are great people and they had an ability. I had it with baseball. What could I do? I couldn't play. So you write letters, begging for a job, any job, and you keep this up for years and years. There had to be a way for me. So I decided to take up a trade. I decided to take up umpiring."

In June, 1967, Mrs. Gera enrolled as a student at the National Sports Academy in West Palm Beach, Florida, a school run by an old-timer named Jim Finley for ballplayers and umpires. The Associated Press sent a

reporter to cover Mrs. Gera's education, and Finley said
she was coming along just fine. "She had the habit of
carrying on conversations with the players," said Finley, "but we broke that by giving her push-ups. . . . I
had expected a tomboy when she signed up, but Bernice is every bit a girl." A few months after her graduation from the Academy, magna cum laude, Mrs. Gera
commented good-naturedly on her experience there. "I
didn't have too much trouble," she said. "The chest protector didn't fit very well. Those things aren't made for
women. And the players tried to give me a hard time."
(Little jokes about Mrs. Gera's chest protector were to
become the leitmotiv of her saga.) Years passed before
Mrs. Gera confessed that the school had actually been
a nightmare. "It was a horrible, lonely experience," she
said. "They all thought there was something wrong with
me." At night, in the dormitory, the men threw beer cans
and bottles at her bedroom door. On the field, the players hazed her, threw extra balls into the game during
a play, spit tobacco juice on her shoes, cursed to try to
shake her up. She would call a runner safe and he would
snarl, "Bad call. I was out." Said Mrs. Gera: "When you
begin, you take an awful lot of abuse. They make you, to
prepare you for the future. I think they overdid it with
me. Tobacco juice. That was unnecessary. It all hinged on
whether I could take it. I took it. But after, I'd go home
and cry like a baby."

A diploma in umpiring was worth nothing at all when
it came to getting a job, and so in 1968 Mrs. Gera began
the first of several lawsuits against professional baseball. Her lawyer, who served without fee, was a New York
politician named Mario Biaggi, who called press conference after press conference to announce action after

action. Finally, in 1969, Mrs. Gera was given a contract by the New York–Pennsylvania Class A League promising her $200 in wages, $300 in expenses, and five cents a mile for a month, beginning with a twilight doubleheader August 1. The sports pages were full of pictures of Mrs. Gera, thumbs up, victorious. But on July 31, the president of the National Association of Professional Baseball Leagues invalidated the contract by refusing to sign it. Mrs. Gera was heartbroken, but she confined her reaction to a string of sports metaphors: "I guess I just can't get to first base. . . . It's a strikeout but I will come up again. The game is not over."

The lawsuit continued. There was a hearing at the New York State Human Rights Commission, where George Leisure, attorney for the baseball interests, said that Mrs. Gera was publicity mad and that furthermore she did not meet any of the physical requirements for being an umpire. Umpires, he said, should be five feet ten inches tall, and weigh 170 pounds. "Being of the male sex is a bona-fide qualification for being a professional umpire," said Leisure. In November, 1970, the Human Rights Commission held that the National League discriminated not only against women but against men belonging to short ethnic groups and would have to "establish new physical standards which shall have a reasonable relation to the requirements of the duties of an umpire." The League promptly appealed the decision, and the legal process dragged on.

Maury Allen of the *New York Post* went into the locker room of the New York Mets at one point during Mrs. Gera's years in chancery and asked some of the ballplayers how they felt about her. He recorded, in response, a number of attempted witticisms about her chest protector, along with a predictable but nonetheless interesting series of antediluvian remarks. "I read the stories about her and she said that she expected people would call her a 'dumb broad,' " said Jerry Koosman. "Hell, that's the nicest thing people would call her. What do you think she'd hear when a batter hit a line drive off a pitcher's cup?" Said Ron Swoboda: "She'd have fifty guys yelling at her in language she wouldn't believe. If she heard those dirty words and didn't react, then they would have to give her a hormone test."

Bernice Gera waited almost two years for the State Court of Appeals to uphold the Human Rights Commission ruling; finally, in the spring of 1972, she once again signed a contract with the New York–Pennsylvania League. In late June, having allowed to reporters that she was "grateful to God and grateful to baseball," she drove to Geneva, New York, for her début. There was a banquet Thursday night and she was cheered over roast chicken. She was ecstatic. "I was in baseball," Mrs. Gera recalled. "I can't tell you. I was on top of the world. And then, the bubble burst."

On Friday, there was a meeting of the League umpires. "That meeting," Mrs. Gera said. "It was like, if you had a group of people in a room and they just ignored you. How can I express it? They made it obvious they didn't want me. How would you feel? You're supposed to work your signals out with your partner. You're a team. You have to know what he's going to do. But my partner wouldn't talk to me. I sat there for six hours. A lot of other things went on that I don't want to discuss because I'm going to write about it someday. I should have realized if they fought me in court they weren't going to welcome me, but I never thought they would do that to me. That was the only way they could get to me, through the other umpires. If they won't work with you, you can't make it."

Saturday night, when Bernice Gera walked out onto the field in her $29 suit, she had come to a decision. She would leave baseball if her fellow umpire would not tell her his signals. Her partner, a lanky young man named Doug Hartmayer, who was also making his professional début, refused even to acknowledge her presence. But the crowd loved her, applauded her emphatic calls, and was amused by her practically perpetual motion. Then, in the fourth inning, a member of the Auburn Phillies came into second base and Mrs. Gera, in an uncharacteristically unemphatic move, ventured a safe call. Seconds later, she realized he was out in a force play, and brought her fist up. The manager of the Auburn team, Nolan Campbell, who had said before the game that Mrs. Gera was "going to have one heck of a time taking the abuse," ran out onto the field and began to shout and chase after her. She ejected him from the game. Campbell was furious. "She admitted she made a mistake," he said later. "I told her, that's two mistakes. The first one was putting on a uniform."

When the game ended, Bernice Gera, trailed by camera crews and a dozen reporters, strode into the clubhouse and announced, "I've just resigned from baseball." Then she wheeled around, left the field, and burst into tears in the back of a friend's car. NBC's Dick Schaap asked Doug Hartmayer how he felt about her quitting. "I was glad," said Hartmayer. "Her job wasn't bad except she changed that call at second base, which is a cardinal sin in baseball." As Schaap later noted, "She committed the cardinal sin of baseball—she admitted she made a mistake."

It is hard to believe that things would not have worked out had Bernice Gera hung in there, stayed on, borne up somehow. It is hard to believe, too, that she could not have been helped by some real support from the women's movement. In any event, Mrs. Gera and the movement did not join forces until three weeks after her debacle, when she attended a meeting at the grubby New York headquarters of the National Organization for Women. "I'm happy to be here with all you girls— I mean women," said Mrs. Gera, and plunged into her new rhetoric. She spoke of the "calculated harassment by the sexist operators who control baseball." She hinted at a boycott of the game. She defended changing her call, quoting from the *Baseball Manual*, a publication that seems to provide the messages in fortune cookies: "To right a wrong is honorable. Such an action will win you respect."

"People are saying I'm a quitter, but I'm not," she said, "not after what baseball put me through. Someone else might have quit earlier but I stayed with it. I would have shined a ballplayer's shoes. That's how much I like baseball."

And so it is over, and Bernice Gera has, if not a profession, a title. She is Bernice Gera, First Lady Umpire. That is how she signs autographs and that is how she is identified at the occasional events she is invited to attend. Bernice Gera, First Lady Umpire, modeled at a fashion show at Alexander's department store, along with several other women of achievement. Bernice Gera, First Lady Umpire, umpired a CBS softball game at Grossinger's and was third-base coach for the wives of the Atlanta Braves at an exhibition game. Bernice Gera, First Lady Umpire, sits on a couch in her Queens apartment and looks back on it all. "People say to me, you quit," she said. "I heard some reports back that I closed the door for all women, that I put women's lib back years. How could I close a door? I was the first woman in baseball. What did I do—close doors or open doors?" It is an interesting question, really, but Bernice Gera prefers not to hear the answer or dwell on the past or deal with what actually happened. "I'm in contact with baseball all the time," she says. "Don't count me out. I expect to be in baseball next year."

January, 1973

Deep Throat

The sign on the door says "Film Productions," and it all couldn't seem blander. The receptionist is a plump, pleasant woman named Frances, who looks like any receptionist in any office. But this is not, Frances assures me, any office. "No way," she says. "I used to work at the *Catholic News*. That was interesting. Then I worked at an ad agency. We had the Rheingold account and Nat 'King' Cole used to come in all the time. That was interesting. But *this* is *really* interesting." This, as it happens, is the office which produced the most successful pornographic film in the short, recent history of mass-market pornographic films. *Deep Throat*, as I write, is currently in its twenty-second record-breaking week at "the mature World Theatre" on Times Square, and is thirty-seventh on the list of *Variety*'s top grossers, having so far taken in some $1,500,000. The film cost $40,000 to make, and its profits are such that Frank Yablans of Paramount Pictures, who speaks in sentences that sound suspiciously like *Variety* headlines, calls it "The *Godfather* of the sex pix."

I am here at the offices of Film Productions because one week ago, on one of those evenings when it was almost impossible to find a movie someone in the group had not seen, we ended up in a packed theatre watching the 7:30 show of *Deep Throat*, ended up there having read in Suzy Knickerbocker's column that Mike Nichols had seen it three times and having heard, from friends, that it was not only the best film of its kind but actually funny. *Screw* magazine had given it 100 points on the Peter Meter. There was an interview with the star of the film, one Miss Linda Lovelace, in *Women's Wear Daily*—"I'm just a simple girl who likes to go to swinging parties and nudist colonies," she said—and a column by Pete Hamill in *New York* magazine. In short, there was an overwhelming amount of conversation and column space concerning the film; not to have seen it seemed somehow . . . derelict.

The plot of *Deep Throat*—that it has one at all is considered a breakthrough of a sort—concerns a young woman, Linda Lovelace playing herself, who cannot find sexual satisfaction through intercourse. "I want to hear bells ringing, dams bursting, rockets exploding," she says. She goes to a doctor and he discovers that her problem is simply that her clitoris is in her throat. (Ah, yes, the famous clitoris-in-the-throat syndrome.) Once diagnosed, she embarks on an earnest program of compensatory behavior—I should say here that her abilities have mainly to do with the fact that, like circus sword-swallowers, she has learned to control her throat muscles to the point where she seems to have no gag reflex whatsoever—and before long, dams burst and rockets explode.

"I do not know what their reasonings were or why," Lou Perry is saying, "but every top motion-picture company in the United States has called us and asked to borrow a print for the weekend." Perry is the producer of *Deep Throat*. He is thirty-five years old, dark-haired, a bit paunchy, and until all this began to happen he was Lou Perino. He is sitting in his office at Film Productions in the midst of what passes for a crisis in the sex-pix business: Hugh Hefner's aide has just called to request a print of *Deep Throat* for Hefner's personal film collection, and all the available prints are in use. "Look," Perry is saying to a tattooed person named Vinny, who works for him, "call Fort Lee. Call Atlanta. This is a very important thing. *Playboy* is giving us a three-page spread in the February issue. We gotta find a print." There are other things on Perry's mind—one is an impending trial on the obscenity of the *Deep Throat* advertising; another is the forthcoming sequel, *Deep Throat II*, which is about to go into production with a $100,000 budget; and a third is the Los Angeles premiere of *Deep Throat*, to be held at the Hollywood Cat in two weeks, complete with searchlights and Linda Lovelace herself. "She's going to do some radio interviews out there," says Perry, "and we think maybe Johnny Carson."

Exactly what Perry was doing prior to entering the pornographic film business he prefers not to say, but he is perfectly willing to tell the story of his big break. "How I got into this," he says, "is I lent—I mean, I invested money in a company that went bankrupt that was into this. We then made two pictures. One was *Sex U.S.A.* The other was called *This Film is All About . . .* That's right. Blank. The original title was going to be a four-letter word, but we realized no newspaper would take the ad. New York papers won't even take the word 'Sex' on movies like this. To give you a for instance, *Sex U.S.A.* in the *Daily News* was printed *Xex U.S.A.* Both these films were documentaries, about events that were happening, sex shows, interviews with people about what did they think about sex shows. *Sex* cost about twelve to fifteen thousand dollars. So far, it's grossed six hundred thousand. The way *Deep Throat* came about was we decided to do another film. We didn't want to do a documentary. There was this film, *Mona*, that we had seen. It was different. It had a story. It was done with what you would call improvisational. We thought of doing possibly the same exact thing, so we decided, let's pick out a subject.

"To be honest about it, we couldn't come up with anything too good. We were just going to do another *Mona*. Then, somehow, Jerry Damiano, the writer and director, he seen this girl at a party. I assume he got fixed up with her. And he came in the next day and he said as he was driving over the Fifty-ninth Street Bridge he was thinking of her. What she had done was fantastic. He's never seen anybody do like she did. So he thought, let's make a picture about this girl.

"We started out with a fifteen-thousand-dollar picture, and then it went up to twenty-two thousand and then thirty thousand and then we said, oh the hell with it, let's go all the way. By the time we finished, we spent forty thousand. I was very worried. How would it be accepted? Before we released it, we had a screening. Personal friends, exhibitors, sub-distributors. I tell you, I was on pins and needles as to what their reaction would be. Well, I've been to many X-rated movie screenings, but this picture—in the screening, when she first gives throat, four or five of the men in the audience said, 'Hurray,' and by the end of the sequence there were fifteen guys standing and they went into a very big applause.

At that point, we knew we had a hit on our hands. *Screw* reviewed it a week before it opened and said it was the best porn film ever made. That had a lot to do with what happened. We opened up against *Cabaret* and the sequel to *Shaft*, and we outgrossed both of them."

It may be a terrible mistake to take *Deep Throat* and its success seriously. These things may just happen. Their success may not mean a thing. The publicity machine marches on, and all that. But I can't help thinking that pornography that has this sort of impact must have some significance. I have seen a lot of stag films in my life—well, that's not true; I've seen about five or six—and although most of them were raunchy, a few were also sweet and innocent and actually erotic. *Deep Throat*, on the other hand, is one of the most unpleasant, disturbing films I have ever seen—it is not just anti-female but anti-sexual as well. I walked into the World Theatre feeling thoroughly unshockable— after all, I can toss off phrases like "split beaver" with almost devil-may-care abandon—and I came out of the theatre a quivering fanatic. Give me the goriest Peckinpah any day. There is a scene in *Deep Throat*, for example, where a man inserts a hollow glass dildo inside Miss Lovelace, fills it with Coca-Cola, and drinks it with a surgical straw—the audience was bursting with nervous laughter, while I sat through it literally faint. All I could think about was what would happen if the glass broke. I always cringe when I read reviews of this sort—crazy feminists carrying on, criticizing nonpolitical films in political terms—but as I sat through the film I was swept away in a bromidic wave of movement rhetoric. "Demeaning to women," I wailed as we walked away from the theatre. "Degrading to women." I began muttering about the clitoris backlash. The men I was with pretended they did not know me, and then, when I persisted in addressing my mutterings to them, they assured me that I was overreacting, that it was just a movie and that they hadn't even been turned on by it. But I refused to calm down. "Look, Nora," said one of them, playing what I suppose he thought was his trump card by appealing to my sense of humor, "there's one thing you have to admit. The scene with the Coca-Cola was hilarious."

Exactly what Linda Lovelace did for a living before becoming the first superstar of her kind is something she prefers not to be explicit about. She will say, though, that she is twenty-one years old, from Bryan, Texas, and that she decided to come to New York almost two years ago. She had met a man she calls J.R., a former Marine, who is now her manager and who taught her the trick of relaxing her throat muscles, and the two of them set off for the big city together. "I was just going to get a job as a topless dancer or something," said Miss Lovelace. "I really didn't think what happened would happen." A few months after arriving in New York, Linda and J.R. went to a party. "J.R. met Jerry Damiano and they got to talking about what I could do," said Miss Lovelace. "And when he saw me, he liked me and the way I looked and he got carried away. The next day he was riding to work across the Brooklyn Bridge and he decided on the whole script for the movie."

Everything that has happened to Linda Lovelace since then is kind of a goof. Making the film was kind of a goof. Its success is kind of a goof. Being recognized in public is kind of a goof. "I totally enjoyed myself making the movie and all of a sudden I'm what they call a superstar," she says. "It's kind of a goof." I am talking to Miss Lovelace long distance—she is living in Texas with J.R.—and we are having a conversation that leaves something to be desired. For instance, Linda Lovelace's idea of candor is to insist that her name really is Linda Lovelace, and her idea of a clever response to the question of whether she has any idiosyncrasies is to say, "I swallow well." As if all this were not enough, it turns out that Linda Lovelace thinks the scene with the Coca-Cola and glass dildo was even funnier than my friend thinks it is. "Actually," she says, "I think the funniest thing that happened when we were shooting was when we did that scene. They were going to shoot a little bit more, but someone said something and I started laughing and the glass dildo went flying into the air and cracked into a million pieces." I am not sure what I expected from this interview—I honestly did not expect Linda Lovelace to be Jane Fonda in *Klute*, nor did I think that she would, as a result of our conversation, see the light and leave the pornographic film business forever. On the other hand, I did not expect what is happening, which is that we seem to be spending as much time talking about me and what Miss Lovelace clearly thinks of as my problems as we are about her and what I clearly think of as her problems. As in this exchange:

"How do you feel about being recognized on the street?" I ask.

"It's kind of a goof," she says.

"But," I say, "Lou Perry told me that it made you a little nervous."

"Why should it make me nervous?"

"I don't know," I say. "I might be nervous if someone

recognized me as the star of a pornographic film. Especially in the Times Square area."

"Would you be nervous," she asks, "if you walked around nude and strangers saw you?"

"Yes."

"See? I wouldn't."

Or in this exchange:

"Why do you shave off your pubic hair in the film?" I ask.

"I always do," Linda Lovelace replies. "I like it."

"But why do you do it?"

"Well," she says, "it's kinda hot in Texas."

That stops me for a second. "Well," I say, "I think it's weird."

"Weird? Why?"

"Well, I don't know anyone who does that."

"Now you do," says Linda Lovelace.

"I don't have any inhibitions about sex," she says. "I just hope that everybody who goes to see the film enjoys it and maybe learns something from it." Like what? "I don't know. Enjoys their sex life better. Maybe loses some of their inhibitions." In the meantime, Linda Lovelace is about to make the sequel. She is under exclusive contract to Film Productions and receives $250 a week when she isn't working and $10,000 plus a piece of the profits for the next film. Does she want to make regular films as well as pornographic films? "Look," she says, "you make a separation between movies and this kind of movie. To me, it's just a movie, like all other movies. Only it has some much better things in it." Like what? "Like me," says Linda Lovelace.

And there we are. Linda Lovelace, "just a simple girl who likes to go to swinging parties and nudist colonies."

And me, a hung-up, uptight, middle-class, inhibited, possibly puritanical feminist who lost her sense of humor at a skin flick. It's not exactly the self-image I had in mind, but I can handle it.

February, 1973

On Consciousness-Raising

I try to remember exactly what the lie was that I made up to tell friends a year ago, when I joined a consciousness-raising group. They would ask me why I had done it, why I had gotten into something like that—a group, an actual organized activity—and I think what I tended to reply was that I didn't see how I could write about women and the women's movement *without* joining a group. Consciousness-raising, according to all the literature, is fundamental to the women's movement and the feminist experience, blah blah blah; it seemed important to me to find out just what the process was about. I said all this as if I were joining something educational, or something that was going to happen to me, as opposed to something I would actively participate in. The disinterested observer, and all that. As I say, this was a lie. The real reason I joined had to do with my marriage.

At our first meeting, we all went around the room explaining why each of us had come. For all intents and purposes, all eight of us were married—the one exception had been living with a man for several years—and, as it turned out, we were all there because of our marriages. Most of the women said that they hoped the group would help them find ways to make their marriages better. Margo, who was in no better shape than the rest of us but tended to have faith in theatrical solutions, said that what she was interested in from the group was mischievous pranks. When we all looked blank, she explained that what she meant by her catchy little phrase was devising experiments like putting hot fudge on your nipples to perk up your sex life. It came around to me, my turn to explain why I was there. I said that I, too, hoped that the group would help me find a way to make my marriage better, but that it was just as likely that I was looking to the group for help in making it worse.

My consciousness-raising group is still going on. Every Monday night it meets, somewhere in Greenwich Village, and it drinks a lot of red wine and eats a lot of cheese. A friend of mine who is in it tells me that at the last meeting, each of the women took her turn to explain, in considerable detail, what she was planning to stuff her Thanksgiving turkey with. I no longer go to the group, for a variety of reasons, the main one being that I don't think the process works. Well, let me put that less dogmatically and more explicitly—this particular group did not work for me. I don't mean that I wasn't able to attain the exact goal I set for myself: in the six months I spent in the group, my marriage went through an incredibly rough period. But that's not what I mean when I say it didn't work.

I should point out here that consciousness-raising was never devised for the explicit purpose of saving or wrecking marriages. It happens to be quite good at the latter, for reasons I would like to go into further on, but it is intended to do something broader and more political—"to develop personal sensitivity to the various levels and forms that the oppression takes in our daily lives; to build group intimacy and thus group unity, the foundations of true internal democracy; to break down in our heads the barrier between 'private' and 'public' (the 'personal' and the 'political'), in itself one of the deepest aspects of our oppression." Those lines are quoted from a mimeographed set of guidelines which were worked out by the New York Radical Feminists and which were read at our group's first meeting, along with a set of rules: each woman must speak from personal experience, the group has no leader, each member takes her turn going around the circle, no conclusions are to be drawn until each woman has spoken, no woman is to challenge another woman's experience. I do not have any idea of what happens in other groups. It took ours just over two hours to break every one of the rules, and just over two months to abandon the guidelines altogether.

In the beginning, none of this seemed terribly important. I loved consciousness-raising. Really loved it. The process sets off a kind of emotional rush, almost a high. There is so much confession, so much support, so much apparent sisterhood. At each meeting, we would choose a topic—mothers, success, sex, femininity, and orgasms were a few we took on at the start—and it was really like being part of a novel unfolding, as every week the character of each woman became clearer and more detailed. There were tears. There were what seemed like flashes of insight. There were cast changes: two women dropped out of the group because their husbands insisted they do so; there were two new members. It all seemed heady, and fun, and yes, voyeuristic, and after every meeting I think each of us felt a kind of pride and relief, not the

kind you're supposed to feel, some sort of high-principled
feminist consciousness or other—we never had that—
but the well-I'm-not-as-bad-off-as-I-thought sort of feeling. Women who were making it with their husbands
only once or twice a week found there were women who
made it with their husbands only once or twice a month.
And so forth.

In the autumn, 1972, *American Scholar* there is a
panel discussion on women by several notable women
writers, followed by a far more interesting commentary by Patricia McLaughlin in which she mentions
consciousness-raising. The problem with it, she says,
"is that discoveries are made, yes. ('You feel that way?
I thought only *I* felt like that.') But what is one to do
with them? Discoveries have reverberations. A new idea
about oneself or some aspect of one's relation to others
unsettles all one's other ideas, even the superficially
unrelated ones. No matter how slightly, it shifts one's
entire orientation. And somewhere along the line of
consequences, it changes one's behavior." All that may
well have happened in Patricia McLaughlin's group, but
it did not happen in mine. No one's behavior changed;
quite the opposite occurred. It almost seemed as if our
patterns were reinforced through the group process. The
tendency among us was always to side with the woman
in the group against her husband, to refuse to see the
part both partners usually play in marital problems, to
refrain even from asking the woman what *she* might
be doing to make things difficult. And as for the discoveries—ah, the discoveries, guaranteed or your money
back—even those had very little impact. In a different time or a different place or under different circumstances, things might have worked out exactly as they're

supposed to. Three or four years ago, say—it must have been electrifying for women to get together and find, for example, that none of them could deal well with anger, or that few of them were having vaginal orgasms, or whatever. In Dubuque, say—perhaps in places like that, when housewives meet for this sort of thing, discoveries pop faster than corn, and women who have never worked go out and find jobs, women who have never shared household duties refuse to wash the dishes, or some such. Had we been single, say, or completely happy with our marriages. . . . But we were all married, living in New York, in 1972. We had read the movement literature. Almost all of us had careers. We were much too sophisticated—or so we thought—to waste time discussing hard-core movement concepts like "the various levels and forms that the oppression takes in our daily lives." What we wanted to talk about was men.

And so, ultimately, it all settled into a running soap opera, with new episodes on the same theme every week. Barbara and Peter, Episode 13 of the Barbara Is Uninhibited and Peter Is a Drag Show: this week Barbara and Peter went to a party and Barbara pulled down her pants and mooned the guests and Peter was furious. Joanna and Dave, Episode 19 of the Will Joanna Ever Get Dave to Share the Household Duties Show: this week Joanna refused to get out of bed and change the channel and Dave hit her and she threatened to kill herself. Claire and Herbie in the Claire Has Sexual Boredom but Loves Her Husband Show: this week a man in the office Claire has the hots for put his hand on her leg while they were having a drink at P. J. Clarke's, but it was time to go home and feed the children and she never did find out whether it was significant or an accident.

And there was also me, with a brand-new episode in my series; and week after week, I felt more and more support from the group and more and more despair about a solution.

A couple of weeks ago, I went to hear Midge Decter speak before the Women's National Book Association. Decter has just published a long, almost unreadable attack on women's liberation and she has been justifiably creamed for it by the critics. The audience at the W.N.B.A. was no more responsive to her, and one of the women in it, in what I suspect was an attempt to make Decter lose even more of her credibility than she already had, asked her what she thought of consciousness-raising. "Consciousness-raising groups are of a piece with a whole cultural pattern that has been growing up," Decter replied. "This pattern begins with the term 'rapping'—which is a process in which people in groups pretend that they are not simply self-absorbed because they are talking to each other." There was a long hiss on that line, but it did not stop Decter. "I personally know of three marriages that broke up because of consciousness-raising," she said.

A year ago, I would have joined the general disdain that greeted that remark. Even now, it kills me to admit that anything Midge Decter says might just possibly be true. But I'm afraid she has a point. Unlike her, I do not consider it a blanket tragedy if a marriage breaks up; several of the marriages I know of that ended after the women entered consciousness-raising would have ended anyway; the breakups cannot really be laid to the groups, and both parties are better off. On the other hand, it seems unquestionably true that many groups tend to get into marriage counseling, and that the process itself tends to lead to exits rather than solutions. I cannot speak for anyone but myself, but it would have been crazy for my marriage to have ended; and yet, back in June, when I left consciousness-raising, it seemed more than likely.*

I suspect Decter is also on the right track when she links the process with the rap. Consciousness-raising is at the very least supposed to bring about an intimacy, but what it seems instead to bring about are the trappings of intimacy, the illusion of intimacy, a semblance of intimacy. There are incredible confidences traded, emotional moments shared, but it is all done in the context of the rap, the shut-up-it's-my-turn-now-it'll-be-yours-in-a-minute school of discussion. The case of the session on turkey stuffing is too classic an example to resist: no woman ever really wants to know what another woman is stuffing her turkey with; she just wants her turn to tell what *she* is planning to do.

What finally happened with my group—and this was, for me, by far the most serious development—was that it became an encounter group. The rules are precise on this point; consciousness-raising is *not* group therapy; there are to be no judgments, no confrontations, no challenges to another woman's experience. But, as I said, all that had begun to crumble by the end of the first meeting, when one of the women in the group was told by three members that her marriage sounded lousy. And I don't want to pretend that I had nothing to do with

---

* I feel that a footnote is called for here, but I'm not exactly sure what to say in it. The marriage *did* end. I don't really want to go into the details of that. But I do want to make the point that when it broke up, it broke up for the right reasons. When it was over, I did not think that I was a victim, or that I-was-perfect-and-he-was-awful, or any of that.

that—I was one of the three women who told her. As time went on, we all fell into the pattern. We felt free to give advice—and not friendly, gentle advice, the kind that is packed with options; this was more your I-think-you're-crazy-to-stand-for-a-minute-more-of-that kind of advice. What was especially interesting about it—and I gather this is fairly common in encounter groups—is that in spite of all this advice, none of us really wanted any one of us to get better. There was one woman in the group whose sex life was so awful that it made us all feel lucky; I think we would have been quite disturbed if she had shown up, one Monday, having straightened the whole thing out. There was another woman in the group who had what I think is called a problem about hostility. She seemed compelled, at every session, to vent her anger against some member of the group. Both these women were playing definite roles for the group, and someone with training and an understanding of group dynamics might have helped them—and us—by pointing this out. But none of us was equipped to do that, and there were no controls whatsoever on anything that happened at the meetings. I am not sure that even with a leader, encounter therapy works; without a leader, it is dangerous.

In June, when our group disbanded for the summer, I left it and went into therapy again. I am not going to write a tribute to therapy here. All I can say is that I was fortunate, I found a brilliant woman therapist, and at the moment I think that things might work out. At the same time, I don't mean to write a wholesale attack on consciousness-raising. I hear of more and more groups every day, and some I hear about sound wonderful. They seem to follow the rules, they give women a real and new sense of pride, they help them change in important ways, they have to do with feminism and politics and the movement as well as with personal trauma. Mine didn't. My group thought the process could be used for something for which it was never intended. And that is the main point I want to make.

March, 1973

Dealing with the, uh, Problem

Leonard Lavin simply does not understand what all this
is about.

Leonard Lavin is the kind of man who believes, almost
to the point of religious fervor, in the free-enterprise system. In capitalism. In advertising. In this great land of
ours. When Leonard Lavin sits in his Melrose Park, Illinois, factory, in the shade of a 75-foot-high can of Alberto
VO5 hair spray, he knows that what he surveys is not
just good but positive proof that America works. In less
than twenty years, he has taken Alberto-Culver, a pid-
dling drug company with sales of $300,000 a year, and
brought it to its current yearly volume of $182 million.
Leonard Lavin is proud of this, proud of every bit of it,
and one of the things he is proudest of is the fact that
there is a product on the market, a product that did not
exist seven years ago and probably would not exist today
but for him, and that product is going to gross over $40
million this year. Forty million dollars a year added on
to the gross national product. Leonard Lavin deserves a
medal for that. Right? And what he is getting instead is
flak.

Leonard Lavin simply does not understand.

• • •

I will try to keep this from becoming gamy, but it is going to be hard. This is an article about the feminine-hygiene spray, and how it was developed and sold. I will try to keep it witty and charming, but inevitably something is going to sneak in to remind you what this product is really about. This product is really about vaginal odor. There are a lot of advertisements on television for the product that are so subtle on this point that some people—maybe not *you*, but some people—might not even know what the product *does*. There are a lot of men who manufacture the product who are so reluctant to talk straight about it that you can spend hours with them and not hear one anatomical phrase. They speak of "the problem." They speak of "the area where the problem exists." They speak of "the need to solve the problem." Every so often, a hard-core word slides into the conversation. Vagina, maybe. Or sometimes, from someone particularly candid or scientific, a vulva or two. But mostly, the discussion of this product from industry spokesmen is vague, elusive, euphemistic. Here, for example, are the words of Larry Foster, a public-relations man for Johnson & Johnson, manufacturers of Vespré and Naturally Feminine. He is speaking here of feminine-hygiene sprays and cunnilingus; I tell you this for the simple reason that he does not.

"What we're talking about here," said Foster, "is first, sex, and second, that segment of sex and how you react to it. Whether or not one needs something like this . . ." He paused. "If you were to really get people honest in terms of their reaction, the reaction is not with the product but with deep-seated feelings, not about sex but that segment of sex." Another pause. "In terms of body odor, feminine odor, in terms of that, each man would give you a difference of opinion, ranging from acceptance of it or disdain of it. Some people would consider it a problem. Others would say, 'What the hell's the difference whether you spray or not?' I don't know why I wax eloquent, but I do think everyone's missing the point."

All this vagueness and euphemism is entirely appropriate, of course, since the name of the product itself is a total euphemism. The feminine-hygiene spray is the term coined by the industry for a deodorant for the external genital area (or, more exactly, the external perineal area). The product has been attacked continuously since its introduction in 1966—by women's liberationists, who think it is demeaning to women; by consumerists, who think it is unnecessary; and by medical doctors, who think it is dangerous. In spite of the widely shared belief among these groups that the product is perhaps *the* classic example of a bad idea whose time has come, and in spite of the product's well-publicized involvement in the recent hexachlorophene flap, the feminine-hygiene spray appears to be here to stay. It is currently being manufactured by more than twenty companies (one industry source claims to have seen some forty different brands) and being used by over twenty million women, and this, according to those in the industry, is just the beginning. Says Steve Bray, who is in charge of Pristeen at Warner-Lambert Company: "It will be as common as toothpaste."

In a time when the young are popularly assumed to be, if not the great unwashed, at least free from the older generation's absurd hang-ups about odors, the sprays are selling most briskly to teen-agers and women in their early twenties. "Secretaries and stewardesses," says the clerk at Manhattan's Beekhill Chemists, which cannot keep the products in stock and which has been having a run of late on a corollary product, the raspberry douche called Cupid's Quiver. Secretaries and steward-esses. It figures. Scratch any trend no one you know is into and you will always find secretaries and steward-esses. They are also behind Dr. David Reuben, contem-porary cards, *Jonathan Livingston Seagull*, water beds, Cold Duck, Rod McKuen, and Minute Rice.

"American women are pushovers for this product," says Dr. Norman Pleshette, a New York gynecologist. "I think it comes down to menstruation, which many are taught is unclean. There are euphemisms for it, like The Curse. This is something instilled in women from girlhood on." Adds Dr. Sheldon H. Cherry, another New York gynecolo-gist: "It's capitalizing on a small minority of women's fears and sensitivities about odors in this area. The average woman certainly does not need the routine use of a femi-nine deodorant. And women who do have odors should see a gynecologist to see if there is a pathological cause."

The success of the feminine-hygiene spray provides a fascinating paradox in that its manufacturers have taken advantage of the sexual revolution to sell some-thing that conveys an implicit message that sex—in the natural state, at least—is dirty and smelly. To make matters more complicated, these same manufacturers are oblivious to the paradox: in their eyes, the mere fact that the sprays are being marketed is a breakthrough, a step forward in the realm of sexual freedom, a solid thrust in the never-ending fight against hypocrisy and puritanism. We didn't invent the problem, they say. It has always been there. The feminine-hygiene spray has just come along to save the day. "Somewhere out there," says Jerry Della Femina, whose advertising agency did the campaigns for Feminique, "there is a girl who might be hung up about herself, and one day she goes out and buys Feminique and shoots up with it, and she comes home and that one night she feels more confident and she jumps her husband and for the first time in her life she has an orgasm. If I can feel I was responsible for one more orgasm in the world, I feel I deserve the Nobel Peace Prize."

How Alberto-Culver Tests FDS for Effectiveness
(A Short but Gamy Section)

A housewife comes to the Institute for Applied Pharmaceutical Research in Yeadon, Pennsylvania, on a Monday morning, at which time she is evaluated by direct olfaction on a scale of eight. What this means, in plain language, is that she simply takes off her clothes, lies down on a bed with a curtain and sheet completely covering the upper half of her body, and a judge takes a nosepiece, places it over her vulvar area, and sniffs. The judge is female, earns up to $1,000 a week, and works also in underarm odor. The housewife is scored: from 0 to 2 means little or no odor; 3–4 denotes a detectable odor though one that is of no concern to the subject; 5–6 is strong odor; and 7–8 is ripe. After the first evaluation, the housewife takes a bath using only soap and water. Six, twelve, and twenty-four hours later, she is sniffed by the judge and evaluated. On Tuesday, the process is repeated. Wednesday and Thursday, she is sprayed with FDS after bathing and the evaluation proceeds. During the four-day period, the housewife sleeps at home but is not allowed to have intercourse. She receives $150 for four days of work. According to the Institute, the test shows that FDS reduces feminine odor more effectively than soap and water—by 74–78 percent after six hours, 53–59 percent after twelve hours, and 38–40 percent after twenty-four hours.

The first feminine-hygiene spray was a Swiss product called Bidex, which was introduced by Medelline in Europe in the early 1960s. Technologically, the product was a step forward: until that point, all sprays had been the wet, sticky variety; the Swiss were the first to use a propellant called fluorocarbon 12 to produce a warm, dry spray. The American rights to Bidex were purchased by Warner-Lambert, which imported it and put it into a small test market under its original name. At the same time, Leonard Lavin, president of Alberto-Culver, saw Bidex during a 1965 trip through Europe, and he brought the concept back to his company and summoned his chief scientist, John A. Cella. Before coming to Alberto-Culver, Cella was part of the original research team on the birth-control pill at G. D. Searle; once, while working with the raw estrogen used in Enovid, he sprouted a pair of breasts. They were only temporary. Cella is a good-natured man who seems to be thoroughly used to the enthusiasms of his boss; still, he admits that the idea of feminine sprays threw him a little. "We were all a little nonplused about it," he recalled. "Oh, well. They never look to me for marketing decisions. Mr. Lavin came back from Switzerland and said, 'This thing will go. Can we do it?' I said, 'I think we can do it.' We had some background research on this going back to 1963 in the general deodorant field, in terms of what you could

deodorize. It was a toiletry, but we were going to treat it
as a pharmaceutical—we realized because of the area
in which it was to be used it would have to have safety
experiments. It is a grooming product, not a pharmaceutical, but it was a breakthrough."

In terms of product development, the feminine-
hygiene spray was not a breakthrough at all. It followed right along in the tradition of mouthwashes
and underarm deodorants and foot sprays, a tradition
Ralph Nader has called the why-wash-it-when-you-can-
spray-it ethic. What the manufacturers of all these products have succeeded at over the years, as economist John
Kenneth Galbraith points out, is in manufacturing and
creating the demand for a product at the same time they
manufacture and create the product. In the area of personal grooming, the new product is considerably easier
to introduce than in other fields. "Year after year," says
Ralph Nader, "in any industry, the sellers become very
acute in appealing to those features of a human personality that are easiest to exploit. Everyone knows what
they are. It's easiest to exploit a person's sense of fear, a
person's sense of being ugly, a person's sense of smelling
badly, than it is to exploit a person's appraisal or appreciation of nutrition, and, shall we say, less emotive and
more rational consumer value."

The underarm deodorant, which was the first product to capitalize on the American mania for odor sup-
pression, was introduced over a hundred years ago, in
1870. A few years later, Mum, the first trademark brand,
came onto the market. It had a primitive formula of
wax which was intended to stop perspiration by simply plugging pores. In 1914, Odo-Ro-No, with a base of
aluminum chloride, became the first nationally adver-

tised brand, and it was followed by dozens of products containing metal-salts bases, which did control perspiration though they were less successful in controlling odor. The big deodorant boom came in the late 1940s, when the less than euphonious term "B.O." was coined, and in the 1950s, when hexachlorophene came onto the market. This drug, which its manufacturers claim inhibits the growth of microorganisms on skin surfaces and thus prevents odors, was discovered in 1939 by a scientist named Dr. William Gump and became the sole property of the New York–based Givaudan Corporation, which sold it by the trainload to the manufacturers of Dial Soap, pHisoHex (the soap used in hospitals by doctors and nurses before surgery), and a wide variety of deodorant products. In the 1960s, the introduction of the aerosol container clinched hexachlorophene's domination of deodorant formulas for the reason that alternative agents, like aluminum salts, could not be used in metal cans. Right Guard, and other "family-type" products, zoomed to the top of sales charts. At the same time, the mouthwash manufacturers introduced pocket-sized spray atomizers, and the first foot-spray powders came onto the market. The American woman had been convinced to spray her mouth, her underarms, and her feet; the feminine-hygiene spray, at this point, was probably inevitable.

Q: *Miss Provine, why are vaginal deodorant
   sprays becoming so popular?*
A: *I believe that we're living in a wonderful new
   era. An era where femininity really counts. And
   the more feminine you feel, the more feminine
   you'll be. The hygiene sprays are popular*

because they're an extension of this feeling. It
tells me that we've come a long way since the
horrible days when women were ashamed of
feeling like women.
—Advertisement for Feminique.

Dorothy Provine, in this case, happens to be right. Women *have* come a long way since the horrible days when women were ashamed of feeling like women. To be exact, women have come full circle. Leonard Lavin is fond of reminding his critics that the tradition for the feminine-hygiene spray goes back to Biblical times; he is absolutely accurate; and he is furthermore totally unaware that he is basing his defense of his product on thoroughly primitive practices, purification rites that originated from physiological ignorance and superstition and that were instrumental in the early forms of discrimination against women. Says Rabbi Ira Eisenstein, editor of the *Reconstructionist* magazine: "To take an ancient concept and apply it to a modern one, especially for commercial purposes, to tie it in with exalted notions, is pure exploitation and misleading."

Early purification rites surrounded the menstrual period, which was a mysterious phenomenon: the female of the species was able to bleed without pain, and elaborate religious customs were devised to cope with this incredible happenstance. The most complicated and widespread of these rites followed childbirth. "Women after childbirth," writes J. G. Frazer in *The Golden Bough*, "are more or less tabooed all the world over." Adds *The New Schaff-Herzog Encyclopedia of Religious Knowledge*: ". . . in childbirth the cause of uncleanness is not the fact of giving birth but the condition resulting which resembles that of the menses."

The assumption that women and their sexual organs are by nature unclean is reflected in widespread practices in primitive societies. Many of these prevailed up to this century and would be quite ludicrous if they were not so barbaric. Delaware Indian girls, for example, were secluded upon their first period, their heads wrapped so they could not see, and were forced to vomit frequently for twelve days; after this, they were bathed, put into fresh clothes, and secluded for two months more; at this point, they were considered clean and marriageable. The Delawares were hardly unique among American Indians: the Pueblos believed a man would become sick if he touched a menstruating woman, and the Cheyennes painted young girls red at puberty and isolated them for four days. In Morocco, menstruating women were forbidden to enter granaries or handle bees. Many Australian and New Guinea tribes forbade menstruating women to look at cattle or at the sun; one stray glimpse, it was believed, could cause milk stoppage, crop failure, plagues, famine, and total disaster.

The purification rites developed by the early Jews are probably the most commonly known today, largely because they are preserved in the Book of Leviticus. In Biblical times, menstruation was regarded as an impurity (it still is by Orthodox Jews) and women were forbidden to enter the Temple or to have intercourse at any time during menstruation and for a week thereafter. Any person who touched a woman—or even her bed linens—during her menstrual period was also considered unclean. After her period ended, the Jewish woman

was required to take a ritual bath, or *mikvah*, and this
was also required to cleanse objects considered idola-
trous, and men who had masturbated or had had noctur-
nal emissions. There are Jewish theologians who insist
that because men as well as women were required to
bathe, the purification rites were not innately discrimi-
natory; however, the status of women in Biblical times
can be measured by the childbirth purification ritual in
the Book of Leviticus (xii), which holds that a woman
who bears a son is unclean for forty days thereafter,
whereas a woman who bears a daughter is unclean for
sixty-six days.

> *As the party goes on people leave Ann alone. And
> she doesn't know why. Ann is never at a loss for
> conversation. It's something else that makes people
> slowly move away. Something that Norforms could
> stop right away. What are Norforms? Norforms are
> the second deodorant—a safe internal deodorant.*
> —Advertisement for Norforms.

Once the basic formula for its feminine-hygiene spray
was settled on (almost all the spray formulas contained
hexachlorophene as the active deodorizing ingredi-
ent, perfume, an emollient, and a propellant), Alberto-
Culver's research department, under Dr. Cella, went to
work testing the safety of the product. Because the spray
was classified by the Food and Drug Administration as a
cosmetic, very little testing was actually required: an eye-
irritation test, an oral-toxicity test, and a skin-patch test
would have been adequate. To its credit, Alberto-Culver
went further; as it happens, though, by the standards set
by its own chief scientist, it did not go nearly far enough.

In an article on deodorants published last year in *American Perfumer & Cosmetics*, Cella itemized the testing he thought was necessary for the sprays, as follows: "Animal skin irritation and sensitization studies, animal vulvar irritation studies, animal vaginal instillation studies using the aerosol concentrates, human repeated insult patch tests on intact and abraded skin, subacute and chronic human-use tests, particle size analysis of the spray, and animal inhalation studies." Cella wrote that efficacy tests would also be desirable, but he added, in a sentence that is a masterpiece of scientific writing: "Efficacy testing in this category presents problems of delicacy which do not encumber the underarm counterparts." Prior to its introduction of FDS in late 1966, Alberto-Culver conducted only three of these tests. One proved that FDS did no injury to the labia and vaginas of twenty rats over a three-day period. A second was a skin-patch test on sixty-seven persons. The third was a use test: thirty-one women were given the product to use at home over a five-week period and showed no irritation.

In the meantime, the market-research and advertising departments of Alberto-Culver were at work developing packaging, fragrance, and a name for the spray. "The first piece of research we did in 1966," said Henry Wittemann, vice-president in charge of advertising services, "was a concept test on the product. If you did it today, there would be different results because today the category exists. The first test we commissioned said that the concept was not appealing, and based on that the research agency recommended that we drop the project. But if you looked at the research carefully, there was a suggestion that women weren't

telling the interviewers what they really thought. The
question came up as to whether women don't really
want to talk about this subject to anyone. We had done
a questionnaire about deodorants with a concept statement saying that a leading manufacturer of toiletries
was planning to come out with a deodorant for the vaginal area. Do you think you need it? Would you use it?
When? With a test like this, you're looking for over seventy percent to express interest. If you don't get that,
chances are you don't have a product that's appealing to
the market. So we decided to go to a research company
that had done work in this area, a company that had
done questionnaires for feminine-hygiene manufacturers like Kimberly-Clark and Johnson & Johnson. These
companies know how to structure questionnaires that
deal with that subject to elicit a true response. So we
did that, went out with a concept statement and samples, and the interest was over seventy-eight percent.
We knew we had a viable concept." Wittemann claims
that at no time during this period was the question of
sexual attitudes explicitly explored; the product, he
claims, was conceived of as a general deodorant, not a
sexual enhancer. (Sexually, the sprays are something
of a bust: they cannot be used right before intercourse
because they tend to cause skin irritation under those
circumstances; furthermore, at least one of the sprays
causes numbness of the tongue.)

"We considered names like Caresse and Care," Wittemann continued, "all the names that might be in
good taste. But every name we thought fit the product
belonged to another product. We were using the code
name 'FD Number One,' for feminine deodorant Number
One. When we were blocked, we just went to the letters

'FSD.' Then it turned out we had to choose 'FDS' because even the letters 'FSD' were taken." One criticism of FDS in recent years has been that its name is so close to F.D.A., a coincidence that might seem to imply government approval. Did that issue ever come up? "Never," Wittemann replied. "The only thing that did come up was an objection by one of our executives, who thought the name sounded too much like FDR."

"I had no idea it would be so controversial," says Leonard Lavin today. "As we developed the product and the research proved to us that there was a need for this product—both from the clinical and consumer viewpoint—we were convinced of what we had. We realized that going to the marketplace with a feminine-hygiene deodorant was not the easiest thing in the world. This was an area, after all, where other products advertised with a certain amount of reluctance. Kotex and Tampax, for example. We leaned over backwards in delicacy, elusiveness, even in design of the package: it was as soft and delicate as possible. If you looked at the first print ads, you would really have to look to find out what the product really did."

FDS was introduced on December 1, 1966. It came in a pale blue and white can, with a lacy white pattern surrounding the label. The drugstore display unit contained a sign, duplicating the first magazine advertisements, that read, "This new product will become as essential to you as your toothbrush." In smaller print: "FDS. The name is FDS. Feminine Hygiene Deodorant Spray. It is new. A most personal sort of deodorant. An external deodorant. Unique in all the world. Essential on special days. Welcome protection against odor—every single day. FDS. For your total freshness."

Ten Very Personal Questions
   1. *Does a woman need more than an under-*
   arm deodorant?
        YES. *A woman, if she's completely honest*
        about it, realizes her most serious problem
        isn't under her arms. . . .
                         —Advertisement for FDS, 1968.

With the exception of Bidex, the Swiss product
Warner-Lambert still had in test market in two cities,
FDS had the feminine-hygiene-spray field to itself for
almost a full year. The drug trade, which is notoriously
unadventurous, did not believe there was any chance for
the product to succeed. Leonard Lavin, who thrives on
the notion of his relatively small company as a little guy
plugging away in an industry of giants, believed implic-
itly in FDS, and he spent hundreds of thousands of dollars animating his belief, advertising in print media,
publishing pamphlets for drugstore displays, creating a
demand for the product by making women understand
how much they needed it. "I don't call it creating guilt,"
said Lavin. "That's your word. I think of what we did as
raising consciousness. That's a less loaded word." There
were almost daily battles to be fought: drugstore owners
would not stock the item; magazines like *Life*, *McCall's*,
and *Seventeen* were reluctant at first to accept ads for
it; television had a ban on advertising for all such products. But by late 1967, Alberto-Culver had sold almost
$4 million worth of sprays, and Warner-Lambert, a
company that could read sales charts as well as any,
decided to move ahead. The name Bidex was changed to
Pristeen and the product went into a wide test-market
pattern prior to national introduction in 1968. "The

name Bidex was already taken under trademark," said Guido Battista, associate director in charge of research and development on toiletries and cosmetics at Warner-Lambert. "But I would have objected to it because of the possibility of misusing the product. It might have seemed to have been intended for internal use. Interestingly enough, some of the information that got to the lay people was that these were vaginal sprays, which they're not."

"Our whole approach," said Warner-Lambert's Steve Bray, "was, women have a vaginal-odor problem and here is a product that will solve the problem. They do, you know. And panty hose contribute to it. Women's liberation says that advertising is creating a need that isn't there. They say it's a nice, natural smell. That's their right. But I would go back and ask them, do women have a vaginal-odor problem? I keep going back to the problem. The problem is there."

Exactly how much of a problem American women were aware of before the sprays were introduced is not clear; what is clear is that feminine-hygiene-spray manufacturers cannot be accused of inventing it. In 1968, a market-research firm hired to investigate consumer reaction to the product gathered a group of housewives for a tape-recorded session that is notable for its embarrassment and coyness about the vaginal area. Said one woman: "I think the new deodorant sprays are sensational. Not that I have a problem down *there*, but sometimes I think I might." Said another: "I prefer sprays to the foams or powders. . . . The sprays eliminate having to touch yourself."

Says Natalie Shainess, a New York psychoanalyst: "Our society has tended since medieval times, when the

odor of the great unwashed was everywhere, to work at
eliminating unpleasant aspects of smell. The sense of
smell is tied up with paranoia—one of the classic paranoid symptoms is the feeling, 'I smell bad. That's why
no one likes me.' The sense of being malodorous is connected with more serious disturbances. These products
further paranoid feelings in women and in men about
women—and the way they're advertised presents a hor-
rendous image, of women being inherently smelly creatures. It undermines the sense of self and ego even as it's
supposed to do something about it."

By 1969, the market for the sprays had grown to
$19.3 million and manufacturers were tumbling in.
The boom in sales came largely because Alberto-Culver
had succeeded in getting the National Association of
Broadcasters to change its code and permit the sprays
to be advertised on television. (The stations themselves
exerted pressure, of course.) The ads were required to be
totally bland and unspecific—the word "vagina" is not
allowed on the air—and they were. A woman walked
down the beach with her child. Or lit the candles for dinner. Or talked, haltingly, about this somewhat mysterious product, she, uh, really liked a lot. Dorothy Provine
emerged from what she calls semi-retirement to endorse
Feminique, and returned to semi-retirement $100,000
richer. The advertising budgets backing the product
mushroomed: in 1970, FDS, which sold somewhere
around $13–14 million worth of the $32 million spray
market, spent $3.5 million advertising it.

What was printed in magazine and newspaper ads for
the sprays was a good deal more blunt than what was on
television. Demure, for instance, offered this: "You don't
sleep with Teddy Bears any more." And "Your Teddy

Bear loved you no matter what." Feminique's early print ad read: "Now that 'The Pill' has freed you from worry 'The Spray' will help make all that freedom worthwhile." FDS, in a more subtle ad, nonetheless promised similar sexual rewards: "Being close was never nicer . . . now is the Age of FDS." Manufacturers who were unwilling to allude to sexuality stressed the importance of including the product as part of the normal deodorant regimen. Said Pristeen, in an ad uncannily similar to an earlier FDS ad: "Unfortunately, the trickiest deodorant problem a girl has *isn't* under her pretty little arms." Or this, from FDS: "Having a female body doesn't make you feminine. It's the extra things you do—like FDS." And yet another from FDS, this one utilizing the tried-and-true approach to upward mobility: "Could you be the last woman to be using just one deodorant?" Pristeen sought out famous women to write articles about women, with Pristeen advertisements tacked onto the end: Suzy Knickerbocker, Angie Dickinson, Mary Quant, and Judith Crist were among them. (For this, Mrs. Crist, along with Dorothy Provine, was chosen Sweet Pea of the Year by *Esquire*'s 1971 Dubious Achievement Awards.)

"The reason I did that ad had absolutely nothing to do with Pristeen," said Judith Crist, the film critic. "It was extremely naïve of me and it was two years ago and I'm ashamed to admit I'm that naïve. They were doing a two-page spread that would have eight pictures of me taken by Richard Avedon, with a two-page headline saying 'Today's Woman.' Then I had approximately eight hundred words to write what I wanted to say about women. I decided to write about women in communications. In the final column, there was a cutoff line and about four inches of space, and then it said something like, 'The modern woman who chooses to be immaculate will use Pristeen, a feminine-hygiene deodorant.' It was going to run in eight women's magazines in one month. It boggled the mind. You were reaching a hundred and twenty-five million people, an audience you couldn't reach even if you were a movie for television. Then there were the photographs with Avedon and the negatives were mine if I wanted them—which was the kind of sitting you could never otherwise afford. And then came a huge fee in addition, and I saw my son getting an extra inning in camp, redoing the living room." The fee for the ad was $5,000.

"What did bother me," Mrs. Crist went on, "was the idea of it being a vaginal deodorant. So I consulted some friends. They said, 'Boy are you ever being sexist. If it were Bond Bread, you'd do it. College presidents do commercials for the right Scotch. Why because it is a feminine-hygiene spray—what difference is a mouth-wash from a vaginal wash? This is small, unenlight-ened thinking if we're going to get silly about vaginas.' But the essential thing was, *I* didn't say, in the ad, 'If you want to be a modern woman, use Pristeen.' What I was saying had nothing to do with Pristeen. Well, it was the dumbest decision I've ever made. It was as if I had waltzed out like Dorothy Provine and said, 'Have you used this marvelous vaginal spray?' Which I hadn't. I thought I would get responses about what I had said about women in the media—to hell with the money, the Avedon pictures, *what I said*. Instead, I got tied up with the spray. There were so many gags I could have thrown up. The students in one of my witty classes gave me an enormous box with a can of Pristeen at the bottom. The

Esquire thing, which was quite embarrassing. Then Rex Reed, feeling betrayed because of my review of *Myra Breckinridge*, retaliated with thorough justification and said, 'Now when she walks down the aisle, people will think, Does She Or Doesn't She.' Which obliged me to retaliate. I got right down to those lower depths, which was the worst part.

"But it was a very educational experience. If Mrs. Gandhi or Golda Meir had posed for a *Playboy* foldout, the results could not have been as bad. It was a learning experience. At my age you don't think you have those."

The first hint from the critics that the sprays might not be merely useless but actually dangerous came in November, 1970, when a Montreal gynecologist named Bernard Davis reported in the *Journal of Obstetrics and Gynecology* that he had treated some twenty to twenty-five patients who had itching, burning sensations in the vulvar area. All of them used the sprays daily. One of the patients, a fourteen-year-old girl, developed "incredibly" swollen labia, and after being treated, the doctor reported, her clitoris and labia remained "peculiarly" abnormal. Davis's letter was answered six months later by Lawrence J. Caruso, a New York gynecologist, who claimed that he had seen many cases of irritation caused by soaps and oils but none whatsoever from the sprays. Caruso conducted a study on twenty-nine of his patients, all of whom used the sprays for six months, and no abnormalities resulted. The study, Caruso said, was conducted "at the request of one manufacturer of a feminine-hygiene-deodorant spray."

The second salvo came in a long, breezily written article in *Medical Aspects of Human Sexuality* in July, 1971.

In it, Bernard Kaye, an Illinois gynecologist, announced that "the great American persuader has struck again!" and went on to report that several of his patients who used the sprays had developed vulvitis; the condition did not recur, he reported, when use of the spray was discontinued. "As an added dividend of the female genital cosmetic industry," Kaye concluded, "it is to be expected that physicians will be seeing *male* genital irritations in greater numbers . . . from exposure to 'Gynacosmetics' [and] . . . from the use of the masculine version of the 'private deodorant.'"

"Honey," said Bill Blass when asked to explain why his line of cosmetics included a so-called private deodorant, "if there's a part of the human body to exploit you might as well get onto it."

Hygiene sprays for men, which are known in the trade as crotch sprays, were introduced in 1970. They have never been advertised on television and today industry sources estimate that $2 million worth of them are sold a year, 5 percent of the feminine-hygiene-spray market. It is commonly assumed by women's liberationists that products that arrive on the market with the kind of minimal testing that characterized the feminine-hygiene spray would never be sold to men—the assumption here being that men, who are in charge of manufacturing and research within industry, would never exploit their fellowmen as recklessly as they do women. Their argument, however true it may be in the case of the birth-control pill, does not hold where crotch sprays are concerned. Revlon, the leading manufacturer in the men's spray market, has three brands—Braggi's Private Deodorant Spray, Bill

Blass's Man's Other Deodorant, and Pub Below the Belt. It put all these products into national marketing with the three tests that are required for cosmetic products sold in spray cans—the eye-irritation, oral-toxicity, and skin-patch tests—plus usage tests. The skin-patch test, according to Dr. Earl W. Brauer, Revlon vice-president in charge of medical affairs, "was not done on the penis but on an area where it can't be tampered with. We do a closed-patch test. The product is kept in place under a closed patch for two days. It's a much higher concentration and we learn much more from such a provocative test." But isn't the skin of the penis different from other skin on the male body? "Yes," said Dr. Brauer. "It's thinner skin and there are more active nerve endings. No patch tests were done on the penis. It's not necessary."

The Food and Drug Administration began looking into the safety of the feminine-hygiene spray on a number of fronts in 1971. It was concerned about the use of the word "hygiene" in connection with the product. There was the general question of the safety of aerosol containers. And there were increasing reports of irritation caused by the sprays. In early 1971, the F.D.A. asked the spray manufacturers for their complaint rates. Four manufacturers replied; their rates ranged from 0 per million packages sold, to 6, which was about standard, to 21 per million. (The product with the highest rate, Johnson & Johnson's Vespré, incidentally, contained over twice as much hexachlorophene as the other sprays. It was reformulated in mid-1971.) Any complaint rate over 5 per million is considered cause for concern by the F.D.A., but it is unlikely that the agency would have moved against the sprays on the mere grounds of effectiveness or excessive irritation.

What finally caused it to take action was the increasing weight of evidence against hexachlorophene.

The earliest indication that there might be serious trouble with the drug actually occurred some six years ago at the Shriners Burns Institute in Galveston, Texas. This hospital, which treats severely burned children, opened in the spring of 1966, and in the first six months six of its patients suffered seizures. "We couldn't find any definite reason for it," said Dr. Duane Larson, chief of staff, "so we looked into our procedure, narrowed it down, and decided it might have something to do with the soap solution we were bathing them in—which was three percent hexachlorophene." Laboratory scientists at the Institute took animals—rats, guinea pigs, pigs, and dogs—and burned their backs and then washed them with a 3-percent hexachlorophene solution. Day after day, the hexachlorophene blood levels in the animals rose higher and higher, and they began to exhibit signs of neurological damage. They were irritable. They all dragged their hind legs. "We tested the cerebral spinal fluid," said Larson, "and were able to determine that hexachlorophene was in it, that it had the property of going through the blood/brain barrier. This was important—a number of drugs don't go into the brain but just stay in the bloodstream." When the animals were autopsied, their brains were extremely swollen.

"We found the same thing with the children," said Larson. "As the blood level of hexachlorophene got higher, they would become irritable and have seizures. I remember one boy in particular who had a small burn on one thigh. He was having neurological problems. His serum level was extremely high—far too high for such a small burn. It turned out the nurse was soaking his dressing in a three-percent hexachlorophene solution to get it off.

"We also measured the hexachlorophene levels of doctors and nurses who scrubbed with soap containing hexachlorophene, and in none could we find a significant level. It seems to be all right for adults if you rinse it off. On the other hand, we do know it goes through normal skin as well as burned skin. We had a patient in Michigan—a baby was brought home from the hospital, a normal baby with no skin lesions, and the mother continued bathing the child in the three-percent hexachlorophene solution that was used in the hospital without rinsing it off. The baby had seizures."

Dr. Larson reported on the Institute's experience, and its decision to discontinue the use of hexachlorophene with burn victims, at a meeting of the American Burn Association in the spring of 1967. His findings were picked up by newspapers at the time, but within a few weeks the issue died down. Then, in 1971, three studies appeared that showed exactly what the Shriners Burns Institute had known for years. The most persuasive of the tests proved that newborn monkeys bathed in a 3-percent hexachlorophene solution for ninety days showed brain changes consisting of extreme swelling in the cerebellum, brainstem, and all the parts of the cord. The 3-percent solution was at that time used to bathe newborns at most American hospitals.

In November, 1971, Jack Walden, a public-relations man for the Food and Drug Administration, sat down with a *Washington Post* reporter and told her that the F.D.A. was looking into the dangers of feminine-hygiene sprays in connection with hexachlorophene. An article to that effect subsequently appeared in the *Post*, and Leonard Lavin of Alberto-Culver reacted to it by demanding Walden's resignation. Whether Lavin thought this would make the hexachlorophene problem go away is not certain; what is certain is that until the very end, every company that was directly affected by the F.D.A.'s concern about hexachlorophene looked upon the investigation as an incredible nuisance. Hexachlorophene was perfectly safe. Everyone knew that. No one had died. Thousands of newborns were bathed in it every day in hospital nurseries; as a result, there had been no staphylococcus outbreaks in American hospitals in years. Just because a few monkeys were brain-damaged did not mean that children would be. "We love hexachlorophene," said Alberto-Culver's Dr. Cella. "It's very valuable," said Warner-Lambert's Battista.

Leonard Lavin, for his part, accepted the hexachlorophene business as a small part of his ongoing battle. First there had been the consumerists—or, as he had referred to them in a letter, "negative-minded consumerist groups who would subject our entire economy to a Marxist purge of everything they object to." Now it was the government, interfering in the smooth processes of private industry. It was just like the cyclamate mess a few years back—there, Lavin insisted, was another perfectly harmless product taken off the market prematurely. He Xeroxed a long article by Vermont Royster in the *Wall Street Journal* which claimed that if aspirin were introduced today, the F.D.A. would ban it. He muttered frequently about Ralph Nader, who had been outspoken on the subject of the sprays. "If Ralph Nader had his way," Lavin said, "he would ban Fritos and soft drinks. I heard him say it myself." He commissioned studies to show the safety of hexachlorophene. Experts

.pored over medical reports about the sprays and jubilantly found errors in them. (One doctor, for example, had claimed in his article to have seen anal infections he traced to the perfume used in scented toilet paper. This was absurd, said Alberto-Culver's Cella: the scent came not from the paper but from the cardboard roll within; the perfume used never came in actual contact with the body.) Gus Kass, a vice-president of Alberto-Culver, delivered a speech in Chicago decrying the attacks on the cosmetics industry by newspapers and magazines. "All of them," said Kass, "are witches' brews of distorted facts, half-truths, or outright falsehoods. . . . What all of the critics fail to understand is that there is no substance to which some person is *not* allergic."

And so it went. There was bound to be some irritation from the feminine-hygiene sprays because there were bound to be some individuals who were allergic to them. And as to the rest of the complaints, the manufacturers said, these had nothing to do with hexachlorophene. Women using the products were simply using them wrong—not holding the spray far enough from their bodies, or spraying just before intercourse, or spraying the actual vaginal area. (There were, to be sure, many reactions to the sprays that were caused by misuse; some manufacturers have recently inserted more explicit instructions in the spray kits.) As for hexachlorophene, most of the sprays contained less than one-tenth of 1 percent—and even if it could be shown that hexachlorophene was dangerous to humans, such a tiny amount would never hurt.

In December, 1971, the F.D.A. took its first action against hexachlorophene, announcing it was no longer recommending bathing of infants in a 3-percent hexa-

chlorophene solution. A month later, when there was a
staph outbreak in a New Haven hospital that had stopped
using pHisoHex, the drug industry was as jubilant as it
could be under the circumstances. But the F.D.A. claimed
that the outbreak could not be traced to the ban and continued to move against the drug. It announced a three-
part proposal: hexachlorophene would be banned from
cosmetics except when it was used as a preservative; all
drugs containing hexachlorophene would be required
to carry warnings; and any drug with more than three-
quarters of 1 percent hexachlorophene would be sold by
prescription only. (Not until seven months later, when
thirty-nine French infants died from the external use of
a baby powder that contained, through a manufacturing
error, 6 percent hexachlorophene, did the F.D.A. make
final its over-the-counter ban on the drug.)

Feminine-hygiene-spray manufacturers could have
fought the proposal at this point. But since the first
reports of F.D.A. concern, sales of the product had
dropped off. A January, 1972, attack in *Consumer
Reports* had not helped. And so, voluntarily, all the
manufacturers removed the drug from the feminine-
spray formulas. Alberto-Culver replaced it with another
antibacterial agent, and then refused to tell the press
what it was. Warner-Lambert removed it entirely (they
claimed it was used only as a preservative), and found
that Pristeen continued to work exactly as it had before.
The industry sat back, quietly, and consoled itself with
memories of the cranberry scare. That had blown over
ultimately, and this would, too. In the meantime, sales of
the product, which had been expected to grow to $53 mil-
lion in 1971, held firm at the $40 million mark. Still, $40
million worth of product wasn't bad. There were women

out there who were loyal, who still wanted to buy. The rest of the public would forget. It always does.

> *Today children in kindergarten are taught the facts of human birth; biology is no longer a taboo subject. But a product that recognizes the existence of the difference between man and woman—and also happens to be relatively new—was sure to become a target in the age of consumerism and women's lib. Soap and water were good enough for grandma, but we think women have changed. Our sales and those of our competitors prove it.*
> —From a form letter written by Leonard Lavin
> to customers requesting information on the
> safety of feminine-hygiene sprays.

Leonard Lavin simply does not understand what all this is about.

March, 1973

The Hurled Ashtray

I once heard a swell story about Gary Cooper. The person I heard the story from did this terrific Gary Cooper imitation, and it may be that when I tell you the story (which I am about to), it will lose something in print. It may lose everything, in fact. But enough. The story was that Gary Cooper was in a London restaurant at a large table of friends. He was sitting in a low chair, with his back to the rest of the room, so no one in the restaurant even knew that he was tall, much less that he was Gary Cooper. Across the way was a group of Teddy boys (this episode took place long long ago, you see), and they were all misbehaving and making nasty remarks about a woman at Cooper's table. Cooper turned around to give them his best mean-and-threatening stare, but they went right on. Finally he got up, very very slowly, so slowly that it took almost a minute for him to go from this short person in a low chair to a ten-foot-tall man with Gary Cooper's head on top of his shoulders. He loped over to the table of Teddy boys, looked down at them, and said, "Wouldja mind sayin' that agin?" The men were utterly cowed and left the restaurant shortly thereafter.

Well, you had to be there.

I thought of Gary Cooper and his way with words the other day. Longingly. Because in the mail, from an editor of *New York* magazine, came an excerpt from a book by Michael Korda called *Male Chauvinism: How It Works* (Random House). I have no idea whether Korda's book is any good at all, but the excerpt was fascinating, a sort of reverse-twist update on Francis Macomber, as well as a pathetic contrast to the Gary Cooper story. It seems that Korda, his wife, and another woman were having dinner in a London restaurant recently. Across the way was a table of drunks doing sensitive things like sniggering and leering and throwing bread balls at Mrs. Korda, who is a looker. Her back was to them, and she refused to acknowledge their presence, instead apparently choosing to let the flying bread balls bounce off her back onto the floor. Then, one of the men sent over a waiter with a silver tray. On it was a printed card, the kind you can buy in novelty shops, which read: "I want to sleep with you! Tick off your favorite love position from the list below, and return this card with your telephone number. . . . " Korda tore up the card before his wife could even see it, and then, consumed with rage, he picked up an ashtray and threw it at the man who had sent the card. A fracas ensued, and before long, Korda, his wife, and their woman friend were out on the street. Mrs. Korda was furious.

"If you ever do that again," she screamed, "I'll leave you! Do you think I couldn't have handled that, or ignored it? Did I ask you to come to my defense against some poor stupid drunk? You didn't even think, you just reacted like a male chauvinist. You leapt up to defend *your* woman, *your* honor, you made me seem cheap and

foolish and powerless. . . . God Almighty, can't you see it
was none of your business! Can't you understand how
it makes me feel? I don't mind being hassled by some
drunk, I can take that, but to be treated like a chattel,
to be robbed of any right to decide for myself whether
I'd been insulted, or how badly, to have you react for me
because I'm *your* woman . . . that's really sickening, it's
like being a slave." Korda repeats the story (his wife's
diatribe is even longer in the original version) and
then, in a *mea culpa* that is only too reminiscent of the
sort that used to appear in 1960s books by white lib-
erals about blacks, he concludes that his wife is doubtless right, that men do tend to treat women merely as
appendages of themselves.

Before printing the article, *New York* asked several
couples—including my husband and me—what our reaction was to what happened, and what we would have
done under the circumstances. My initial reaction to the
entire business was that no one ever sends me notes like
that in restaurants. I sent that off to the editor, but a few
days later I got to thinking about the story, and it began
to seem to me that the episode just might be a distilla-
tion of everything that has happened to men and women
as a result of the women's movement, and if not that, at
least a way to write about etiquette after the revolution,
and if not that, nothing at all. Pulled as I was by these
three possibilities, I told the story over dinner to four
friends and asked for their reaction. The first, a man,
said that he thought Mrs. Korda was completely right.
The second, a woman, said she thought Korda's behavior
was totally understandable. The third, a man, said that
both parties had behaved badly. The fourth, my friend

Martha, said it was the second most boring thing she had ever heard, the most boring being a story I had just told her about a fight my college roommate had with a cabdriver at Kennedy Airport.

In any case, before any serious discussion of the incident of the hurled ashtray, I would like to raise some questions for which I have no answers. I raise them simply because if that story were fed into a computer, the only possible response it could make is We Do Not Have Sufficient Information To Make An Evaluation. For example:

Do the Kordas have a good marriage?

Was the heat working in their London hotel room the night of the fracas?

Was it raining out?

What did the second woman at the table look like? Was she as pretty as Mrs. Korda? Was she ugly? Was part of Michael Korda's reaction—and his desire to assert possession of his wife—the result of the possibility that he suspected the drunks thought he was with someone funny-looking?

What kind of a tacky restaurant is it where a waiter delivers a dirty message on a silver tray?

What about a woman who ignores flying bread balls? Wasn't her husband justified in thinking she would be no more interested in novelty cards?

Did Michael Korda pay the check before or after throwing the ashtray? Did he tip the standard 15 percent?

Since the incident occurs in London, a city notorious for its rampant homoerotic behavior, and since the table of drunks was all male, isn't it possible that the printed card was in fact intended not for Mrs. Korda but for Michael? In which case how should we now view his response, if at all?

There might be those who would raise questions about the ashtray itself: was it a big, heavy ashtray, these people might ask, or a dinky little round one? Was it glass or was it plastic? These questions are irrelevant.

In the absence of answers to any of the above, I would nonetheless like to offer some random musings. First, I think it is absurd for Mrs. Korda to think that she and she alone was involved in the incident. Yes, it might have been nice had her husband consulted her; and yes, it would have been even nicer had he turned out to be Gary Cooper, or failing that, Dave DeBusschere, or even Howard Cosell—anyone but this suave flinger of ashtrays he turned out to be. But the fact remains that the men at the table *were* insulting Korda, and disturbing his dinner, as well as hers. Their insult was childish and Korda's reaction was ludicrous, but Mrs. Korda matched them all by reducing a complicated and rather interesting emotional situation to a tedious set of movement platitudes.

Beyond that—and the Kordas quite aside, because God Almighty (as Mrs. Korda might put it) knows what it is they are into—I wonder whether there is any response a man could make in that situation which would not disappoint a feminist. Yes, I want to be treated as an equal and not as an appendage or possession or spare rib, but I also want to be taken care of. Isn't any man sitting at a table with someone like me damned whatever he does? If the drunks in question are simply fools, conventioneers with funny paper hats, I suppose that a possible reaction would be utter cool. But if they were truly insulting and disturbing, some response does seem called for. Some wild and permanent gesture of size. But on whose part? And what should it consist of? And how tall do you have to be to bring it off? And where is the point that a mild show of strength becomes crude macho vulgarity; where does reserve veer off into passivity?

Like almost every other question in this column, I have no positive answer. But I think that if I ever found myself in a similar situation, and if it was truly demeaning, I would prefer that my husband handle it. My husband informs me, after some consideration, that the Gary Cooper approach would not work. But he could, for example, call over the captain and complain discreetly, perhaps even ask that our table be moved. He could hire a band of aging Teddy boys to find out where the drunks were staying and short-sheet all their beds. Or—and I think I prefer this—he could produce, from his jacket pocket, a printed card from a novelty shop reading: "I'm terribly sorry, but as you can see by looking at our dinner companion, my wife and I have other plans."

I'm going out to have those cards made up right now.

April, 1973

Truth and Consequences

I read something in a reporting piece years ago that made a profound impression on me. The way I remember the incident (which probably has almost nothing to do with what actually happened) is this: a group of pathetically naïve out-of-towners are in New York for a week and want very much to go to Coney Island. They go to Times Square to take the subway, but instead of taking the train to Brooklyn, they take an uptown train to the Bronx. And what knocked me out about that incident was that the reporter involved had been cool enough and detached enough and professional enough and (I could not help thinking) cruel enough to let this hopeless group take the wrong train. I could never have done it. And when I read the article, I was disturbed and sorry that I could not: the story is a whole lot better when they take the wrong train.

When I first read that, I was a newspaper reporter, and I still had some illusions about objectivity—and certainly about that thing that has come to be known as participatory journalism; I believed that reporters had no business getting really involved in what they were writing about. Which did not seem to me to be a problem at the time. A good part of the reason I became a newspaper reporter was that I was much too cynical and detached to become involved in anything; I was temperamentally suited to be a witness to events. Or so I told myself.

And now things have changed. I would still hate to be described as a participatory journalist; but I am a writer and I am a feminist, and the two seem to be constantly in conflict.

The problem, I'm afraid, is that as a writer my commitment is to something that, God help me, I think of as The Truth, and as a feminist my commitment is to the women's movement. And ever since I became loosely involved with it, it has seemed to me one of the recurring ironies of this movement that there is no way to tell the truth about it without, in some small way, seeming to hurt it. The first dim awareness I had of this was during an episode that has become known as the *Ladies' Home Journal* action. A couple of years ago, as you may remember, a group of feminists sat in at the offices of *Journal* editor John Mack Carter to protest the antediluvian editorial content of his magazine; to their shock, Carter acceded to their main demand, and gave them ten pages of their own in the *Journal*, and $10,000. Shortly thereafter, I was asked if I would help "edit" the articles that were being written for the section— I put edit in quotes, because what we were really doing was rewriting them—and I began to sit in on a series of meetings with movement leaders that I found alternatingly fascinating, horrifying, and hilarious. The moment I treasured most occurred when the first draft of the article on sex was read aloud. The article was a conversation by five feminists. The first woman to speak began,

I thought, quite reasonably. "I find," she said, "that as I have grown more aware of who I am, I have grown more in touch with my sexuality." The second woman— and you must remember that this was supposed to be a conversation—then said, "I have never had any sensitivity in my vagina." It seemed to me that the only possible remark a third person might contribute was "Coffee, tea, or milk?"—there was no other way to turn it into a sensible exchange. Anyway, when the incident happened, I told it to several friends, who all laughed and loved the story as much as I did. But the difference was that they thought I was telling the story in order to make the movement sound silly, whereas I was telling the story simply in order to describe what was going on.

Years pass, and it is 1972 and I am at the Democratic Convention in Miami attending a rump, half-secret meeting: a group of Betty Friedan's followers are trying to organize a drive to make Shirley Chisholm Vice-President. Friedan is not here, but Jacqui Ceballos, a leader in N.O.W., *is*, and it is instantly apparent to the journalists in the room that she does not know what she is talking about. It is Monday afternoon and she is telling the group of partisans assembled in this dingy hotel room that petitions supporting Chisholm's Vice-Presidential candidacy must be in at the National Committee by Tuesday afternoon. But the President won't be nominated until Wednesday night; clearly the Vice-Presidential petitions do not have to be filed until the next day. I am supposed to be a reporter here and let things happen. I am supposed to let them take the wrong train. But I can't, and my hand is up, and I am saying that they must be wrong, they must have gotten the wrong information, there's no need to rush the petitions, they can't be due until Thursday. Afterward, I walk out onto Collins Avenue with a fellow journalist/ feminist who has managed to keep her mouth shut. "I guess I got a little carried away in there," I say guilt- ily. "I guess you did," she replies. (The next night, at the convention debate on abortion, there are women report- ers so passionately involved in the issue that they are lobbying the delegates. I feel slightly less guilty. But not much.)

To give you another example, a book comes in for review. I am on the list now, The Woman List, and the books come in all the time. Novels by women. Nonfiction books about women and the women's movement. The apparently endless number of movement-oriented and movement-inspired anthologies on feminism; the even more endless number of anthologies on the role of the family or the future of the family or the decline of the family. I take up a book, a book I think might make a column. It is *Women and Madness*, by Phyllis Chesler. I agree with the book politically. What Chesler is saying is that the psychological profession has always applied a double standard when dealing with women; that psy- chological definitions of madness have been dictated by what men believe women's role ought to be; and this is wrong. Right on, Phyllis. But here is the book: it is badly written and self-indulgent, and the research seems to me to be full of holes. If I say this, though, I will hurt the book politically, provide a way for people who want to dismiss Chesler's conclusions to ignore them entirely. On the other hand, if I fail to say that there are problems with the book, I'm applying a double standard of my own, treating works that are important to the movement dif- ferently from others: babying them, tending to gloss over their faults, gentling the author as if she and her book were somehow incapable of withstanding a single carping clause. *Her heart is in the right place; why knock her when there are so many truly evil books around?* This is what is known in the women's movement as sisterhood, and it is good politics, I suppose, but it doesn't make for good criticism. Or honesty. Or the truth. (Furthermore, it is every bit as condescending as the sort of criticism men apply to books about women these days—that unconsciously patronizing tone that treats books by and about women as some sort of sub-genre of literature, outside the mainstream, not quite relevant, interesting really, how-these-women-do-go-on-and-we-really-must-try-to-understand-what-they-are-getting-at-whatever-it-is.)

I will tell you one more story to the point—though this one is not about me. A year and a half ago, some women from the Los Angeles Self-Help Clinic came to New York to demonstrate do-it-yourself gynecology and performed an abortion onstage using a controversial device called the Karman cannula. Subsequently, the woman on whom the abortion had been performed developed a serious infection and had to go into the hospital for a D and C. One of the reporters covering the story, a feminist, found out about the infection, but she decided not to make the fact public, because she thought that to do so might hurt the self-help movement. When I heard about it, I was appalled; I was more appalled when I realized that I understood why she had done it.

But I cannot excuse that kind of self-censorship, either in that reporter or in myself. I think that many of us in this awkward position worry too much about what the movement will think and how what we write will affect the movement. In fact, the movement is nothing more than an amorphous blob of individual women and groups, most of whom disagree with each other. In fact, no amount of criticism of the movement will stop its forward momentum. In fact, I am intelligent enough to know that nothing I write really matters in any significant way to any of it. And knowing all this, I worry. I am a writer. I am a feminist. When I manage, from time to time, to overcome my political leanings and get at the truth, I feel a little better. And then I worry some more.

May, 1973

Baking Off

Roxanne Frisbie brought her own pan to the twenty-fourth annual Pillsbury Bake-Off. "I feel like a nut," she said. "It's just a plain old dumb pan, but everything I do is in that crazy pan." As it happens, Mrs. Frisbie had no cause whatsoever to feel like a nut: it seemed that at least half the 100 finalists in the Bake-It-Easy Bake-Off had brought something with them—their own sausages, their own pie pans, their own apples. Edna Buckley, who was fresh from representing New York State at the National Chicken Cooking Contest, where her recipe for fried chicken in a batter of beer, cheese, and crushed pretzels had gone down to defeat, brought with her a lucky handkerchief, a lucky horseshoe, a lucky dime for her shoe, a potholder with the Pillsbury Poppin' Fresh Doughboy on it, an Our Blessed Lady pin, and all of her jewelry, including a silver charm also in the shape of the doughboy. Mrs. Frisbie and Mrs. Buckley and the other finalists came to the Bake-Off to bake off for $65,000 in cash prizes; in Mrs. Frisbie's case, this meant making something she created herself and named Butterscotch Crescent Rolls—and which Pillsbury promptly, and to Mrs. Frisbie's dismay, renamed Sweet 'N Creamy

Crescent Crisps. Almost all the recipes in the finals were renamed by Pillsbury using a lot of crispy snicky snacky words. An exception to this was Sharon Schubert's Wiki Wiki Coffee Cake, a name which ought to have been snicky snacky enough; but Pillsbury, in a moment of restraint, renamed it One-Step Tropical Fruit Cake. As it turned out, Mrs. Schubert ended up winning $5,000 for her cake, which made everybody pretty mad, even the contestants who had been saying for days that they did not care who won, that winning meant nothing and was quite beside the point; the fact was that Sharon Schubert was a previous Bake-Off winner, having won $10,000 three years before for her Crescent Apple Snacks, and in addition had walked off with a trip to Puerto Vallarta in the course of this year's festivities. Most of the contestants felt she had won a little more than was really fair. But I'm getting ahead of the story.

The Pillsbury Company has been holding Bake-Offs since 1948, when Eleanor Roosevelt, for reasons that are not clear, came to give the first one her blessing. This year's took place from Saturday, February 24, through Tuesday, February 27, at the Beverly Hilton Hotel in Beverly Hills. One hundred contestants—97 of them women, 2 twelve-year-old boys, and 1 male graduate student—were winnowed down from a field of almost 100,000 entrants to compete for prizes in five categories: flour, frosting mix, crescent main dish, crescent dessert, and hot-roll mix. They were all brought, or flown, to Los Angeles for the Bake-Off itself, which took place on Monday, and a round of activities that included a tour of Universal Studios, a mini-version of television's *Let's Make A Deal* with Monty Hall himself, and a trip to Disneyland. The event is also attended by some 100 food editors, who turn it from a mere contest into the incredible publicity stunt Pillsbury intends it to be, and spend much of their time talking to each other about sixty-five new ways to use tuna fish and listening to various speakers lecture on the consumer movement and food and the appliance business. General Electric is co-sponsor of the event and donates a stove to each finalist, as well as the stoves for the Bake-Off; this year, it promoted a little Bake-Off of its own for the microwave oven, an appliance we were repeatedly told was the biggest improvement in cooking since the invention of the Willoughby System. Every one of the food editors seemed to know what the Willoughby System was, just as everyone seemed to know what Bundt pans were. "You will all be happy to hear," we were told at one point, "that only one of the finalists this year used a Bundt pan." The food editors burst into laughter at that point; I am not sure why. One Miss Alex Allard of San Antonio, Texas, had already won the microwave contest and $5,000, and she spent most of the Bake-Off turning out one Honey Drizzle Cake after another in the microwave ovens that ringed the Grand Ballroom of the Beverly Hilton Hotel. I never did taste the Honey Drizzle Cake, largely because I suspected—and this was weeks before the *Consumers Union* article on the subject—that microwave ovens were dangerous and probably caused peculiar diseases. If God had wanted us to make bacon in four minutes, He would have made bacon that cooked in four minutes.

"The Bake-Off is America," a General Electric executive announced just minutes before it began. "It's family. It's real people doing real things." Yes. The Pillsbury Bake-Off is an America that exists less and less, but exists nonetheless. It is women who still live on farms, who have six and seven children, who enter county fairs and sponsor 4-H Clubs. It is Grace Ferguson of Palm Springs, Florida, who entered the Bake-Off seventeen years in a row before reaching the finals this year, and who cooks at night and prays at the same time. It is Carol Hamilton, who once won a trip on a Greyhound bus to Hollywood for being the most popular girl in Youngstown, Ohio. There was a lot of talk at the Bake-Off about how the Bake-It-Easy theme had attracted a new breed of contestants this year, younger contestants— housewives, yes, but housewives who used whole-wheat flour and Granola and sour cream and similar supposedly hip ingredients in their recipes and were therefore somewhat more sophisticated, or urban, or something-of-the-sort than your usual Bake-Off contestant. There were a few of these—two, to be exact: Barbara Goldstein of New York City and Bonnie Brooks of Salisbury, Maryland, who actually visited the Los Angeles County Art Museum during a free afternoon. But there was also Suzie Sisson of Palatine, Illinois, twenty-five years old and the only Bundt-pan person in the finals, and her sentiments about life were the same as those that Bake-Off finalists presumably have had for years. "These are the beautiful people," she said, looking around the ball-room as she waited for her Bundt cake to come out of the oven. "They're not the little tiny rich people. They're nice and happy and religious types and family-oriented. Everyone talks about women's lib, which is ridiculous. If you're nice to your husband, he'll be nice to you. Your family is your job. They come first."

I was seven years old when the Pillsbury Bake-Off began, and as I grew up reading the advertisements for it in the women's magazines that were lying around the house, it always seemed to me that going to a Bake-Off would be the closest thing to a childhood fantasy of mine, which was to be locked overnight in a bakery. In reality, going to a Bake-Off *is* like being locked overnight in a bakery—a very bad bakery. I almost became sick right there on Range 95 after my sixth carbohydrate-packed sample—which happened, by coincidence, to be a taste of the aforementioned Mrs. Frisbie's aforementioned Sweet 'N Creamy Crescent Crisps.

But what is interesting about the Bake-Off—what is even significant about the event—is that it is, for the American housewife, what the Miss America contest used to represent to teen-agers. The pinnacle of a certain kind of achievement. The best in field. To win the Pillsbury Bake-Off, even to be merely a finalist in it, is to be a great housewife. And a creative housewife. "Cooking is very creative." I must have heard that line thirty times as I interviewed the finalists. I don't happen to think that cooking is very creative—what interests me about it is, on the contrary, its utter mindlessness and mathematical certainty. "Cooking is very relaxing"—that's my bromide. On the other hand, I have to admit that some of the recipes that were concocted for the Bake-Off, amazing combinations of frosting mix and marshmallows and peanut butter and brown sugar and chocolate, were practically awe-inspiring. And cooking, it is quite clear, is only a small part of the apparently frenzied creativity that flourishes in these women's homes. I spent quite a bit of time at the Bake-Off chatting with Laura Aspis of Shaker Heights, Ohio, a seven-time Bake-Off finalist and duplicate-bridge player, and after we had discussed her high-protein macaroons made with coconut-almond frosting mix and Granola, I noticed that Mrs. Aspis was wearing green nail polish. On the theory that no one who wears green nail polish wants it to go unremarked upon, I remarked upon it.

"That's not green nail polish," Mrs. Aspis said. "It's platinum nail polish that I mix with green food coloring."

"Oh," I said.

"And the thing of it is," she went on, "when it chips, it doesn't matter."

"Why is that?" I asked.

"Because it stains your nails permanently," Mrs. Aspis said.

"You mean your nails are permanently green?"

"Well, not exactly," said Mrs. Aspis. "You see, last week they were blue, and the week before I made purple, so now my nails are a combination of all three. It looks like I'm in the last throes of something."

On Sunday afternoon, most of the finalists chose to spend their free time sitting around the hotel and socializing. Two of them—Marjorie Johnson of Robbinsdale, Minnesota, and Mary Finnegan of Minneota, Minnesota—were seated at a little round table just off the Hilton ballroom talking about a number of things, including Tupperware. Both of them love Tupperware.

"When I built my new house," Mrs. Johnson said, "I had so much Tupperware I had to build a cupboard just for it." Mrs. Johnson is a very tiny, fortyish mother of three, and she and her dentist husband have just moved into a fifteen-room house she cannot seem to stop talking about. "We have this first-floor kitchen, harvest gold and blue, and it's almost finished. Now I have a second kitchen on my walk-out level and that's going to be harvest gold and blue, too. Do you know about the new wax

Congoleum? I think that's what I put in—either that or Shinyl Vinyl. I haven't had to wash my floors in three months. The house isn't done yet because of the Bake-Off. My husband says if I'd spent as much time on it as I did on the Bake-Off, we'd be finished. I sent in sixteen recipes—it took me nearly a year to do it."

"That's nothing," said Mrs. Finnegan. "It took me twenty years before I cracked it. I'm a contest nut. I'm a thirty-times winner in the *Better Homes & Gardens* contest. I won a thousand dollars from Fleischmann's Yeast. I won Jell-O this year, I'm getting a hundred and twenty-five dollars' worth of Revere cookware for that. The Knox Gelatine contest. I've won seven blenders and a quintisserie. It does four things—fries, bakes, roasts, there's a griddle. I sold the darn thing before I even used it."

"Don't tell me," said Mrs. Johnson. "Did you enter the Crystal Sugar Name the Lake Home contest?"

"Did I enter?" said Mrs. Finnegan. "Wait till you see this." She took a pen and wrote her submission on a napkin and held it up for Mrs. Johnson. The napkin read "Our Entry Hall." "I should have won that one," said Mrs. Finnegan. "I did win the Crystal Sugar Name the Dessert contest. I called it 'Signtation Squares.' I think I got a blender on that one."

"Okay," said Mrs. Johnson. "They've got a contest now, Crystal Sugar Name a Sauce. It has pineapple in it."

"I don't think I won that," said Mrs. Finnegan, "but I'll show you what I sent in." She held up the napkin and this time what she had written made sense. "Hawaiian More Chant," it said.

"Oh, you're clever," said Mrs. Johnson.

"They have three more contests so I haven't given up," said Mrs. Finnegan.

• • •

On Monday morning at exactly 9 a.m., the one hundred finalists marched four abreast into the Hilton ballroom, led by Philip Pillsbury, former chairman of the board of the company. The band played "Nothin' Says Lovin' Like Somethin' from the Oven," and when it finished, Pillsbury announced: "Now you one hundred winners can go to your ranges."

Chaos. Shrieking. Frenzy. Furious activity. Cracking eggs. Chopping onions. Melting butter. Mixing, beating, blending. The band perking along with such carefully selected tunes as "If I Knew You Were Coming I'd Have Baked a Cake." Contestants running to the refrigerators for more supplies. Floor assistants rushing dirty dishes off to unseen dishwashers. All two hundred members of the working press, plus television's Bob Barker, interviewing any finalist they could get to drop a spoon. At 9:34 a.m., Mrs. Lorraine Walmann submitted her Cheesy Crescent Twist-Ups to the judges and became the first finalist to finish. At 10 a.m., all the stoves were on, the television lights were blasting, the temperature in the ballroom was up to the mid-nineties, and Mrs. Marjorie Johnson, in the course of giving an interview about her house to the *Minneapolis Star*, had forgotten whether she had put one cup of sugar or two into her Crispy Apple Bake. "You know, we're building this new house," she was saying. "When I go back, I have to buy living-room furniture." By 11 a.m., Mae Wilkinson had burned her skillet corn bread and was at work on a second. Laura Aspis had lost her potholder. Barbara Bellhorn was distraught because she was not used to California apples. Alex Allard was turning out yet another Honey

Drizzle Cake. Dough and flour were all over the floor. Mary Finnegan was fussing because the crumbs on her Lemon Cream Bars were too coarse. Marjorie Johnson was in the midst of yet another interview on her house. "Well, let me tell you," she was saying, "the shelves in the kitchen are built low. . . . " One by one, the contestants, who were each given seven hours and four tries to produce two perfect samples of their recipes, began to finish up and deliver one tray to the judges and one tray to the photographer. There were samples everywhere, try this, try that, but after six tries, climaxed by Mrs. Frisbie's creation, I stopped sampling. The overkill was unbearable: none of the recipes seemed to contain one cup of sugar when two would do, or a delicate cheese when Kraft American would do, or an actual minced onion when instant minced onions would do. It was snack time. It was convenience-food time. It was less-work-for-Mother time. All I could think about was a steak.

By 3 p.m., there were only two contestants left—Mrs. Johnson, whose dessert took only five minutes to make but whose interviews took considerably longer, and Bonnie Brooks, whose third sour-cream-and-banana cake was still in the oven. Mrs. Brooks brought her cake in last, at 3:27 p.m., and as she did, the packing began. The skillets went into brown cartons, the measuring spoons into barrels, the stoves were dismantled. The Bake-Off itself was over—and all that remained was the trip to Disneyland, and the breakfast at the Brown Derby . . . and the prizes.

And so it is Tuesday morning, and the judges have reached a decision, and any second now, Bob Barker is going to announce the five winners over national television. All the contestants are wearing their best dresses and smiling, trying to smile anyway, good sports all, and now Bob Barker is announcing the winners. Bonnie Brooks and her cake and Albina Flieller and her Quick Pecan Pie win $25,000 each. Sharon Schubert and two others win $5,000. And suddenly the show is over and it is time to go home, and the ninety-five people who did not win the twenty-fourth annual Pillsbury Bake-Off are plucking the orchids from the centerpieces, signing each other's programs, and grumbling. They are grumbling about Sharon Schubert. And for a moment, as I hear the grumbling everywhere—"It really isn't fair." ..."After all, she won the trip to Mexico"—I think that perhaps I am wrong about these women: perhaps they are capable of anger after all, or jealousy, or competitiveness, or something I think of as a human trait I can relate to. But the grumbling stops after a few minutes, and I find myself listening to Marjorie Johnson. "I'm so glad I didn't win the grand prize," she is saying, "because if you win that, you don't get to come back to the next Bake-Off. I'm gonna start now on my recipes for next year. I'm gonna think of something really good." She stopped for a moment. "You know," she said, "it's going to be very difficult to get back to normal living."

July, 1973

Crazy Ladies: I

Washington is a city of important men and the women they married before they grew up. Is that how the saying goes? Something like that, anyway. All those tidy little summations of local phenomena—California is fine if you're an orange; first prize one week in Philadelphia, second prize two weeks in Philadelphia—turn out, after close inspection, to be even more accurate than they seemed at first hearing. But the one I wanted to talk about is the one about Washington.

I don't know a great deal about life in Washington for women—I spent a summer there once working in the White House, and my main memories of the experience have to do with a very bad permanent wave I have always been convinced kept me from having a meaningful relationship with President Kennedy—but that doesn't stop me from making generalizations about the place. Because it has always seemed obvious that life for women in Washington combined the worst qualities of the South and small-town life. Washington is a city of locker-room boys, and all the old, outmoded notions apply: men and women are ushered to separate rooms after dinner, sex is dirty, and they are still serving onion-soup dip. A married woman with any brains and personality at all is faced with a Hobson's choice: she can be her husband's appendage, and pay that price—and we have Joan Kennedy as the classic example of a woman who has. Or she can be a crazy lady.

I should clarify what I mean by crazy lady. In my youth—which ended about eight years ago—I occasionally had a date with someone who was very straight. Which is to say, square. In most relationships, I tend to be the straight one, cautious, conservative, not crossing on the Don't Walk, but whenever I was confronted with someone even squarer than I was, whenever I was confronted with a relationship where the role of the crazy person was up for grabs, I would leap in, say outrageous things, end the evening lying down in Times Square with a lampshade on my head. I wasn't a patch on Zelda Fitzgerald—I would never have leaped into the Plaza fountain for fear of ruining my hair—but I was in there doing my damnedest.

The crazy lady I have been thinking about apropos of all this is Barbara Howar. Mrs. Howar is not really crazy in any context where real craziness exists—in New York, she would just be another outspoken, somewhat bitchy woman. But Washington is a city that is an all-purpose straight man: you don't have to be a terribly funny joke to get laughs in Washington, and you don't have to be a terribly crazy person to seem about as loony as they come. Just jump into the Supreme Court fountain. Or refuse to go off with the ladies after dinner. Or have an affair. That's about all it takes.

Barbara Howar, who has written a book about her experiences in Washington, *Laughing All the Way* (Stein & Day), was a socialite who hooked up with Lynda Bird and Luci Baines in some inexplicable way having to do with wedding trousseaus and became a social light in the Johnson Administration. In an era not noted for its sophisticates, she became notorious for her sharp-tongued remarks, some of which were occasionally mistaken for wit and some of which were actually witty. Then she was dumped shortly before Luci's wedding, in a tacky and hilarious episode which confronted her with a true moral dilemma: should she warp her six-year-old daughter for life by withdrawing her from the role of flower girl in the ceremony, or warp her for life by letting her go on with it? After resolving this dilemma (she let her go on with it) and living through a decent period of social ostracism, Mrs. Howar emerged once again to resume her role as the town's Peck's Bad Girl.

As she recalls in her memoir, "I was filled with an uncontrollable desire to shock—to say or do anything that would raise voices and eyebrows or boredom's threshold. I had a natural ability to alienate people I found dull. I would rudely cut short any matron lady who dwelled too long on her wonderful children, her indispensable housekeeper, or her husband's unheralded political abilities. I once interrupted a woman deep into her monologue about the great Lone Star State with, 'If I hear one more exaggeration about Texas, I'm going to throw up on the Alamo.' I became incautious in my description of Texas habits, asking one gentleman sporting a hammered-silver belt studded with ersatz stones: 'Did you make it at summer camp?' And to a Dallas lady in reference to the Tex-Mex delicacy she had proudly served for dinner: 'Did you get this recipe off the back of a Fritos bag?'"

I liked *Laughing All the Way*—it happens to be far
more charming than what I just quoted would indicate;
it also happens to be fun to read. But I was surprised
to find it as fascinating as I did, because what Barbara
Howar has written, and I don't think it was uninten-
tional, is almost a case study of a kind of woman and a
kind of misdirected energy. And while I'm not sure any
lesson or moral can be drawn from it—or if it can, I'm
not about to do it—her floundering attempts to make a
life and identity for herself are genuinely, and surprisingly, moving.

Barbara Howar came to Washington just out of finishing school and the South and went to work on Capitol Hill. She was pretty and blond and energetic and,
as we used to say in high school, popular. As she writes,
"I never wearied of flying on private planes to the Ken-
tucky Derby with groups that included Aly Khan, of
first nights of Broadway musicals. . . . But the tedium
of clerical work dulled the excitement of my social life.
I started doing bizarre things—my personal indicator
of unrest—painting mailboxes shocking pink, leaping
fully clothed into the Supreme Court fountain. One day
I woke up disposed to do the only thing I had not yet
tried: marriage." She married very well: her husband
was a builder, heir to an Arab fortune, and she entered
into the life of being his wife, working at charities, being
photographed at luncheons, having parties and a family. Then 1964 came along, and because it was the thing
to do that year, she went to work for the campaign of
President Johnson.

It is altogether possible that had Barbara Howar
married someone she was more capable of being an

appendage of, none of what followed would have happened. Or it would have happened much later. In any event, she went off as Lady Bird Johnson's hairdresser on the campaign swing of the South, met a Johnson aide with whom she had an affair, and charmed the President to the point that he was soon holding her hand (and falling asleep) during White House movie screenings and whirling her about the dance floor at State functions. "I was *that* woman dancing with *the* President . . . ," Mrs. Howar recalls. "It never occurred to me that I could distinguish myself in more admirable fashion." *Women's Wear Daily* began to follow her everywhere, *Life* magazine profiled her, and Maxine Cheshire watched as she danced on a tabletop in a white dress with gold chains she said "cut into my tender young flesh . . . just a little number the Marquis de Sade whipped up for me. . . .

"There simply was no shutting me up. I had to tell every newspaper and magazine that Mrs. Johnson, a lady who spent every waking minute planting trees in ghettos and sprinkling tulip bulbs around settlement houses that had no plumbing, was 'off base' with her Beautification Program, that it was 'like buying a wig when your teeth are rotting.' I had to say in print that Mrs. Johnson's rich New York friends 'would be better advised to donate their money to countless endeavors like fighting street crime, and that to celebrate their philanthropy I would gladly wear a bronze plaque saying: TODAY I WAS NOT RAPED OR MUGGED THROUGH THE KIND GENEROSITY OF THE LASKER/LOEB FOUNDATIONS.'"

The affair with the Johnson aide continued and became a full-fledged Washington scandal; she left her husband and went off with her lover for a week in Jamaica. "In the sultry, alien surroundings of the Caribbean," she writes, in one of the more melodramatic sections of the book, "harsh reality became larger than my fantasy of finding peace by changing marriages. I became morbidly depressed for the first time in my life. I missed the children, my home, everything familiar and comfortable. I was melancholy and homesick, maudlin in my confusion, I wanted something to make me happy, something to give me reason not to care that half my life was over and that I had no real zest for finishing out the rest. Guilty and restless as before, I saw the future now as even more menacing. I wanted it all and I wanted out. It was the woman's primal feeling of being trapped, unable to live without marriage because it was all I knew, but incapable of projecting myself happily into more of the same. My anxieties grew. I had doubts about who I was and what I wanted to be. Why was I even in Jamaica?" At about this moment, Mrs. Howar's reveries were interrupted by a group of detectives, who burst in on her and the Johnson aide, ripped the strap on her nightgown, and took pictures. Mrs. Howar returned to Washington, reconciled for a time with her husband, and was promptly dropped by the Johnsons.

At this point, Barbara Howar's story became a morality tale. Her son gets spinal meningitis and almost dies. She finally leaves her husband. She develops a social conscience through a relationship with Bobby Darin, the singer, and becomes a star on a local television news show, where her standard operating procedure was to fling her newly acquired set of facts on life in the slums at her guests. "It was a long while," she writes, "before I learned that if there was anything worse than a bigoted keeper of the status quo, it was a recycled socialite with a newly aroused public conscience." Mrs. Howar complains, in what are straight women's movement terms, that her remarks on the air were not taken seriously because she was a woman. "If my male counterparts made strong critical statements, they were 'blunt' or 'forceful'; similar candor from television women is 'cutting,' 'catty,' and 'bitchy.'" She is right about the problems—though probably not in her own case. A typical moment in Mrs. Howar's television career was this remark, made as a criticism of the space program's all-white personnel: "If N.A.S.A. can train a monkey to operate the controls of a rocket, they can train a black man."

Laughing All the Way ends with a description of Mrs. Howar's disastrous and final experience in television, co-hosting a show with Mrs. David Susskind, and a marvelous chapter on her mother's death. "I am enormously saddened to understand that I would not be on my way to real peace if my mother were still alive," she writes. I don't know whether she is on her way to real peace—I would like to have heard a little more about that—but she *has* written a pretty good book about Barbara Howar. Which is more than I can say about her friend Willie Morris, who has also written a book about Barbara Howar this year, a novel called *The Last of the Southern Girls*. There is a point to be made here about borrowing material, and there is another point to be made about fact and fiction and the difference between them, but I don't want to get into that. I do want to say that I read Morris's book when I was almost finished with this column, and I note that we make some of the same points about Washington and women. I also note that he has the quote right. Washington is a city of men and the women they married when they were young. That's how it goes.

August, 1973

The Pig

Every so often, you turn a corner and Life, or the times, or the public-relations mechanism that makes the world go round throws out a hero you have to live with for a while. The point here is not about heroes but heroines. And long before the Bobby Riggs–Margaret Court tennis match took place near San Diego in May, 1973, it was clear to me that Margaret Court, the heroine who had been thrown not just my way but at the entire female population of the world, was going to leave something to be desired. The symbolism of the match was haywire enough to begin with—Riggs has always played a woman's game, Court a man's—and it was to get even more muddled before the actual confrontation. But beyond that, it seemed quite likely that of all the big women players now on the circuit, Margaret Court would be the one least likely to come through. I'm not just talking about winning the match—although God knows that would have helped. But there were the nerves. Margaret had nerves. Muscle spasms under pressure. She, of course, insisted they were simply magnesium deficiencies and potassium deficiencies; everyone else insisted they were nerves. *Just like a woman.* And then there was her style.

I suppose it's not really fair to bring up style; style has nothing to do with tennis, nothing to do with anything really, but it mattered to me. I mean, here is Bobby Riggs, the Lip, the hustler, saucy Bobby Riggs with his dyed red hair and his never-ending monologue and his relentless promotions (the copper-bracelet promotion, the Head tennis-clothes promotion, the 415-vitamin-pills-a-day promotion, the land-development-that-sponsored-the-match promotion, the building-project-where-Bobby-lived promotion); here is Bobby Riggs, clown prince of the Old Boy tennis circuit, great copy, and he is standing on the court of the San Vicente Country Club in San Diego Country Estates posing for photographs with Margaret Court. It is Friday afternoon, two days before the Mother's Day match, and he is whispering to Margaret, taunting her about the weight of the tennis balls and the question of her nerves and the despicable quality of women's tennis and the pressure of having all the women counting on her on Sunday. And here is Margaret. Nervous. Smiling uneasily. Occasionally offering a demure reply to Bobby or the press. "I like a challenge," she is saying. "I love the game. It's been very good to me." Like that. I didn't want *that*. I wanted some lip. I wanted some aggression. I wanted some fight. I wanted satisfaction. And what I got, what all of us got instead, was a lady.

It all began a little over two years ago, when former Wimbledon champion Bobby Riggs made a few derogatory comments about women's tennis in *Sports Illustrated* and issued a challenge to Billie Jean King: "You insist that top women players provide a brand of tennis comparable to men's. I challenge you to prove it. I contend that you not only cannot beat a top male player but that you can't beat me, a tired old man." As it happens, Billie Jean King did not say precisely that; what she did say was that women's tennis was more entertaining than men's, and that women deserved equal prize money. "Women play about twenty-five percent as good as men," Riggs countered, "so they should get about twenty-five percent of the money men receive." Nothing much came of Riggs's initial challenge, but this year Tony Trabert, the pro at San Diego Country Estates, prodded Riggs to try again, and after Mrs. King turned him down, he sent telegrams challenging six other top women players and offering $5,000 of his own money and $5,000 put up by the land-development corporation to the winner. Margaret Court was first to respond. "I'd still rather play Billie Jean," Riggs said later, "because she's really the ringleader of the liberation movement. She's the revolutionary. Margaret Court is such a nice person—I don't want to say by contrast." Margaret Court, thirty years old, Australian, mother of a fourteen-month-old boy, is such a nice person by contrast that she doesn't even think women deserve the same prize money as men. "I don't feel there's a depth in the women's game," she said. "There are so many good men. There are only six or eight good women. If you have a thirty-two-draw tournament, you're going to give some youngster a thousand dollars to lose in the first round, and she doesn't deserve it. I don't think it's good for the game. The money will come. The depth will come. At the moment, we're rushing it a little."

Margaret Court trained for the match in Berkeley, working out quietly with her coach, a South African named Dennis Van der Meer. Occasionally reporters would come to the court for an interview and she would reluctantly grant one. Her answers were short and genteel; she was visibly uncomfortable with the press. "Margaret really doesn't enjoy this," her husband, Barry, would explain. Meanwhile, every day, Riggs played five sets, jogged two miles, swallowed 415 vitamin pills, and gave out interviews. Hundreds of interviews. Any reporter who called or showed up got more than he came for. "This is so much fun," Riggs said during one interview, "that I wish it were postponed so we could go on like this another six weeks."

By the weekend of the match, Riggs had worked his remarks into a finely honed performance, with set lines that varied only slightly from press conference to press conference. "This," he would announce, in a wonderfully unsyntactical sentence, "is the match of the century between the battle of the sexes." When even that description seemed inadequate, he would shout, "This is the most important match ever played in tennis!" After the match, he concluded at the top of his lungs that he had just played the most significant sporting event of all time. He would stand, or sit, surrounded by sports reporters, and spin a simple question into a thirty-minute monologue, inserting rhetorical questions to stretch it out, waving his copper bracelet in the air for a plug or dropping in a remark about "beautiful San Diego Country Estates." The delivery would begin slowly, usually with his old-person routine ("I'm a fifty-five-year-old man with one foot in the grave"), heavily studded with a series of impotence jokes ("The flesh won't do what the mind tells it to," and "Why shouldn't they let me into the women's tournaments—everyone knows there's no sex after fifty-five"). Then Riggs would build, gradually, ignore interrupting questions, pitch his high voice even higher, and suddenly he would be speaking so quickly that no one could quite get it down or get a word in. A typical Riggs monologue, this one recorded in the *Los Angeles Times*, went like this:

"It's pretty fantastic to think I am playing the match of the century and the battle of the sexes. This match is going to be more important than the Wimbledon, Forest Hills, or a fifty-thousand-dollar match between Laver and Rosewall. Why? Because Margaret Court is carrying the banner for women all over the world and I'm carrying the banner for all the old guys who have always felt superior to women, and they'll want to see an old guy win because then they'll feel superior, too, and I'll be doing a very good thing for all the men all over the world and they won't give in to the women's lib quite so easily. She's got twenty-five years on me. She's bigger, stronger, more agile. She's got better shots. Does everything better on a tennis court. She's the best woman player in the world. What's she going to do if she can't even beat a fifty-five-year-old guy with one foot in the grave? What are people going to think of women's tennis after that? She's going to have a lot of pressure on her. I love tension. Not that there will be that much on me. I thrive— I have always played my best under tension. Whereas just the opposite is true with her. We're going to be playing in front of the biggest audience ever to see a tennis match, right here at San Diego Country Estates."

It was difficult to distinguish how much of Riggs's remarks were put on, how much mere hysteria, and how much utterly sincere babble, but I finally concluded after hearing the routine some two dozen times that underneath all that surface male chauvinism was heartfelt male chauvinism, heightened, in this case, by Riggs's bitterness toward open tennis.

All the older men tennis players are dismayed that open tennis, with its huge prize money, came too late for them to take advantage of it. That women are playing open tennis, too, and in some cities even beginning to outdraw the men's tour, that a player like Margaret Court can earn $100,000 a year—this is almost more than a man like Riggs can bear. Instead of playing in high-stakes tournaments, Riggs has been forced in the past twenty-five years to play the kind of tennis he really prefers, hustling opponents with poodles tied to his legs, umbrellas and suitcases in hand, top hat on his head.

Stories of Riggs's hustling have been legendary in the sports world, and the press managed to dredge most of them up again for this match. What few in the press realized, though, was that they were being conned at least as cleverly as Mrs. Court. Eighteen of the twenty-four reporters covering the match picked Margaret Court to win, most of them in straight sets. Explanations of sentimentality and sheer stupidity aside, the reason for all this faulty judgment had mainly to do with the amazing total performance Riggs put on the week before the match. Whenever the press watched him practice, he played well under his game. Whenever he was interviewed, he discoursed at length on his failing strength. He spent days fighting for a lightweight ball, lost in a flip he referred to as "the flip of the century," and spent days sulking about how the weight of the balls would permanently cripple his game. After the match, of course, he confessed he had wanted the heavy-duty balls all along and had just made the fuss to throw Mrs. Court off.

The scene over the weight of the balls was just one of

several incidents that served to cloud the already murky
male-female issues. Most men would have wanted to flip
for heavy-duty balls, while women prefer lightweight
ones; Riggs uses the lighter aluminum racket while
Court plays with wood; Riggs's game is all lobs and slices
and spins and twists, while Court plays the serve-and-
volley technique favored by strong male players. What
happened as a result was that the press covering the
match, all of whom were male except for me, became far
more interested and threatened by the women's liberation implications of the relationship between Margaret
Court and her husband than by the totally confusing
implications of the match itself.

"Look at that," one reporter said to me, pointing to
Barry Court, who was carrying the Courts' young son
Danny. "He always carries the baby. Margaret never carries the baby." In fact, Mrs. Court carried the baby as
often as her husband did when she was off court; this
was never registered by the press, who persisted in referring to Barry Court, a tall Australian who manages his
wife's career, as "the baby-sitter." Sunday night, after Mrs.
Court had been trounced by Riggs, I was walking back to
my room and bumped into Brent Musberger of CBS. "Do
you know who the real winner of today's match was?" he
asked. Yes, I thought, I know exactly who the real winner
was. Bobby Riggs. That, however, was obviously not the
answer Musberger was going for. "Who?" I asked. "Barry
Court," he replied. "What are you talking about?" I asked.
"It's simple," he explained. "Now she'll really need him.
Now she'll really have to depend on him." The notion that
Mrs. Court's defeat by a male would somehow alter her
relationship with her husband—who has been married
to her for six years and presumably came to terms with

the bargain at least that long ago—seemed a peculiarly
male fantasy. On the other hand, it may be my peculiarly
feminist fantasy to believe that Barry Court is happy in
his life.

And finally, there was the match. No point in dwelling too long on that. Riggs bounced down to the court in
a sky-blue workout suit that looked like a pair of Doctor Dentons; he presented his opponent with a bouquet
of twenty-four roses that were arranged exactly like a
funeral spray. Margaret Court appeared in a specially
designed yellow-and-green tennis dress with the word
"Margaret" stitched into its high collar; it was exactly the
sort of dress Queen Elizabeth would choose to play tennis in. The match began, and by the time the first three
games were over, Riggs was in total control: his lovely
lollipop game and his psych-out had Margaret blowing
her first serves, failing to rush the net, missing shots she
had no business missing. "She's just not bright enough,"
said the man next to me, who happened to be Pancho
Segura. The match ended with Riggs winning 6–2, 6–1. "I
played awful," said Mrs. Court afterward. "He hit softer
than many of the girls I've been playing. I couldn't get my
timing. It was one of the worst matches I've played in a
long long time." In the end, Margaret provided a perfect
illustration of Radcliffe president Matina Horner's thesis on women fearing success. About the only thing she
failed to do was cry.

And we were left with Bobby Riggs. Margaret Court
went off to her room—the baby was sick, her husband
explained—and Riggs held the press conference alone.
Two hours later, when I left San Diego Country Estates,
he was still talking. He was planning to enter the Virginia Slims tournament and would even consider wear-

ing a dress. He was knocking women's tennis. He was contemplating a match against Billie Jean King.* "Tell her she has to play for fifty thousand dollars a side," he said. "And she's got to put up the money. I'm not putting up any more free shots. I've done enough for these women." He was describing the last-minute bets he had made and won. He was plugging his vitamin pills and waving his copper bracelet. He was pumping for senior tennis. "The girls say they should get as much money as men," he was saying. "Well, if girls should get as much as men, us seniors should get as much as the girls. Look at this. One of the best woman players beaten by a fifty-five-year-old guy with one foot in the grave." Every so often, you turn a corner and Life, or the times, or the public-relations mechanism that makes the world go round throws out a hero you have to live with for a while.

September, 1973

---

* The Riggs-King match was held in September, 1973. I never wrote anything about it afterward—partly because I didn't want to repeat myself and partly because I had mixed feelings about the outcome. I knew that it was a triumph for women's tennis, and it was even a small triumph for the women journalists at it—we won $800 from Riggs. But when the circus was over, I felt sorry for Riggs. I thought he was a harmless goniff, and I was sad that his fifteen minutes were up—it had been fun.

Dorothy Parker

Eleven years ago, shortly after I came to New York, I met a young man named Victor Navasky. Victor was trying relentlessly at that point to start a small humor magazine called *Monocle*, and there were a lot of meetings. Some of them were business meetings, I suppose; I don't remember them. The ones I do remember were pure social occasions, and most of them took place at the Algonquin Hotel. Every Tuesday at 6 p.m., we would meet for drinks there and sit around pretending to be the Algonquin Round Table. I had it all worked out: Victor got to be Harold Ross, Bud Trillin and C. D. B. Bryan alternated at Benchley, whoever was fattest and grumpiest got to be Alexander Woollcott. I, of course, got to be Dorothy Parker. It was all very heady, and very silly, and very self-conscious. It was also very boring, which disturbed me. Then Dorothy Parker, who was living in Los Angeles, gave a seventieth-birthday interview to the Associated Press, an interview I have always thought of as the beginning of the Revisionist School of Thinking on the Algonquin Round Table, and she said that it, too, had been boring. Which made me feel a whole lot better.

I had never really known Dorothy Parker at all. My

parents, who were screenwriters, knew her when I was a child in Hollywood, and they tell me I met her at several parties where I was trotted out in pajamas to meet the guests. I don't remember that, and neither, I suspect, did Dorothy Parker. I met her again briefly when I was twenty. She was paying a call on Oscar Levant, whose daughter I grew up with. She was frail and tiny and twinkly, and she shook my hand and told me that when I was a child I had had masses of curly black hair. As it happens, it was my sister Hallie who had had masses of curly black hair. So there you are.

None of which is really the point. The point is the legend. I grew up on it and coveted it desperately. All I wanted in this world was to come to New York and be Dorothy Parker. The funny lady. The only lady at the table. The woman who made her living by her wit. Who wrote for *The New Yorker*. Who always got off the perfect line at the perfect moment, who never went home and lay awake wondering what she ought to have said because she had said exactly what she ought to have. I was raised on Dorothy Parker lines. Some were unbearably mean, and some were sad, but I managed to fuzz those over and remember the ones I loved. My mother had a first-rate Parker story I carried around for years. One night, it seems, Dorothy Parker was playing anagrams at our home with a writer named Sam Lauren. Lauren had just made the word "currie," and Dorothy Parker insisted there was no such spelling. A great deal of scrapping ensued. Finally, my mother said she had some curry in the kitchen and went to get it. She returned with a jar of Crosse & Blackwell currie and showed it to Dorothy Parker. "What do they know?" said Parker. "Look at the way they spell Crosse."

I have spent a great deal of my life discovering that my ambitions and fantasies—which I once thought of as totally unique—turn out to be clichés, so it was not a surprise to me to find that there were other young women writers who came to New York with as bad a Dorothy Parker problem as I had. I wonder, though, whether any of that still goes on. Whatever illusions I managed to maintain about the Parker myth were given a good sharp smack several years ago, when John Keats published a biography of her called *You Might As Well Live* (Simon & Schuster). By that time, I had come to grips with the fact that I was not, nor would I ever be, Dorothy Parker; but I had managed to keep myself from what anyone who has read a line about or by her should have known, which was simply that Dorothy Parker had not been terribly good at being Dorothy Parker either. In Keats's book, even the wonderful lines, the salty remarks, the softly murmured throwaways seem like dreadful little episodes in Leonard Lyons's column. There were the stories of the suicide attempts, squalid hotel rooms, long incoherent drunks, unhappy love affairs, marriage to a homosexual. All the early, sharp self-awareness turned to chilling self-hate. "Boy, did I think I was smart," she said once. "I was just a little Jewish girl trying to be cute."

A year or so after the Keats book, I read Lillian Hellman's marvelous memoir, *An Unfinished Woman* (Little, Brown). In it is a far more affectionate and moving portrait of Parker, one that manages to convey how special it was to be with her when she was at her best. "The wit," writes Hellman, "was never as attractive as the comment, often startling, always sudden, as if a curtain had opened and you had a brief and brilliant glance into what you would never have found for yourself." Still, the

Hellman portrait is of a sad lady who misspent her life and her talent.

In one of several unbelievably stupid remarks that do so much to make the Keats biography as unsatisfying as it is, he calls Parker a "tiny, big-eyed feminine woman with the mind of a man." There are only a few things that remain clear to me about Dorothy Parker, and one of them is that the last thing she had was the mind of a man. *The Portable Dorothy Parker* (Viking) contains most of her writing; there are first-rate stories in it—"Big Blonde," of course—and first-rate light verse. But the worst work in it is characterized by an almost unbearably girlish sensibility. The masochist. The victim. The sentimental woman whose moods are totally ruled by the whims of men. This last verse, for example, from "To a Much Too Unfortunate Lady":

> *He will leave you white with woe*
> *If you go the way you go.*
> *If your dreams were thread to weave,*
> *He will pluck them from his sleeve.*
> *If your heart had come to rest,*
> *He will flick it from his breast.*
> *Tender though the love he bore,*
> *You had loved a little more. . . .*
> *Lady, go and curse your star,*
> *Thus Love is, and thus you are.*

What seems all wrong about these lines now is not their emotion—the emotion, sad to say, is dead on—but that they seem so embarrassing. Many of the women poets writing today about love and men write with as much wit as Parker, but with a great deal of healthy anger besides. Like Edna St. Vincent Millay's poetry, which Parker was often accused of imitating, Dorothy Parker's poetry seems dated not so much because it is or isn't but because politics have made the sentiments so unfashionable in literature. The last thing I mean to write here is one of those articles about the woman artist as some sort of victim of a sexist society; it is, however, in Parker's case an easy argument to make.

And so there is the legend, and there is not much of it left. One no longer wants to be the only woman at the table. One does not want to spend nights with a group of people who believe that the smartly chosen rejoinder is what anything is about. One does not even want to be published in *The New Yorker*. But before one looked too hard at it, it was a lovely myth, and I have trouble giving it up. Most of all, I'm sorry it wasn't true. As Dorothy Parker once said, in a line she suggested for her gravestone: "If you can read this, you've come too close."

October, 1973

A Star Is Born

A few months ago, I got a phone call from a man at CBS named Sandy Socolow. I have known Sandy Socolow ever since college, when I was a copy girl at CBS for a summer and he was working for Walter Cronkite. A few years later, he and his wife, Nan, and their children and I all lived in the same New York apartment house, One University Place. As a matter of fact, the night of the 1965 blackout Nan Socolow and I spent a rather ragged evening together. I had groped my way down to her apartment, having nowhere better to go, having no idea that I ought to be doing something memorable that night to tell my children about, and Nan suggested we play canasta. I had forgotten how, but she taught me. She won the first game. I wiped her out in the second. After it, Nan looked up and said, "It's too bad you have to leave." Anyway, I have a fondness for Sandy Socolow in spite of the fact that his wife is a sore loser, and I was glad to hear from him.

"Let's have lunch," he said. "I want to talk to you about your future in television and mine."

"I hate television," I said.

"Let's have lunch anyway," he said.

A few weeks passed between the phone call and the lunch, and during that time I read that CBS was revamping its morning news show and was looking for an anchorwoman and anchorman. I became more interested in the lunch. I really do hate television—last year I did a pilot for a talk show for women, and when it was through, and, as far as I was concerned, perfect, the head of the company that produced the show saw it and said I had a quality on screen not unlike Howard Cosell. The show was cut to pieces, I was fired, and an entire other person was dubbed in my place. All in all, it was not a happy story, and it left me almost certain I never wanted anything serious to do with the medium again. I say *almost* certain, because the only desire I was left with, the only ambition the experience did not manage to kill, was for Barbara Walters's job. I have always wanted Barbara Walters's job. The CBS thing seemed about as close to it as I was ever going to get.

So Sandy Socolow and I had lunch. I told him I had read about the job in the papers. "That's what I was calling you about," he said. It was a nice lunch. Soft-shell crabs. Rice pudding with a lot of raisins in it. I had some ideas. He had some ideas. He said he'd call me after he looked at an old tape of me on *The Dick Cavett Show*. He also said that his wife would be delighted to hear I was separated from my husband, because she had a lot of extra men.

The next day Nan Socolow called.

"Are you free for dinner Tuesday night?" she said.

"Sure," I said.

"Good," she said. "We're having dinner with a man who's a writer, and we'd like you to come, but it's not a fix-up."

"Fine," I said.

"I really want to make that clear," she said. "It's not a fix-up."

"What are you trying to tell me?" I asked. "Is he gay?"

"No," said Nan. "It's not that. It's just that we have to have dinner with him, and we have to have dinner with you, and I thought we'd kill two birds with one stone."

I passed on the dinner.

A few days later—June now—Sandy Socolow's secretary called quite frantically to set up a lunch. He had apparently seen my Cavett tape and was still interested. I went to the lunch to find Sandy and Lee Townsend, the producer of the show, Gordon Manning, one of the heads of CBS News, and Hughes Rudd, who had just been given the job of anchorman on the new morning show. Part of the purpose of the lunch was to see whether Hughes and I had chemistry. We had chemistry. I have always liked Hughes—he is funny and dry. I like Sandy. I liked Lee Townsend. As for Gordon Manning—when I first came to New York, I ran copy at *Newsweek*, where he was executive editor, and I was forever bearing memos from him that he had written "nifty" across the top of. I am constitutionally incapable of truly relating to anyone whose favorite adjective is nifty. Still, it was a pretty good lunch. Lamb chops. Crème caramel. It was also a seductive lunch, and I left it wanting the job. I also left it knowing that if I got it, it would probably be the worst thing that ever happened to me, the worst hours, the end of my privacy, my private life, my writing. "If you take the job," the man who used to be my husband said to me, "the only person in New York you'll be able to have an affair with is Hughes Rudd." I thought about that, and about the other drawbacks, and I knew that I would never have the courage or good sense to turn it down. It made me crazy.

"What do you want to do?" asked my psychoanalyst in the middle of it all.

"I want them not to offer it to me so I won't have to make a decision," I said.

"That's ridiculous," said my psychoanalyst.

"I'm not sure it is," I said.

It got to be the middle of June. The *Esquire* issue on women, which I had worked on, was on the stands. CBS booked me onto the *Morning News* show, ostensibly to give the magazine a plug but actually to audition me. I got up at 6 a.m., tried not to think about what life would be like if I had to be awake at that hour five days a week, put on my most grown-up dress, and went over to be interviewed by John Hart.

"You did fine," he said after it was over. "I hope you win."

"Who else is up for it?" I asked.

"Well," he said, "the front runner is Sally Quinn."

There is no way, particularly at this point, particularly since the outcome of this contest is no secret, for me to convey the exact pain I felt at that moment. It had something to do with my stomach and something to do with dizziness. For one thing, I knew it was all over, that I would never get the job. For another—and I'll go into this in a minute—it seemed hopelessly ironic.

"Gordon Manning is really hot for her," said John Hart.

"That doesn't surprise me," I said.

There has been altogether too much written about Sally Quinn, here and elsewhere, in recent months; I am sorry to add to it, but a story's a story. Sally Quinn and I were friends. She came to my house a couple of times. I went to her house a couple of times. She helped me out on a story I wrote about Henry Kissinger. I had known Sally two or three years, had seen her over a dozen times, but until the A. J. Liebling Counter-Convention last May, I had never heard her discuss her philosophy of reporting. I never even knew she had one.

As it turned out, she did. She appeared on a panel at the convention, leaned into the microphone, and went on huskily and at some length about being a woman reporter. She said that the essence of reporting was manipulation—through flirtation, the insinuation of availability, a few too many drinks for the interview subject, whatever means were necessary. "Being blond," she said very very slowly, "doesn't hurt." I found all of it incredibly offensive, and said as much to one of Sally's rivals on the *Washington Post*, who quoted me to that effect. Then I spent a few weeks trying to figure out why I had been so upset. At first, it seemed to me it was because I thought what she was saying was demeaning to the profession and to women in it. Then I realized that that wasn't really true, that the profession would some-how survive her remarks. My second thought, and this came during a period of what I like to think of as mental health, was that I had been upset because I thought that Sally's remarks were demeaning to herself. I saw her at a party in June and said as much.

"You don't really work that way," I said, "and when you say that you do, you're just putting yourself down."

"I do work that way," Sally said. "And so do you. We all do."

As it happens, I don't work that way. I have never

worked that way. I am uncomfortable flirting, it requires a great deal of energy and ego, and I manage to do it only a couple of times a year, and not with interview subjects.

But the conversation at the party went on, and we got around to the line about being blond. "If what you meant to say by that," I said, "is one of life's cruel truths, which is that it is better to look good than bad in this world, you picked the one way of saying it that was the most self-aggrandizing and least likely to make anyone hear what your point was."

Sally conceded that there might be some truth to that, that she had chosen her words badly, and I went off thinking I had at least made a small point. Later on, I realized I was wrong. I was reading Pauline Kael's review of Norman Mailer's *Marilyn*, and it suddenly hit me that what Sally Quinn had meant to say when she said, "Being blond doesn't hurt," was simply this: being blond doesn't hurt. I also realized later, much much later, what it was that had bothered me so much about her performance that day. When John Hart told me that she was the front runner for the job, I realized that what had gotten to me was that Sally Quinn was right. Her way worked. Mine didn't. Lillian Hellman said it all a good deal better than I could have, in an interview I had with her this summer. We had gotten to talking about women. "Dashiell Hammett used to say I had the meanest jealousy of all," Miss Hellman said. "I had no jealousy of work, no jealousy of money. I was just jealous of women who took advantage of men, because I didn't know how to do it."

Well, you know how it all ended. Sally Quinn got the job. *New York* magazine wrote an article about her. Sally Quinn said the only reason the magazine had published the article, which was not entirely complimentary, was that Clay Felker, the editor, had offered her a job and she had turned it down. "You were going to be a star," Sally said Felker said to her, "and you should have let me make you one." Clay Felker says he never said that to Sally Quinn, but that's not the point. The point is he is capable of saying it. I know, because a few nights after I read in the *New York Times* that Sally had gotten the job—CBS never bothered to tell me—Clay came to my new apartment and looked around. "Oh, Nora," he said. "You shouldn't have to live like this." And he made me an offer.

And I figured, what the hell.

I figured, why not leave *Esquire* magazine.

I figured there are worse things in this world than letting Clay Felker make you a star.

And here I am.

October, 1973

Women in Israel:
The Myth of Liberation

Tel Aviv—A number of important and unimportant
things seem to fly right out the window in a country like
Israel in time of war. One of them is partisan politics,
which vanished about a month ago and is now making
a tentative and slightly unwelcome comeback now that
there is a tentative and slightly unwelcome cease-fire.
Another is public transportation—the city buses take
the troops to war, and most of them are still sitting out
in the Sinai Desert waiting to bring them back. A third
is room service—or service of any kind, for that matter.
"There's a war on" is the all-purpose excuse. It is offered
by the El Al steward to explain why no one on the plane
except Abba Eban is being served alcoholic beverages,
and it is offered by the hotel operator to explain why it
has taken her a full ten minutes to answer the telephone.

Yet another casualty of war—at least for the time
being—has been the women's movement here. The wom-
en's liberation movement in Israel could, without too
much trouble, be packed into a small suite in the Dan
Hotel. But in spite of its numbers, it has had considerable impact. Publicity has helped, and there has been a
great deal of it, much of it sympathetic and provoking.

And while the religious laws of Israel, which govern all family and marital matters, are not particularly outrageous in the context of life in the Middle East, there are people here who prefer to think of themselves as part of the Western world, and in that context the laws are extraordinarily backward.

One example of this has become known as the Case of the Mistaken *Mamzerim*. Under religious law, the children of a married woman and a man she is not married to are considered *mamzerim*, or bastards, and they are not allowed to marry Jews who are legitimate—are not, in fact, allowed to marry anyone but other *mamzerim*. (Significantly, this law does not apply to the illegitimate children of married men and single women.) Last year, when there was time to be concerned with such matters, the country spent several months mesmerized by a fascinating case of *mamzerism*. Many years before, a Polish-Jewish woman had eloped with a gentile. They were married and moved to Israel, and he converted to Judaism. Then they were divorced. The woman remarried, this time to a Jew, but she forgot to tell the rabbi who performed the ceremony that she had been divorced. She had children—a son and a daughter. Twenty years later, both children joined the army, and the son went to apply for a marriage certificate. In the course of going through his papers, the rabbinical authorities discovered his mother's failure to mention her divorce. They promptly ruled the second marriage invalid, declared the offspring *mamzerim*, and said that the son could not marry his intended. Not surprisingly, there was a huge public outcry, and the case was appealed to one of the chief rabbis, Shlomo Goren, who is something of a diplomat as chief rabbis go. After holding a hearing, Rabbi

Goren managed to find a way to declare the mother's first marriage illegal (and hence, her second marriage legal), on the ground that her first husband, although a convert, had clung to Christian ways. This fact was established conclusively in court when neighbors testified that they had seen him through the bathroom window sitting in the tub drinking vodka and eating pork. The *mamzerim* were pronounced legitimate after all.

Cases of this sort pop up with some frequency, and they have done much to help the women's movement attract attention to the injustice of the religious laws. Before the war began, the movement had attained, if not actual momentum, a fairly constant chugging pace—it had begun to hold demonstrations, file lawsuits against employers, and organize consciousness-raising groups. Now, though, these concerns seem rather trivial against the background of crisis in the Middle East, and members of the two main women's liberation groups in Jerusalem and Tel Aviv seem a bit puzzled as to whether their cause, which had historically done better in times of peace and prosperity, is at all relevant. And the interesting thing is not just that it is in many ways more relevant than ever, but that the war may, quite by accident, bring about substantial improvements for women here.

There is, of course, a prevalent belief in Israel, as well as in the rest of the world, that this country is some sort of paradise for women. To begin with, there is Golda Meir, and her extraordinary achievements are constantly used as an argument against the need for liberation—as in "How can you say women are discriminated against when we have a woman Prime Minister?" In fact, Golda is simply Golda, and she is frequently referred to, in a line that is regarded as a witticism, as "the only man in the Cabinet." What is more to the point is that she is not only the only woman in the Cabinet, but also the only woman who has *ever* served in the Cabinet. Mrs. Meir has never shown any active interest in women's rights—she is a classic example of the successful woman who believes that because she managed to rise to the top, anyone can. Furthermore, her coalition government—like others before it—cooperates with the religious party. The rabbis keep quiet about military spending, and in exchange the politicians keep their hands off the religious laws.

The second factor that contributes to the myth concerns women and the army. Israel is the only country in the world with compulsory military service for women. What is not as well known is that women in the Israeli Army do the clerical and service tasks and leave the important work—which is to say, the fighting and killing—to the men. This was not always true. Before the establishment of the state, women were routinely used as soldiers—first in the Jewish Brigade, next in the underground, and then in the War of Independence. But after 1948, the population increase and religious influence combined to push the women into minor roles— they are not even used as drivers behind the lines, a job frequently given to WACs and the like in supposedly less liberated armies. The women in the Israeli Army today are regarded with exactly the same sort of protective instincts men have always felt toward women in time of war. In the first days of the 1973 war, there was a recurrent rumor here that six women in the Israeli Army had been captured, raped, and killed by the Syrians. The Israelis who repeated it seemed far more outraged by the fate of these women, who turned out not to exist, than by that of the hundreds of men who died fighting in the Golan Heights. It is one of the paradoxes of a male-dominated society that the price of a woman's life is seen to be higher than that of a man's.

The price of her work is not. In 1970, the average yearly income of a woman in communications was 61 percent of a man's—and in just three years this figure has dropped to 42 percent. A woman working in a public service earns 67 percent of a man's salary. Although half the university graduates are women, they are only 2 percent of the full professors in universities, 7 percent of the lawyers, and 5 percent of the engineers. (In contrast, women make up 38 percent of the medical profession.) Women in Israel tend to be employed in jobs that have always been female strongholds—secretarial work and teaching, for example. More important, barely 30 percent of the women between the ages of fifteen and sixty-five work full-time. This, in large part, is due to the widespread prejudice among both Oriental and Western Jews against working women, a prejudice that is reinforced by the rabbis and results in minimal day-care facilities and no legal abortions.

The rabbis oversee all affairs having to do with marriage and divorce—and they do this with 3,000 years of Biblical tradition, much of which would be sheer balderdash if it were not so grotesquely sexist. An Israeli woman is required to go to a *mikvah* before her wedding—and it is estimated that 90 percent of the women married in this unorthodox country comply. The *mikvah* is the ritual bath originally based on primitive beliefs about the uncleanness of female genitalia following the menstrual period; the baths are staffed by older women, some of whom persist in believing that ordinary hygiene will not do the trick and who are notorious for passing on a series of updated superstitions about what they call "the dirty days." One particularly common example of this nowadays is the belief that a woman who touches her husband during her period will cause him to be killed in the next war. A woman who does not want to go to a *mikvah* has two choices: she can bribe someone to sign a paper saying she has been to one, or she can go to Cyprus to be married by a justice of the peace. This practice has become so commonplace of late that the leader of Cyprus is often referred to as Rabbi Makarios.

"According to civil law, women are equal to men," says Shulamit Aloni, the lawyer and politician who is the leading spokeswoman for women's rights here. "But I have to go to a religious court as far as personal affairs are concerned. Only men are allowed to be judges there— men who pray every morning to thank God He did not make them women. You meet prejudice before you open your mouth. And because they believe women belong in the home, you are doubly discriminated against if you work."

No woman may testify in a religious court: hence, no woman may be divorced without her husband's consent. Several years ago, a woman whose husband had been jailed for child-molesting asked for a divorce; he refused, and there the matter rested. A woman without children who is widowed may not remarry without the consent of her husband's unmarried brother or, failing that, a formal exemption from the rabbinical court. Some three hundred cases have been disputed under this law since the 1967 war, and there will be hundreds more as a result of this last conflict. But the most oppressive of the religious laws—and the one most relevant to the current political situation—is the law of *agunot*, which holds that a deserted wife may not remarry under any circumstance. Under Jewish religious law, this prohibition is absolute. What this means is that a woman whose husband is believed dead but whose body has not been recovered may never ever remarry. (However, from time to time, a woman who appeals is sometimes given permission to become a widow.)

Cases arising under the law of *agunot* are often incredibly complicated. After World War II, a Jewish woman who had been in the concentration camps with her husband emigrated to Israel. She believed that her husband had been killed in the camps, and after seven years he was declared dead under an exception to the law of *agunot*. She remarried and had children; thirteen years later, her first husband arrived in Israel, and the children of the second marriage were ruled to be *mamzerim*.

This law accounts in large part for the unusual concern and energy the Israeli Army brings to the often dangerous task of recovering the bodies of its soldiers. Until two years ago, when an Israeli submarine carrying over seventy men sank without a trace, no blanket deviation from this law was ever tolerated. But Rabbi Goren, obviously caught up in his role as a demi-Solomon, went into action and managed to provide a true measure of relief by ruling that the wives of the missing could remarry. The good rabbi will undoubtedly be forced to do something of the sort again: at this point, the discrepancy between Israeli and Arab estimates of the number of prisoners of war held by the Arabs is so vast that it is altogether possible that some four hundred Israeli soldiers' bodies may never be recovered. This will result

in some four hundred not-quite-widows, and that is too
many not-quite-widows for the law of *agunot* to stand
up to. None of the women in Israel in or out of the movement want to go through a war to weaken an oppressive
law; in a coalition government of this sort, however, that
seems to be the only way.

Another and more far-reaching irony that may result
from this war is that the status of women in the work
force may improve substantially. The general election,
which is now scheduled for December 31, is expected
to produce at least a slight shift in favor of the right-
wing, or more hawkish, political parties—and this in
turn may lead to a situation where far more Israeli
men are kept mobilized. Whether or not this occurs, a
large number of men will be kept at the front simply
to hold the cease-fire lines on the West Bank: in the
short run, at least, the Israeli government will probably find it necessary to lure some women out of the
home and into the factories. (The Israeli G.N.P. is off 40
percent since the beginning of the war.) If more women
are needed in the labor force, the government will have
to do something about day care for the middle-income
women. There is even some talk now about the possibility of setting up a special reserve force for women—not
to fight in the army, but to take their husbands' places
in the economy during war.

"One of the reasons women's lib isn't catching on as
much as it should," said Ruth Rasnic, a translator who
is a member of the Tel Aviv women's liberation group,
"is because of this great military myth we have here.
The myth is essential—only I think women should take
a much more active part in it. Whether women want

to work in peacetime is up to them, but they should be made to take part in the economy during a war, because war is inevitable."

And so war and an increased mobilization—which Israeli women do not want—may lead to a situation that improves the status of women here. It is the kind of twist of logic that seems entirely fitting in a country whose citizens take so much delight in calculating every possible consequence of every situation. Besides, like everything else that has flown out the window of late, logic has been in short supply, and for the moment, at least, all is confusion.

November, 1973

The Littlest Nixon

She comes down the aisle, and the clothes are just right, Kimberly-knitted to the knee, and she walks in step with the government official, who happens to be H.E.W. Secretary Caspar Weinberger, and her face is perfect, not smiling, mind you—this is too serious an event for that—but bright, intent, as if she is absolutely fascinated by what he is saying. Perhaps she actually is. They take their places on the platform of the Right to Read Conference at Washington's Shoreham Hotel, and he speaks and she speaks and the director of Right to Read speaks. Throughout she listens raptly, smiles on cue, laughs a split second after the audience laughs. Perhaps she is actually amused. On the way out, she says she hopes she will be able to obtain a copy of the speech she has just sat through. Perhaps she actually thought it was interesting. There is no way to know. No way to break through. She has it all down perfectly. She was raised for this, raised to cut ribbons, and now that it has all gone sour, it turns out that she has been raised to deal with that, too.

The Washington press corps thinks that Julie Nixon Eisenhower is the only member of the Nixon Administration who has any credibility—and as one journalist put it, this is not to say that anyone believes what she is saying but simply that people believe *she* believes what she is saying. They will tell you that she is approachable, which is true, and that she is open, which is not. Primarily they find her moving. "There is something about a spirited and charming daughter speaking up for her father in his darkest hour that is irresistibly appealing to all but the most cynical." That from the *Daily News*. And this from NBC's Barbara Walters, signing off after Julie's last appearance on the *Today* show: "I think that no matter how people feel about your father, they're always very impressed to see a daughter defend her father that way."

There *is* something very moving about Julie Nixon Eisenhower—but it is not Julie Nixon Eisenhower. It is the *idea* of Julie Nixon Eisenhower, essence of daughter, a better daughter than any of us will ever be; it is almost as if she is the only woman in America over the age of twenty who still thinks her father is exactly what she thought he was when she was six. This idea is apparently so overwhelming in its appeal that some Washington reporters go so far as to say that Julie doesn't seem like a Nixon at all—a remark so patently absurd as to make one conclude either that they haven't heard a word she is saying or that they have been around Nixon so long they don't recognize a chocolate-covered spider when they see one.

I should point out before going any further that I have a special interest in Presidents' daughters, having spent a good thirty minutes in my youth wanting to be Margaret Truman. And even back then, I knew it was not a perfect existence—Secret Service men trailing you everywhere, life in a fishbowl, and so forth. Still, whatever the drawbacks, it seemed clear that if you were the President's daughter, you at least got to date a lot. The other attraction to the fantasy, I suppose, had to do with the fact that the role of the President's daughter is the closest thing there is in America to being a princess, the closest thing to having stature and privilege purely as a result of an accident of birth. It is one of life's little jokes that both America and Britain have suffered through remarkably similar princesses in recent years: the Johnson girls, the Nixon girls, and Princess Anne are all drab, dull young women who have managed to acquire enough poise and good grooming to get through the public events their parents do not have time to attend.

Julie and Tricia were born just as their father was beginning public life. They grew up in Washington as congressman's daughters, senator's daughters, and Vice-President's daughters. Then they moved to California to be gubernatorial candidate's daughters, and later to New York to be Presidential contender's daughters. After graduating from the Chapin School, Tricia went on to Finch College, Julie to Smith. There she began dating, and married—not a commoner, but a President's grandson. (David Eisenhower, with his endless tables of batting averages and illogical articles on the American left, is the perfect Nixon son-in-law. Still, he is not stupid. Last summer, after working as a sportswriter for the Philadelphia *Bulletin*, he was asked if he had any observations on the American press. "Yes," he reportedly said. "Journalists aren't nearly as interesting as they think they are.")

Marriage—which might logically have been expected

to move Julie into a more removed and private existence—
has instead strengthened and intensified her family
connections and political role. During college, the Eisenhowers spent their summer vacations in a third-floor
suite at the White House and took time off from school
to campaign for Nixon's re-election. These days, they see
Julie's parents several times a week; the Nixons often
sneak off to eat with Julie and David in the $125,000 two-
bedroom Bethesda home that Bebe Rebozo bought and
rented to the Eisenhowers, presumably at well below its
market price.

A few months ago, Julie took a full-time job at $10,000
a year at Curtis Publishing, where she is assistant editorial director of children's magazines and assistant editor of the *Saturday Evening Post.* She announced at the
time that the children's magazine field attracted her
because it would be impossible for her, as the President's
daughter, to write for adult magazines on sensitive political subjects. An upcoming article for the *Saturday Evening Post*, however, while hardly on anything sensitive
or political, is nonetheless on a topic that could not be
more calculated to draw attention to her position: it is a
profile of Alice Roosevelt Longworth, who is now eighty-
nine and in the seventy-third year of her career as a
President's daughter.

Julie, of course, is nothing like Alice Roosevelt, or
any of the other flibbertigibbet Presidents' daughters
in the history of this country. In the months since the
Watergate hearings began, she has become her father's
principal defender, his First Lady in practice if not in
fact. "It was something I took on myself," she said. "I
just thought I had a story to tell, that there were certain
points I could make, and I was very eager to do it. The

idea that my father has to hide behind anyone's skirts is of course ludicrous." In any case, Julie's skirts were the only ones available: Pat Nixon is uncomfortable in press and television interviews, and Tricia is in New York. (Washington rumor has it that her husband, Edward Cox, and the President do not get on.) "And that leaves me," said Julie.

It has left her to make two appearances on the *Today* show, a television hookup with the BBC, a guest shot on Jack Paar's show. She has survived Kandy Stroud of *Women's Wear Daily* and lunch with Helen Thomas of the U.P.I. and Fran Lewine of the A.P. Odd little personal details about the President have slipped out during these interviews—whether deliberately or not. She has said that her father sometimes doesn't feel like getting up in the morning, that he took the role of devil's advocate in a family discussion on whether he should resign, that he often sits alone at night upstairs in the White House playing the piano. During her last appearance with Barbara Walters, whose interviews with her have been dazzling, she even came up with a sinister-influence theory of her own to explain everything: "Sometimes I think we were born under an unlucky star."

Her performances are always calm and professional and poised, her revelations just titillating enough, and after all, she's only a girl—and the combination of these has tended to draw attention away from the substantive things she is saying and the way she is saying them. Julie Eisenhower has developed—or been coached in— three basic approaches to answering questions. The first is not to answer the question at all. During her BBC appearance, an American woman living in England phoned in to say, "I would like Mrs. Eisenhower to know that her father's actions have made our position abroad untenable . . . it would be better if he came forward and answered questions himself instead of putting you in his place." Julie replied, "I'd like to ask . . . how she thinks my father can answer more on Watergate without pointing the finger at people who have not been indicted." This answer—in addition to skirting the question and making Nixon look like a man whose sole thought is of the Constitution—utterly overlooks the fact that almost everyone connected with Watergate has been called to testify, a good many have been indicted, and some have even been convicted.

The second approach is to point to the bright side. Thus, when she is asked about Watergate, she talks instead of her father's successes with China, Russia, and the Middle East crisis. When she is asked about the number of Presidential appointees who have been forced to resign, she mentions Henry Kissinger and Ron Ziegler, whom she once called "a man of great integrity." "And I'd go beyond that," she said once. "I'd say that many of these people we're talking about, these aides, were great Americans, really devoted to their country, and they didn't make any money on Watergate, they didn't do anything for personal gain. They made mistakes, errors in judgment. I don't think they're evil men."

The third, and most classic, of Mrs. Eisenhower's techniques is simply to put the blame elsewhere—on the press. She combines the Middle American why-doesn't-the-press-ever-print-good-news theme with good old-fashioned Nixon paranoia. I spoke with her the other day for five minutes, and she spent most of that time complaining that her mother had met the day before with a group from the Conference on the Role of Women in the Economy, and not one word about it had been printed in the papers. "Instead we get all these negative things," she said. When she was asked recently what she thought of Barry Goldwater's charge that her father's credibility was at an all-time low, she replied: "Barry Goldwater also had a press conference during this whole period . . . and he said that the press were hounds of destruction. I don't think he meant all of the press, but, um, Goldwater *is* a quotable man, isn't he? I didn't hear *that* on the networks. But when he says [my father's] credibility is at an all-time low, that *is* on the networks."

The only questions that stump Julie Eisenhower at all are the ones that concern her father's personality. She has said that she is sick of telling reporters what a warm, human person he is—a fact that fortunately has not stopped reporters from pressing her to give examples. One story she produced recently to show what a card her father can be in his off moments concerned the time her husband, David, took the wheel of Bebe Rebozo's yacht—and the President, in response, appeared on deck wearing not one but two life preservers. "He is quite a practical joker," she said on another occasion. "He likes to tease and he likes to plan surprises when he can. Things like getting birthday candles for a cake that don't blow out. You know, all nice and lit and you sit there huffing and puffing and they don't go out. . . . Things like that."

There is no point in dwelling too heavily on the implications of a daughter who has managed to play a larger role in her father's life than his wife seems to. And there is also no point in wondering what is going to happen to Julie Eisenhower's view of her father if the fall actually comes. It is safe to say that breeding will out, and all the years of growing up in that family will protect her from any insight at all, will lead her to conclude that he was quite simply done in by malicious, unpatriotic forces. What is clear, though, is that Julie Nixon Eisenhower is fighting for herself and her position as hard as she is fighting for her father and his. She once said that if her father was forced out of office, she would "just fold up and wither and fall away." What is more likely is that she will deal with that, too, vanish for a couple of years, and then crop up in politics again. That, after all, is what Nixons do, and that, in the end, is all she is.

December, 1973

Divorce, Maryland Style

The *Ladies' Home Journal* is after her. *Cosmopolitan* is after her. I am after her. All of us think that there is something to the story of Barbara Mandel, something positively paradigmatic. After all, what happened to Barbara Mandel last year happens to thousands of American women. After thirty-two years of marriage, her husband left her for another woman. Moved into a hotel. Called a lawyer. It happens every day. The difference, in this case, was that Barbara Mandel's husband was Marvin Mandel, the governor of the state of Maryland. And Barbara Mandel was having none of it.

It is safe to say that there was no way Marvin Mandel could have left his wife that would have made her happy; nonetheless, he managed to leave her in a way that was bound to humiliate her as completely as possible. To begin with, he did not even tell her himself. Well, that's not entirely fair: for two years he had been telling her he wanted a divorce, and for two years she had been telling him she would never give him one. But he never told her he was actually moving out; the morning he did, July 3, 1973, he arranged an appointment for her with the family doctor and had him break the news. His press secretary read her the statement over the telephone. And when Barbara Mandel called her husband to beg him to hold off, he informed her that it was too late; the press had already been given the statement.

"I would like to announce that I am separated from Mrs. Mandel," it read. "My decision and separation are final and irrevocable, and I will take immediate action to dissolve the marriage. . . . I am in love with another woman, Mrs. Jeanne Dorsey, and I intend to marry her. Mrs. Mandel and I have had numerous discussions about this matter and she is completely aware of my feelings, of my actions, and of my intentions. . . . Mrs. Mandel and I no longer share mutual interests nor are our lives mutually fulfilling. . . ."

There was not a mention of the good years, the old times spent growing up as childhood sweethearts in northwest Baltimore. There was not a mention of what she had done for him, all those hands she shook, all those ward heelers' names she memorized, all those rooms in the governor's mansion she repainted. He was leaving her. He was leaving her publicly. He was stripping her of her only weapon—the threat of exposing his liaison—by announcing it himself. Barbara Mandel, First Lady of Maryland—that was how she signed the souvenir ashtrays and the 8" x 10" glossies—reacted by refusing to go.

"The governor crawled out of my bed this morning," she told the reporters she telephoned that afternoon. "He has never slept anyplace but with me. I think the strain of the job has gotten to him. I'm surprised. Marvin has not discussed this with me. I don't know what in the world he's talking about. I hope the governor will come to his senses on this. You don't take thirty-two years of

married life and throw them down the drain." Mrs. Mandel added that she thought her husband "should see a
psychiatrist." In the meantime, she said, she would wait
for him in the mansion.

So far, a fairly ordinary American tragedy. A woman
invests her life in her husband's career, and he pays
her back by leaving her. A woman grows up in a society
where the only option seems to be to dedicate herself to
her husband. "My case is just different because I helped
to make him governor," Mrs. Mandel said.

But, of course, that was a big difference—and that
is where the case departs abruptly from the paradigm.
Barbara Mandel responded to her husband's rejection
not just as a wounded wife but as a seasoned politician.
She carefully leaked tidbits of information to selected
reporters. She allowed one reporter to negotiate on her
behalf with the governor's chief aide. Her statement on
July 3—which seems on the surface quite hysterical—
carefully left the governor a face-saving way to return:
he could simply admit that she was right, the pressures
of the job *had* gotten to him; now he had come to his
senses. Hell hath no fury, it is true; at the same time, it
was clear that part of Mrs. Mandel's fury came not just
from the fact that there was another woman involved,
but also from the suspicion that the other woman wanted
to use her husband and his position exactly as much as
Mrs. Mandel did.

Marvin Mandel was a young Baltimore lawyer in
1952 when he first entered the state legislature. He was
diligent and hard-working; in addition, he was thoroughly introverted. His outgoing wife—who was known
as Bootsie, a nickname that she inexplicably rhymes
with "footsie"—campaigned and went everywhere with

him; she provided the warmth and earthiness he was chronically unable to convey. Mandel rose to become speaker of the House of Delegates. In 1969, after Spiro Agnew left the governorship to become Vice-President, the Mandels moved into the fifty-three-room Georgian governor's mansion in Annapolis. By this time, the governor's relationship with Mrs. Dorsey had been common knowledge around the State House for years; one of Mrs. Dorsey's four children recently told the *Washington Post* that his mother had been seeing Mandel since 1960. Mrs. Dorsey, now thirty-six, was divorced a few years ago from another Maryland legislator; she is a Democrat who served as police commissioner during a stint on her town board. ("I'm not a big story," she told the *Post*'s Judy Bachrach recently, "and there's no reason why I should open my private life to you. Now, frankly, there is a big story and it's right here in Leonardtown. We have this terrific sewage problem.")

Bootsie Mandel was never in the tradition of great first ladies—but compared with her predecessor, she did an energetic, creditable job, and she became more involved in it as her isolation from the governor increased. "God damn it, I'm nothing around here," she told one of her husband's supporters early in his first term. "Before he was governor, I used to drive him everywhere. Now he has a state trooper. I used to help him with his speeches. Now he has a speechwriter. What good am I?" What good she did had mainly to do with the mansion. She refurbished it, printed up lavish programs describing its interior, appeared at charity luncheons to announce that twice-a-week tours through it were available.

At the same time, she had a habit of getting everything she did slightly wrong. At one point, she discovered that a portrait hanging in the mansion had a label attributing it to Hogarth; she promptly insured it for $300,000, scheduled a ceremony and surprise announcement, and was informed by a prominent art historian that the painting wasn't a Hogarth at all. Several years ago, she confounded the entire state legislature by inviting the wives to the annual party celebrating the legislature's adjournment; the party had traditionally been an event for the politicians to be with whatever women they had been seeing on the sly during the session. Said one Baltimore assemblyman: "You cannot overestimate the panic that went through this place that day."

Governor Mandel's relationship with Mrs. Dorsey became increasingly open. In December, 1970, his unmarked state police car hit another car in Prince Georges County and the driver of the other car was killed. The governor refused to say what he was doing in an unmarked car after midnight; then he said he had been at a secret political meeting. Reporters checked and could not find any other politicians who had been to a meeting with the governor that night. When they asked whether he hadn't in fact been returning from St. Marys County, where Mrs. Dorsey lived, he declined comment. At about that time, Mrs. Mandel apparently found out that the situation was serious and began to pump friends for information. Sometimes she asked straight out; more often, she attempted an approach she seemed to believe was devious. "What do you think the Jewish community would say about a governor who left his wife for another woman?" she asked the wife of one of her husband's associates.

Within a few weeks of the governor's walkout, Mrs. Mandel realized she had made a terrible mistake. She had counted on her friends to side with her—and they sided with the governor and his power. She had counted on major political repercussions—but there was only a brief flurry of mail support from middle-aged women. She had counted on seeming to be a force for morality— and instead she became an object of ridicule. "She was playing cards in a game that had ended," said one Maryland politician. "It had ended in American politics, in American life, even ended in her narrow circle. Divorce just doesn't mean that much anymore."

Bootsie carried on. She alerted the press as to her comings and goings. She appeared at a Washington literary party and identified herself as the woman who had knocked Elizabeth Taylor and Richard Burton's breakup off the front page. She spoke to a group of Democratic women, many of whom cried as she vowed to continue as first lady. "I want you to know that I am a very proud woman," she said, "very very proud of everything I've done since I've been a little girl. Life does not always work out the way you want it. . . ."

In the end, what kept Barbara Mandel in the governor's mansion as long as she stayed was not the pathetic hope that her husband would return—she had long given up on that—but the fact that her presence there was the only wedge she had to negotiate a substantial money settlement. Mandel's first offer to his wife, she told friends, was $6,250 a year, a quarter of his yearly salary as governor. Her lawyer ultimately negotiated a six-figure settlement. And on December 20, with a crowd of reporters standing outside the wrought-iron gates, Barbara Mandel moved out, with her hope chest, love seat, artificial flower centerpieces, and eight wardrobe boxes of clothing. "Five and a half months have passed and our marriage has not returned to normal," she said. "Therefore, with deep regret, I am leaving the mansion."

She moved to a two-bedroom apartment in Baltimore—in the same complex where her married son and daughter live—and when I reached her on the telephone, she told me she preferred not to say anything. "I'm very busy," she said. Doing what? I asked. "Just the normal things," she said, "the normal things you have to do for yourself."

"I'll tell you a story," one of her friends said a few days ago. "The day after Marvin moved out, last July, Bootsie went to the family cemetery. She sat looking at the graves, and she wished that he were dead. She felt she would have been better off as a widow. I can't help thinking she was right."

January, 1974

Rose Mary Woods— the Lady or the Tiger?

It all depends on whom you talk to. Everything does, as it happens, but the case of Rose Mary Woods depends so much on whom you talk to that the more people you talk to, the more confused everything becomes. People in Washington talk to each other about Rose Mary Woods a great deal these days, and the conversations always end up sounding like the third-to-last chapter in an Agatha Christie mystery. Loose ends. Nothing but loose ends. The Uher tape recorder. The mysteriously elliptical testimony of J. Fred Buzhardt. The White House allegation that the subpoena did not cover the Haldeman conversation. The weekend at Camp David. The weekend in Key Biscayne. The role of Stephen Bull. And at the center of it all is Rose Mary. Dear, sweet, considerate, thoughtful, devout, loyal, put-upon Rose Mary. Tough, cunning, crafty, complicated, powerful, fanatical Rose Mary. Which one is Rose Mary: the lady or the tiger? It all depends on whom you talk to.

"Everybody on God's earth is against her," Charles Rhyne is saying. "The power of the judiciary, the White House lawyers, the prosecutors, the tape experts. There's never been a setup like this one. How can she stand up against all this by herself? She's got the grand jury, the Common Cause people, the milk people, the Watergate committee—all of them are after her." Charles Rhyne is Rose Mary Woods's lawyer, has been since the day after Thanksgiving, two days after Miss Woods, who has been Richard Nixon's personal secretary some twenty-three years, was told she had better go out and find a lawyer of her own, because the White House lawyers would not represent her on this one. The problem, of course, had to do with an eighteen-and-a-half-minute gap on a White House tape made June 20, 1972, three days after the Watergate break-in. And the reason the White House lawyers cast Rose Mary Woods out to pay her own legal fees was that they thought she might well be responsible for every buzzing second of it. Charles Rhyne is outraged by the whole business. He is a former president of the American Bar Association, the lawyer Central Casting sends out when you ask for Integrity, a man of impeccable connections (most of whom he appears with in photographs on his office wall), a classmate and good friend of Richard Nixon's from Duke Law School, and his North Carolina-accented voice becomes positively mellifluous as he assures the press that his client was sold down the river. To prove it, he pulls out a transcript of a conference held the day before Thanksgiving, November 21, 1973, when White House counsels J. Fred Buzhardt and Leonard Garment finally went to Judge John J. Sirica to tell him they had discovered a gap on the tape.

"Judge, we have a problem," Buzhardt began that day. "In the process of preparing the analysis . . . one of the tapes, the intelligence is not available for approximately eighteen minutes. You can't hear the voices. . . . Under the circumstances, we know at this point that it looks quite serious. It doesn't appear from what we know at this point that it could be accidental."

"Does not appear?" Sirica asked.

"Does not appear from the information we have at this point," Buzhardt said. "At its worst, it looks like a very serious thing, Your Honor. If there is an explanation, quite frankly, I don't know what it is at the moment. . . ."

"Who was the last one that actually listened to this particular tape?" Sirica asked.

"The original? The original, according to the record, was first checked out to Miss Woods."

"Was it all right before it was checked out to Miss Woods?" Sirica asked.

"We don't know . . ." Buzhardt said. "I guess she is the only one [who] listened to it. . . . Then the circumstance is even a little worse than that, Your Honor."

"I don't know if it could get much worse," said Sirica.

"Just wait," said Leonard Garment.

"As you know, Your Honor," Buzhardt went on, "the notes were subpoenaed, too. We found Mr. Haldeman's notes on this meeting. . . . The notes reflect that the discussion was about Watergate. . . . When you get past the Watergate typed notes . . . that is where the tape picks up. . . . Maybe I am out of line for saying this, but quite frankly I think Miss Woods ought to have time to reflect on this and she ought to have time to secure counsel."

The meeting ended with Sirica's scheduling a hearing for the following Monday, November 26. Leonard Garment accepted a subpoena for Rose Mary Woods to appear there—and telephoned her to say he was doing so. He returned to the White House and sent it over to her with a note. "Here is the subpoena we discussed earlier," it read. "Love, Len."

" 'Love, Len,' " Charles Rhyne says, shaking his head. "Her own lawyers plead her guilty, then say she ought to get counsel of her own, then accept a subpoena for her when they've admitted they aren't her lawyers any longer, and then send it over and sign it with love. Of course, I didn't know anything about this in the beginning. The day after that meeting, on Thanksgiving Day, I was called by General Haig and he asked me to come down. He told me that Rose had been told to get a lawyer and was very upset. I've known Rose twenty-three years. I called her and told her to calm down, that I'd come down the next morning.

"So on Friday I go down and speak to Haig and he sends me over to see Garment and Buzhardt. 'She did it,' they said to me. 'No question about it. We ran tests on the lamp and the typewriter. So sorry. We don't know what you can do for her.' I went over to see Rose. She was enormously upset. I've never seen Rose upset. She said she didn't know what was going on. 'For the last week,' she said, 'everyone's been treating me like a leper.' 'Well, Rose,' I said, 'I've talked to Garment and Buzhardt and they say you knocked eighteen and a half minutes off this tape.' She just blew up. She said she'd known me a long long time and she was going to tell me everything. She would not accept responsibility for that. She hadn't done it. She wouldn't say she'd done it. She would not let them say she'd done it. She told me about the accident she had had October first with the tape, that she might have knocked four minutes off it. 'But,' she said, 'what really haunts me is that I never heard a word on that part of the tape.' I talked to her for three or four hours. I listened to the tape. And I said to her, 'I believe you.'

"This poor secretary, without any government money, all alone," said Rhyne. "I stand between her and the world."

Aunt Rose. That is what Tricia and Julie call her. She is family. Dick and Pat and Tricia and Julie and David and Bebe and Rose. She baby-sat for the girls. She exchanged clothes with Pat. Her brother Joe, a former F.B.I. man who served as sheriff of Cook County, used to wear Richard Nixon's hand-me-down suits. She attends family dinners in the White House. The President relaxes with her. He kids her—and it is not even labored. He becomes openly irritated with her—and he does that only with people he is close to. She is the person his own relatives call when they want to get through to him: the night of the first debate against Kennedy in the 1960 election, Nixon's mother, Hannah, called Rose Woods—not Pat Nixon—to say she thought her son looked a bit under the weather. Rose has been through it all. She took dictation for the telegram he wanted sent to General Eisenhower withdrawing from the 1952 ticket after the slush-fund charges—and she would have torn it up herself but for the fact that Murray Chotiner did it instead. She was in the car when they were stoned in Caracas, in the kitchen in Moscow; she followed him to Los Angeles and New York during the long out-of-office stretch. "I was his, I suppose you could say, personal secretary, aide, waste-basket emptier, anything else," she testified recently. "I was the only person who worked for him at that time."

"When I heard about it," said a man who used to work in the White House, "when I heard that Rose Woods had to go out and get a lawyer, I thought, Well, that's it. They have now reached the point where they're having hand-to-hand combat in the Oval Office."

The relationship between Rose Mary Woods and Richard Nixon is a complicated one. He counts on her. He respects her judgment on political matters, particularly where people are concerned. She is not afraid to disagree with him, even to snap back at him. In *Six Crises*, Nixon calls her "one of my most honest critics," and says, "She has that rare and unique characteristic that marks the difference between a good secretary and a great one—she is always at her best when the pressures are greatest." The emotional content of their relationship fascinates people.

"She's a little like the choir member in the Baptist church who falls in love with the minister," says one administration insider. "It's the classic Christian fantasy of the virgin and God—and obviously a part of the fantasy is that nothing ever happens. It just remains a kind of worship."

"Have you ever been in love?" asks another man who considers himself a friend to both Nixon and Miss Woods. "Really in love? Over a long period of time? She's been in love with Nixon—though not at all in a sexual sense—for over twenty years. Have you ever played poker? She's an extremely good poker player in the political world. She's smart, tough, ruthless, experienced, all the things you have to be. And she plays on behalf of Nixon, not on behalf of herself.

"Rose has provided him with the feeling that there was support for him and his cause, emotional sustenance at times when there really wasn't anyone else—not even Pat. At various times, Pat laid down the law and said, 'No more politics.' Rose always encouraged him to persevere. Another thing she does is to provide him with emotional and intellectual justification. During the period prior to the 1968 convention, she was always ready with criticisms of his rivals. In the fall of 1967, Lyn Nofziger, Reagan's press agent, broke the story of the homosexual ring that was active at the top level of Reagan's administration. Rose had found out about it a few weeks before, and I remember a dinner with her and Nixon where she presented that to us, saying, in effect, that that was what one could expect from Reagan, that he would be so careless about his staff selection he couldn't possibly be a good President."

There has always been a slight tinge of the martyr in the way Miss Woods operated with Nixon. In early 1969, when she was engaged in a power struggle with H. R. Haldeman and became so disturbed by it that she considered leaving her job, she never once mentioned what was going on to the President. And according to Charles Rhyne, the President has never once referred to, much less reassured his secretary about, her legal problems since the gap was found on November 14, when she claims she told him that she might well be responsible for four or five minutes of it, but would not take the blame for the full eighteen. Rose Woods presumably would never think to bring the question up herself. The only family or administration member who has spoken up for Rose since then has been Julie Nixon Eisenhower, who called her "a woman of complete integrity. She would never commit a criminal act."

Rose Mary Woods went to work for Nixon on February 21, 1951, just after he had been elected to the Senate. She is red-headed, well groomed, with a peaches-and-cream complexion. She gives the impression of being quite petite, and her friends say that she is somewhat frail physically and has suffered periodic bouts of pneumonia from overwork. She has literally worked seven-day, hundred-hour weeks, fifty-two weeks a year for twenty-three years—and in many ways she is not at all unique. There are thousands of women like her in Washington, women who come here as girls, get secretarial jobs on Capitol Hill, devote their lives to politicians, and end up elderly spinsters, living on their government pensions in apartments full of political knickknacks.

"They are a special twentieth-century breed," Helen Dudar wrote in the *New York Post*, "those ladies who guard the boss's door and fend off the telephone calls and read his mail; women largely without private lives because the real world is right there in the vortex spinning around the great man; women usually without husbands because the job takes most of their time and energies; women with small fiefdoms of their own encompassing sub-secretaries, the Xerox machine, the messenger service, and some nervous stenographers. Selfless, happily job-enslaved, eager to be useful, they are the vestal virgins in the temples of business and politics, the Indispensables, the private secretaries."

"It's a very exciting life," said Doris Jones, secretary to former Nixon aide Robert Finch and a close friend of Miss Woods's. "You get caught up in it. You get so busy. The next thing you know, you turn around and you're forty-five or fifty years old and unmarried, and you hadn't intended for it to work out that way at all. I know I never did."

• • •

Rose Mary Woods came to Washington from Sebring, Ohio, where she was born fifty-five years ago, the middle child of five children. Her parents were devout Catholics; her father worked at the Royal China Company, first as a potter, then as foreman, finally as personnel director. Her parents died a few years ago, and Miss Woods refers to them frequently: her father, she says, was a temperamental Irishman, while her mother was a calm, pacific woman. "Rose is a strange combination of Irish fire and quiet determination," says Robert Gray, a public-relations executive at Hill & Knowlton, who is Miss Woods's most frequent escort. "She often says, 'I've got to pray to God to let my mother's cool head prevail, and not my father's temper.'"

But for a series of misfortunes, Rose Mary Woods would probably have grown up to lead a traditional small-town Midwestern life. But in her last year at McKinley High School, she contracted a mysterious disease. "I weighed eighty-two pounds," she once said. "It was a growth. It may well have been cancer. Nobody knows. They X-rayed it and it disappeared. I wasn't able to work when I first got out. I wasn't able to go to school." Ultimately, she recovered and went to work as a secretary at Royal China; she became engaged to a young man who died. In 1943, she came to Washington. "I had a sister here who had a very tragic personal problem and I was the only one who could come." The sister was employed at the Office of Censorship, and Miss Woods went to work there, too. After the war, she joined the International Training Administration and then a committee on Capitol Hill run by Christian Herter. There she came to the attention of Richard Nixon, then a young congressman, and he to hers. She has often said that she was very much impressed by him before she even knew him, because he kept such neat expense accounts.

In the 1950s, Miss Woods lived on California Street in Washington, first in an apartment she shared with an elderly woman, then in a studio apartment of her own. She had almost no time for the few activities she favors—dancing, duckpin bowling, entertaining—and her moments of leisure were mostly spent grabbing sandwiches with other Capitol Hill secretaries. These women—who are still close to her—paint a picture of Rose Mary Woods and her life that is low-key and muted. They emphasize her devout Catholicism, her sacrifices, the thoughtful favors she does for friends, her total integrity. They believe every word she has testified, assure you she would never have done anything like what she has been accused of. "She'd probably lay down her life for Richard Nixon," says her friend Winnie De Weese, who used to be with the Republican Policy Committee, "but she would never lie for him."

Another close friend, Eloise De La O, former secretary to Senator Clinton Anderson, says, "I called her the night I heard she had gotten a lawyer. She said to me, 'You know, Eloise, my boss would never ask me to do anything like that.' She is a good Christian, a good Catholic, a practicing Catholic. You don't do things like that if that's the kind of person you are. Somebody is trying to do something to her."

The men who have known Rose Woods over the years tell a slightly different story. "There was a story about her dancing the tango alone one night at San Clemente," said one man. "Don't let it confuse you. Don't make the mistake of thinking of her as a sad, fragile, overworked secretary. She's a complicated woman who's been at the center for twenty-five years." And the men tend to be far more cynical about just what Rose might have done. One, a former White House aide who considers her a dear friend, was asked what he thought when he first read about the gap.

"My first thought," he said, "was that I hoped my secretary would be that loyal."

The women in the office have seen little of Rose Woods but her extraordinary stenographic skills, but the men have seen her function as an almost legendarily firm Nixon appendage. Following Nixon's 1960 defeat, several Republican leaders claimed that Miss Woods had kept them from communicating with the candidate during the election. Senator Styles Bridges, who was chairman of the Senate Republican Policy Committee, telephoned at the end of the campaign, and, as the late columnist George Dixon reported at the time, reached Miss Woods.

"The Vice-President is very busy," she told him.

"I just want to tell him," Bridges said, "that our reports show your boss is not doing too well."

"We disagree with you," Miss Woods replied. "Our reports are different."

In 1968, after Nixon was nominated, former Republican National Committee Chairman Leonard Hall made a courtesy call to the candidate to offer congratulations. Hall had been Nixon's campaign manager in 1960, but he had spent the last year working for two Nixon rivals— Governor George Romney and Governor Nelson Rockefeller. Hall got as far as Rose Mary Woods. She listened to him, said she would give Nixon the message, and ended the conversation with a flat "Don't call us, we'll call you."

"Rose is Nixon's memory," says a former White House aide. "She knows who was with him when the chips were down. She reacts purely politically to people. *What have you done for him lately?* During the Watergate hearings, she was complaining about Senator Baker for asking such tough questions, and she said, 'How dare he do that? We went into his district twice to help him.'" Another Washingtonian tells the story of a local Republican politician Miss Woods deliberately kept off the White House party list because she had heard that during the 1968 convention the man had put a picture of Nixon out on his front lawn with a sign reading, "Would you buy a used car from this man?"

After Nixon's defeat in 1960, Miss Woods followed him to Los Angeles, where he ran for, and lost the race for, governor of California, and then to the New York law firm Nixon, Mudge, Rose, Guthrie & Alexander. She lived on East 50th Street, in a cheerful apartment with a paper rose on the front door, and her friends were happy for her because they felt that for the first time she had some balance in her life. She gave dinner parties. She dated frequently. She was able to afford pretty clothes— her evening dresses are elaborate, with ostrich feathers and the like. She went to the theatre. She made new friends.

When prominent Republicans came to New York, they checked in with Rose. When young Republicans came to New York, they went to see her—and every third time, she gave them a few minutes with The Boss. After 1966, when Nixon decided to try again for the Presidency, she and Pat Buchanan, now a White House aide, were the only people on his staff, and she had considerable influence and total control over access to Nixon. But as the

1968 campaign got under way, her power diminished. And immediately after the election, she came up against the President's new chief of staff, H. R. "Bob" Haldeman.

The fight between her and Haldeman was, at its simplest, over office space. It began with his decision not to let her have Evelyn Lincoln's old office, directly connected to the Oval Office, and it went on for months as he tried unsuccessfully to move her out of the White House entirely and into the Executive Office Building across the alley. But, at bottom, the dispute was over something far more substantive: both wanted to control access to the President. They went to the mat, and the President went with Haldeman. "Rose kept saying she didn't want to go to the President with her problems because he was too busy," said Eloise De La O. "Her office was moved, down the hall. Wouldn't you think the President would be aware of it? It seems to me that if all of a sudden my secretary was moved, I'd notice. But she said she didn't want to worry him. She is so loyal." Significantly, Miss Woods never blamed Nixon for choosing Haldeman over her and instead focused her anger solely against the chief of staff.

The politicians and friends who had always counted on Rose as a way to the President's ear found themselves up against the Berlin Wall, and Rose found herself increasingly excluded from the meetings she had expected to be part of. "Suddenly, she never seemed to be there," said one Republican politician. "She was always off typing or something. After the election, I had a meeting with the President. I was waiting outside, and Haldeman came out and said to come in and meet Dr. Kissinger. I went in. Haldeman, Kissinger, and Nixon were there talking, and Bob was making notes. Then they left and the two of us started to talk. I was just telling the President what the mood was in a couple of states I'd been to—nothing confidential—when Nixon pushed a buzzer. Something I'd said had triggered something in his head. Bob Haldeman came in and took the notes on it on his yellow pad. It struck me not only as a little odd, but also inefficient—he didn't even take shorthand."

In February, 1969, Haldeman managed to keep Miss Woods's name off the list of people who were to accompany the President on his first official trip to Europe, and she was devastated. "It was a classic example of Haldeman's sadism," said one former aide. "She never complained and never raised an objection. But a few days before the trip, the President was leaving the White House and Haldeman walked him out to the helicopter. Nixon must have mentioned something about it, because Haldeman came back to tell Rose that she was going on the trip after all. It was a great victory, although she hadn't done anything." And in 1971, Haldeman and John Ehrlichman made yet another attempt to remove Miss Woods from power. At that point, she was demoralized; she was almost the only old-time Nixon aide who had survived Haldeman's machinations. "Hans and Fritz said she was drinking," said one observer, "and that it had undermined her health. They went to work and started telling Nixon that she was unreliable. Of course, it was their sadistic pressure that had driven her to it. But she pulled herself together and snapped out of it."

"There was a natural clash between Haldeman's zero defects system and Rose's theory that life was more complicated," said another observer. "Haldeman wanted a zero defects system to avoid mistakes, and Rose had the natural insight that that was the way to have a mega-mistake. She provided ways and means of access, and he resented it."

Rose Woods's office is two from the Oval Office, and there she has a staff of three secretaries who handle high-level clerical tasks. The Christmas card list. Letters to the President's friends and supporters. Requests from V.I.P.s. Miss Woods—who is paid $36,000 a year—has continued to perform her customary duties for the President. She is in the office every morning by 8:05 and often works well into the evening hours. "Her work is essentially mountains of mail," says Rhyne, "keeping in contact with people who know the President personally, handling indeterminate numbers of phone calls. It drives you nuts to look at the stack of messages on her desk. The President has continued to use her to do exactly what she did before. I can't see any big change in that. He has not cut her loose. But so far as I know, they've had only one conversation about the tape—on November 14—and nobody has broached the subject with her since. It seems the guy is so intent on what he's doing he doesn't concern himself with anything else. This is a very interesting aspect of the picture."

Miss Woods has always typed most of the President's speeches—and not just his drafts, but the speechwriters' drafts. "I've seen her edit mistakes out of copy that would have gotten everyone in trouble," said one of those speechwriters. "She is also something of an artist. You know how e e cummings writes poetry? She takes a draft of a speech and does a similar thing to it, breaks it up into phrases on the page, makes it much more easy to read, and, incidentally, makes it almost impossible to put back together as prose." Miss Woods also controls the lists for White House parties and prayer breakfasts—which gives her a great deal more power over patronage than might be supposed. And she has functioned as a sort of White House ombudsman, listening sympathetically to complaints from other employees who hope she will go to the President with them. When she goes out at night, she is constantly cornered by Nixon supporters who press letters to the President upon her, ask her to give him messages, give her something they've clipped for him.

Her apartment at the Watergate is a two-bedroom cooperative, furnished by a decorator in beige and brown, and trimmed with some of the mementos she has picked up on her trips with the President—elephants from every country she has been to, a chest from China, an ikon from Spain. There are also lots of flowers—friends have been sending them lately—and they have also been sending posters of a cat hanging from a tree limb, with a printed message: "Hang in there, Baby." She reportedly has enough of them to wallpaper a room.

Rose Mary Woods is hanging in, but her friends say it has been difficult. "Of course she's depressed," says a New York friend, Claudia Val. "Anyone would be, under the circumstances." She is not speaking to Leonard Garment and J. Fred Buzhardt, and apparently a number of people in the White House are not speaking to her. Recently, she called her dear friend Miss De La O, and asked, half-humorously and half-bitterly, "Are *you* still speaking to me?" The antipathy she has always felt for the press has increased; she is not used to being in the public print, even less used to hostile questions from reporters. A few months ago, Miss Woods stood up at a dinner party to toast the President as "the most honest

man I have ever known," and reporters continually bad-
ger her with the remark. After one of her recent court
appearances, a journalist asked her if she would stand
by the statement, and Miss Woods lost her temper. "That
is a rude, impertinent . . ." she replied. "The answer is
yes." Hill & Knowlton executive Gray has tried—strictly
in a private capacity—to make sure she goes to a lot of
parties and keeps busy, and he also made certain she
bought a Christmas tree this year. "This wasn't the year
for her not to have one," he said.

Until mid-November, Rose Mary Woods's troubles
were not particularly serious; or if they were, she at least
felt she was being taken care of by the family. Haldeman
was gone, and she had been named executive assistant
to the President. She had been asked to give a deposi-
tion in the Common Cause lawsuit. (She had sole possession of the secret list of corporate donors to the 1972
campaign—the list is known as "Rosemary's baby"—and
used it for party invitations.) The Watergate committee
was thinking of subpoenaing her because of her knowledge of the Howard Hughes $100,000 contribution, but
had not gotten around to it. There was the milk case,
and the fact that she has had a peripheral involvement
in the President's murky finances—in 1968 he gave her
stock options he held in a Florida land deal, and she dou-
bled her money. But her problems were the President's
problems. And then, on November 14, the White House
lawyers sat down to play the tape and found the buzz.
They could not duplicate it—and they entered Miss
Woods's office without her permission in an attempt to
reproduce it.

Miss Woods's version of her role in the mystery of
the buzz is as follows. On September 28, the President

asked her to go to Camp David for the weekend to transcribe the tapes. She canceled her plans, and on Saturday morning she and the President's appointments
secretary, Steve Bull, went up to Dogwood Cabin, and
Bull began marking which sections of the tapes Miss
Woods was to transcribe. At 10:10 a.m.—apparently in
response to a question from Bull—General Haig called
and explained to Miss Woods that the subpoena of the
June 20 tape covered only the conversation between the
President and John Ehrlichman and that she should not
bother listening to the one between the President and
Haldeman. Miss Woods sat down to work, but she had
a difficult time: the quality of the tape was bad and the
Sony tape recorder she was using was cumbersome. Saturday afternoon, President Nixon came into the cabin,
jiggled the tape back and forth several times, and said
he didn't know how she could hear anything on it. Miss
Woods worked until 3 a.m. Sunday morning, and got up
three hours later to work until 5 p.m., when she joined
the Nixons for dinner. "It is one of the few [Sundays]
in my life I did not attend Mass," Miss Woods testified,
"because I was trying to finish this job."

On Monday, October 1, she resumed work on the June
20 tape back at the White House. Technical Services
brought her a Uher 5000 tape recorder they had purchased that day. Sometime around 2 p.m., she was listening to the beginning of the Haldeman conversation—just
to verify that Ehrlichman had left the room, she says.
The telephone rang. When she got off the phone—four
to five minutes later—she realized she had pushed the
record button down. She put the tape into reverse and
heard the buzz. As soon as she saw the President was
alone, she went into his office, the Oval Office, and told

him she had made a mistake. "He said there is no problem," Miss Woods testified, "because that is not a subpoenaed tape."

Miss Woods's version continues. In early November, she was told she would be testifying before Sirica, and on November 7, she met with White House lawyers Leonard Garment and Sam Powers—who have said they did not know about the accident at that point. They told her to answer the questions yes and no, and not to volunteer anything. Miss Woods does not remember being so instructed, but she says it was her impression that her testimony was to cover only the subpoenaed tapes. She appeared in court November 8, and she calmly and deftly told the story of the weekend at Camp David, described at some length how difficult a job it was, and said she had worked on a conversation that seemed to her to be "two to three hours" long "between the President and Ehrlichman, chiefly, and Haldeman, briefly." She added: "It was a very dull tape, frankly."

"Were there any precautions taken to assure you would not accidentally hit the erase button?" prosecutor Jill Wine Volner asked.

"Everybody said be terribly careful," Miss Woods replied. "I mean, I don't think I want this to sound like I am bragging, but I don't believe I am so stupid that they had to go over it. . . . I was told if you push that button it will erase, and I do know even on a small machine you can dictate over something and that removes it and I think I used every possible precaution not to do that."

"What special precaution did you take? . . . " Mrs. Volner asked.

"What precautions?" Miss Woods replied. "I used my head. It is the only one I had to use."

From November 26 through 28, Miss Woods appeared
once again before Sirica, this time represented by
Charles Rhyne, and she finally told the story about the
accident and posed for a series of ridiculous pictures at
her desk. Judge Sirica asked her why she had not mentioned the accident when she first appeared in court.

"I would say, Your Honor," she replied, "that I would
today, but I didn't then. I think, if you may remember,
that I was petrified; it was my first time ever in a court-
room, and I understood that we were talking only about
the subpoenaed tapes. And I think all I can say is that I
am just dreadfully sorry."

A few questions: How did the President know off the top
of his head that that part of the tape was not subpoenaed unless he was already concerned about it? Why did
Technical Services buy a new Uher when they had four
identical models sitting in the basement not in use? Why
did Miss Woods have to listen ahead to make sure Ehrlichman had left the room if Steve Bull had marked the
part of the tape she was to transcribe? Why did the White
House legal staff think the Haldeman conversation was
not subpoenaed when the language of the August 13 revision of the subpoena read: "Respondent met with John
Ehrlichman and H. R. Haldeman in his old Executive
Office Building office on June 20, 1972, from 10:30 a.m.
until approximately 12:45 p.m."? Why did Miss Woods
mention that she had worked on "Ehrlichman, chiefly,
and Haldeman, briefly" if she did not believe the Haldeman section was covered? How could it have taken her
thirty-plus hours at Camp David to transcribe only an
hour of conversation—and why did she originally think
the conversation was "two or three hours long"? Why did

she claim to have had the Uher for several hours before the accident when she had had it for only an hour? Why did she think she went in to see the President alone in the Oval Office when White House logs show that on October 1 she saw the President in his Executive Office Building office while he was with his doctor?

In an article in the *New Republic*, Walter Pincus suggests that Miss Woods was telling the truth November 8, and invented the story of the accident some time later. "But in so doing," Pincus writes, "she had no intention of taking the blame for the entire . . . gap." That is possible. It is also possible that Miss Woods heard the Haldeman section of the tape, knew it was damaging, and erased it deliberately. It is possible she erased the entire eighteen and a half minutes accidentally. It is possible she erased the initial four minutes accidentally and then someone who hoped to stick her with it erased the rest. It is possible that the erasure was already on the tape and Miss Woods was deluded into thinking she had done it. It is possible that the President—or someone working on his behalf—erased the tape and Miss Woods agreed to take part of the blame, never dreaming she would be sold out by the White House legal staff. It is even possible that the experts are wrong in saying that the gap was caused by five to nine separate and deliberate erasures; a faulty diode may have done it. At this point, no one knows—and it is possible that, like many other aspects of the whole Watergate mess, no one will ever know.

And in the meantime, we are left with Rose Mary Woods. The loyal secretary who did it for The Boss? Or the loyal secretary who was set up? The tiger or the lady?

"I was thinking about her last night," Eloise De La O

was saying. "Here all these things are happening and there isn't a thing any of us can do for her. It's a maze of things you just can't figure out. I don't know how she's going to get out of it. But I pray for her. And I know she's praying very hard."

March, 1974

No, But I Read the Book

I suppose it is completely presumptuous for me to write
even one word on the saga of Pat and Bill and Lance
and Kevin and Grant and Delilah and Michele Loud.
Last year, I managed to miss every single episode of *An
American Family*. But I did catch the Louds on the talk
shows, and it seemed to me at the time that, with the
possible exception of Tiny Tim, no group of people had
ever passed so quickly from being celebrities to being
freaks. I was amazed at the amount of time they lin-
gered on, being analyzed in print, taking up space on the
air, stealing valuable time from any number of people
I would prefer to have read about or seen, even including Shecky Greene. Finally, though, like a toothache, the
Louds went away. And the other day, when Pat Loud's
book arrived in the mail, I felt terrible that I had not
spent the months of their absence grateful for it; it is
always easier to have a toothache return when you have
at least had the sense to appreciate how wonderful it
was not to have had one.

Pat Loud: A Woman's Story was written by Mrs. Loud
with Nora Johnson, and the publicity director at Cow-
ard, McCann & Geoghegan assures me that its style—

which is slick and show-biz rat-a-tat-tat—reflects Mrs. Loud's way of speaking exactly. "Gloria was a lamb chop." "Rose gardens he doesn't walk through." Like that. The book itself is sad and awful, and at times quite fascinating and moving. All these adjectives ring a bell: it seems to me that they were applied to the television series as well. In fact, the only thing about Pat Loud's book that is different from the television series that propelled her into her book contract is that no one who reads it will ever wonder Why She Did It. She did it because she wanted to tell her side. She did it because she had very little else to do. And she did it because she has come to believe that her brand of letting-it-all-hang-out candor is valuable to others in her position. Will she ever learn?

"Every other writer and cocktail circuit sociologist is contemplating the problem of the 46-year-old mother-housewife who suddenly isn't needed anymore," Mrs. Loud writes. "But most of these 'problem women' never had what has saved me, at least so far, from that devastating moment of truth: instant fame." The television show may not have saved Pat Loud from the truth—her own head seems to have done that job perfectly well. But the experience certainly confused her, and confused the issues involved to boot. Pat Loud's book is not the straight I-found-myself-through-divorce women's lib confessional; her case is too unusual. Rather, it is a rambling, perplexing, contradictory account by a woman who is trying, and failing, to make some sense out of a series of events that probably defy sensible explanation.

The real story of the Loud marriage, as told in this book, is a good deal more complicated and tacky, mainly tacky, than what I gather came out in the television series. The Louds and their five children lived in Santa Barbara, California, Pat working hard at being Supermom, Bill at his strip-mining-equipment business. As the marriage went on and the number of children increased, Mrs. Loud began finding telltale clues around the house. First a love letter to Bill from another woman, then a loose glove in his suitcase, lipstick on his handkerchiefs, a brochure from a Las Vegas hotel. The love letter enraged her so that she packed her four children into the family car—she was pregnant with the fifth— and drove off into the night. As it turned out, she did not get very far; Mrs. Loud, who has no selectivity index whatsoever, explains: "When I'm pregnant, I have the trots all the time, and sometimes it's really essential to get to a john fast . . . and there wasn't any gas station.... So finally I turned around and went home." In 1966, she found a set of her husband's cuff links, engraved "To Bill, Eternally Yours, Kitty," and all hell broke loose. Her husband assured her he had bought the cuff links in a pawn shop, but she did not believe him. So she snuck off, had an extra set of his office keys made, and while he was off on a business trip she went to look through his files.

"It was all there," she writes, "as though it had been waiting for me for years—credit card slips telling of restaurants I'd never been to and hotels I'd never stayed at, plane tickets to places I'd never seen, even pictures of Bill and his girls as they grinned and screwed their way around the countryside."

Bill Loud returned from his business trip. Pat Loud slugged him, in front of the children. He slugged her back, in front of the children. They both went to see a psychiatrist. They both stopped seeing the psychiatrist. They spent night after night getting drunk as Bill Loud recited the intimate sexual details of his infidelities. The subject of open marriage was introduced. Pat Loud began going to local bars during lunch and picking up businessmen. "We would have a few drinks and some tortillas," she recalls. "Then we would let nature take its course." She threatened divorce. He started seeing his women again. And in the midst of this idyllic existence, Craig Gilbert, a film-maker with a contract from public television, came into their home and told them he was looking for "an attractive, articulate California family" to do a one-hour special about.

It is impossible to read this book and not suspect that Craig Gilbert knew exactly what he was doing when he picked the Louds, knew after ten minutes with them and the clinking ice in their drinks that he had found the perfect family to show exactly what he must have intended to show all along—the emptiness of American family life. Occasionally, in the course of this book, Pat Loud starts to suspect this, nibbles around it, yaps like a puppy at the ankles of truth, then tosses the idea aside in favor of loftier philosophical pronouncements. "If he knew it," she concludes, "it was not necessarily because he actively smelled it about us, but because he knew in a way what we didn't—that life is lousy and it's tragic and it's supposed to be and you can pretend otherwise if you want, but if you do, you're wrong."

Gilbert had no trouble persuading the Louds to cooperate. Bill had always been outgoing and exhibitionistic. Pat, for her part, saw the show as a way to appear as she had always wanted to—the perfect mother, cheerfully beating egg whites in her copper bowls. When Gilbert informed them that the show was going to be so good that he would shoot enough for five specials and then twelve, the Louds consented, apparently without a tremor of anxiety.

"Of course," Pat Loud writes, "if you're going to be in print or on the radio or TV, you can't help thinking of all the people who will read or see you, and the first ones I thought of were all Bill's women. There they would sit in frowzy little rented rooms scattered about California, Oregon, Washington, and Arizona, little gifts from Bill here and there, a memento from some trip or something he'd bought them, pathetic scraps of forgotten pleasure in their failed and lonely worlds. Their bleached blond hair would be falling sloppily out of its hairpins and their enormous breasts would be falling equally sloppily out of their torn, spotty negligees as they clutched their glasses of Scotch and rested their fat ankles on footstools to relieve their aching, varicose veins. . . . In pathetic, panting interest they would turn on their televisions to look at the Louds, and they would weep. . . . If they'd had Bill for a few hours or days, if they'd had a few sessions of what they probably thought of as blinding ecstasy, I had had him a thousand times more."

Pat Loud offers a number of other explanations as to why her family agreed to Gilbert's proposal—the one she seems to believe most firmly is that anyone would have. But she is less sure about why the reaction to the show was so enormous. "What nerve have we touched?" she asks at one point. "I would like to know; I would really like to know." I suspect I know. I think the American public has an almost insatiable need to feel superior to people who appear to have everything, and the Louds were the perfect vehicle to fill that need. There they were, a beautiful family with a beautiful house with a beautiful pool, and one son was a homosexual, the rest of the children lolled about, uninterested in anything, and the marriage was breaking up. All of it was on television, in *cinéma vérité*—a medium that at its best (I'm thinking of the Maysleses' *Salesman* and the Canadian Film Board's *Lonely Boy* and *The Most*) has always tended to specialize in a certain amount of implicit condescension.

It is on the subject of the making of the series that Pat Loud is most interesting. *Cinéma vérité* film-makers have always insisted that after a time, their subjects forget the cameras are there, but as Pat Loud makes clear, it's just not possible. "You can't forget the camera," she writes, "and everybody's instinct is to try and look as good as possible for it, all the time, and to keep kind of snapping along being active, eager, cheery, and productive. Out go those moments when you're just in a kind of nothing period. . . . You don't realize how many of those you have until you're trying not to have them. . . . And what you also don't realize is that you *have* to have them—they're like REM sleep."

Ultimately, Pat Loud seems to have come to believe that she owed more to the film-makers than she did to herself or her husband; any concept of dignity or privacy she may have had evaporated in the face of pressure from them. Again she nibbles around the edges of this, almost but not quite getting it, but the suggestions of what happened are there: the illiterate Californians trying to impress the erudite Easterners; the boring, slothful family attempting to come up with a dramatic episode to justify all that footage; the woman who had always tried to please men—first her father, then her husband—now transferring it all to Craig Gilbert.

And when, in the course of events, Pat Loud decided

she wanted a divorce, Craig Gilbert convinced her that she owed it to him, to all of them, to do it on the air. "If I decided to divorce during the filming," Mrs. Loud says Gilbert told her, "I must be honest enough to do it openly and not confuse the issue further by refusing to allow it to be shot." Again she almost has it, almost sees how she was conned, and then falls into utter nonsense. "Couldn't it be," she asks, "that since circumstance and fate had put me in a position to rip away the curtain of hypocrisy, that maybe, just maybe, we could help other families face their problems more honestly?" And then she switches gears, and makes sense again: "A psychiatrist told a friend of mine recently that in his experience he'd found that there is almost always a third force present when divorce finally happens. The miserable marriage can wobble on for years on end, until something or somebody comes along and pushes one of the people over the brink. . . . It's usually another man . . . or another woman . . . or possibly a supportive psychiatrist; in my case, it was a whole production staff and a camera crew. . . ."

And so the marriage and the television series ended, and along came the notoriety. And now there is the book, and there will be more: more talk shows, more interviews. It all seems sad; there is no way to read this book and not feel that this bumbling woman is way over her head. She has made a fool of herself on television, and now she is making a fool of herself in print. She does not understand that it is just as hard to be honest success-fully as it is to lie successfully. And now, God help her, she has moved to New York. She will get a job, she tells us at the end of the book, and perhaps she will be able to fulfill her fantasy. Here is Pat Loud's last fantasy. She's at this swell New York cocktail party, "exchanging terribly New York in-type gossip about who's backing what new play and who got how much for the paperback rights to Philip Roth's latest," and there is this man who takes her to dinner, and then to bed, and they have a wonderful affair. "I'm not saying he would solve everything, or pick up the pieces, or even make me happy. Nor is he as important as a good job. But the nice thing about fantasies is that you don't have to explain them to anybody. They are absolutely free." There she goes again, almost making sense, talking about the importance of work, and the need not to look to anyone for the solution of her problems, and then she blows it all. "They are absolutely free." That's the thing about fantasies. They're not absolutely free. Sometimes you pay dearly for them. Which is something Pat Loud ought to have learned by now. Will she ever?

March, 1974

Crazy Ladies: II

It was, as these things go, a fairly ordinary week. One Flying Wallenda. Two midgets who claimed to be the world's smallest married couple. An anthropologist who insisted that people who eat bear meat become more aggressive than people who eat eggs. A tiger who chewed up the carpet. And the requisite number of folk singers, politicians, writers, actors, doctors, palm readers, and tax experts who travel the country filling up the air time on local television talk shows. Not that any of them mattered to me. The reason I was there—and the reason a great many more people than usual watched *The Panorama Show* in Washington the week of April 1—was that Martha Mitchell was the co-host. Martha of the late-night phone calls, Martha the black-and-blue political prisoner, Martha who lives alone now while her husband commutes between his Essex House suite and his trial in the federal courthouse, Martha whose own daughter has chosen to spend most of her time with her father—Martha was making her first public appearance since "the mess," as she refers to it, began. From Monday through Friday, she sat under the lights, doing a perfectly creditable job, and I sat there in

the studio watching and waiting—I'm not sure for what.
A few bitchy remarks about Richard Nixon, maybe. A
couple of tidbits about her own state of mind. An insight
or two about political wives, or about how-the-mighty-
have-fallen, or some such. I had never confused Martha Mitchell with Diogenes, never thought she knew a
great deal about Watergate, never found her anything
but a rather frowzy, excessive, blathering woman who
never (until the Watergate break-in) said anything that
I found remotely sympathetic. I did not expect to find
her charming, and I did not expect to find her canny,
and I certainly did not expect to find her moving. All
of which she was. At the end of the week, one reporter
who covered the show suggested in print that the staff
of *Panorama* had taken advantage of Martha, had used
her, had held her up as a freak, had titillated the public
with coy and tasteless references to her sanity. It seemed
to me more complicated than that. Martha Mitchell has
always used the media at least as well as they have used
her. She even told a story about it on the show. She was
asked by host Maury Povich about her late-night phone
calls to the press.

"A lot of them were planned," she explained. "I'd call
in the daytime and say, 'Now this is my story, let's put
it out at midnight.' Sometimes they'd ask where I was
calling from, and I'd say the balcony of Watergate. Now
it's not in any way possible to get a telephone out on the
balcony of Watergate, but that was just a little come-on
to make it more interesting."

"You mean you could determine when a story would
be broken?" Povich asked.

"Well," she said, "I learned pretty early on in the

game what you have to do to get a story on the wires or printed. That's what I did."

"I thought it was all off the top of your head," said Povich.

"Well," said Martha Mitchell, "I try to be dumb."

The Panorama Show got exactly what it wanted from Martha Mitchell—a lot of publicity and attention. And she got from it the chance to prove that she wasn't crazy. In the end, it was a fair trade.

It is, of course, extremely easy to become known in Washington as a crazy lady. Even Marion Javits is thought of there as a crazy lady. But Martha Mitchell's reputation as one was earned. She always reveled in the image she created as the slightly dizzy dame whose husband could not control her. In fact, she rarely said anything he did not approve of; nonetheless, the image worked perfectly. But in June, 1972, it all caught up with her. No one ever takes crazy ladies seriously. And so when she called U.P.I.'s Helen Thomas to claim that she was being held prisoner in a California motel and injected with drugs against her will, the press dutifully reported the claim and did virtually nothing to check it out. She was telling the truth—but almost no one knows that, even now. It is almost impossible to think of another politician's wife who could have gone through such an experience and had so little serious attention paid to it. When John Mitchell resigned as the President's campaign manager shortly afterward, the White House had an easy time convincing the press—and the public—that he had done so in order to look after his wife. Now, almost two years later, the Mitchells are separated; he is facing an apparently endless series of court

battles; and she is living alone in a Fifth Avenue cooperative where—she notes sadly—she has never even had a
chance to use the dining room.

Mrs. Mitchell's appearance on *Panorama* was negotiated by the show's producer, Jane Henry Caper, through
a mutual friend; she was paid just above the $480
AFTRA scale. There were no explicit ground rules set for
the appearance, but Povich, the host of the show, deliberately stayed away from any direct questions about John
Mitchell and his legal difficulties, and he waited until
midweek to ask her directly about her own problems.
He need not have waited. Martha Mitchell may not be
a brilliant woman, but her instincts are first-rate; she
knew exactly when to laugh off a question and when to
take the opening to make a point about herself.

At the beginning of the week, though, it seemed
likely that Mrs. Mitchell would provide only indirect
hints about her state of mind. She did get off a couple
of zingers at the President—particularly when she told
of converting her husband to Republicanism. "The day I
talked my husband out of calling the President Tricky
Dick, I could shoot myself," she said. But the most interesting moment on Monday's show came when she turned
to Helen Gahagan Douglas, who ran unsuccessfully for
the Senate against Richard Nixon in 1950. "Well, Helen,"
she said, "I want to ask you something. I think you went
through a certain smear campaign in those years. How
do you overcome a smear campaign? How do you explain
it to your children?" It was a wonderful question; unfortunately, Mrs. Douglas did not answer it, and the show
went on to far more mundane things—including an
extended series of misunderstandings between the two
women. As Diana McLellan put it in the *Washington*

Star, Mrs. Douglas and Mrs. Mitchell "hit it off immediately, in the splendid way of two very polite women, each of whom insists on believing that the other is in total agreement with her, no matter how diametrically opposed she is."

"What worries you as you walk around?" Mrs. Douglas asked Mrs. Mitchell. "What do you see that distresses you?"

"I have got to the point, Helen, where I can't read the papers," replied Martha. "Everything worries me. What worries me more than anything is the example this country is setting for the younger people."

"That's true," Mrs. Douglas grimly agreed, apparently thinking Mrs. Mitchell was referring to the Nixon Administration.

"For instance," Martha went on, "this streaking. I see a TV show the other night and there go nudes in front of me. What is now left? Why should children go out and streak?"

The subject of streaking came up with some frequency during the week, and Martha continued to be baffled by it. "Where did it start?" she asked. "At one of the Ivy League colleges?" It was a perfect subject for her: one of her gifts as a co-host is that except when she wants to make a point about herself, she asks exactly the kinds of unsophisticated questions any Middle American housewife would, and has absolutely no embarrassment about revealing how naïve she is. "This conversation is too technical for me," she sighed during what was in fact a rather technical explanation of tax shelters. "I'm not sure what you're explaining," she said to two housing officials who had been totally unintelligible for fifteen minutes. "What does this mean?" she asked after reading a completely meaningless weather report. "Is it going to rain or isn't it?"

The first reference to her mental health came up on Wednesday—and she chose to take it lightly. Pat Loud was on the show, and she remarked that since moving to New York she had seen more crazy people than she ever had in her life.

"Don't you think that's because American people have too much leisure?" asked Martha.

"No," said Pat Loud. "I don't think so."

Povich turned to Mrs. Mitchell. "I don't know whether I should, but I will bring this subject up," he said. "There were nasty rumors about you, Martha, when you left Washington, in this circumstance, and I was wondering how you lived with that."

"Well," said Martha, "don't you see, I'm still crazy. It doesn't take very long to find that out. But, you know, I'm happy. They say that crazy people are happier than anyone else. Look at me."

On Thursday, Helen Thomas and *Time* magazine's Bonnie Angelo came on as guests—and Martha, surrounded by the closest thing she has to friends these days, relaxed. Povich fumbled in with a question—this time to Miss Thomas—about Martha's sanity, and Martha listened as Miss Thomas defended her. "Martha Mitchell hit this town like a bombshell," she recalled, and as she talked, Martha Mitchell seemed to become sadder—which was understandable, since Helen Thomas sounded a little as if she were talking about a dead person. Povich asked how the telephone connection between the two of them began. "You know, it always amazes me," said Martha. "Why am I associated with a telephone when we've had two Presidents of late who've done nothing but telephone all night long? I mean, why should they pick on a poor woman? Look at Johnson. Look at Richard Nixon. I have more funny stories to tell about Richard Nixon telephoning the apartment at two or three in the morning, and I'm going to tell them sometime."

"How about right now?" said Bonnie Angelo.

"No," said Martha. "I'm saving it for my book."

Miss Angelo asked how Martha felt about the press.

"I want to say, from the bottom of my heart, that I think that I wouldn't be sitting here today if it weren't for the press," she said. "They have literally saved me from an asylum, and from I don't know what. And I can take it one step further. If I hadn't made that telephone call to Helen in California, the people that were behind all this, that were holding me a prisoner, would not have taken into consideration that the press knew that if anything happened to Martha Mitchell, Helen would have been there looking for me. It literally saved my life."

Bonnie Angelo pointed out that the White House planted the rumors about Martha's crack-up and told reporters she was the reason Mitchell resigned.

"Poor John," said Martha. "Poor John had to take care of me." She smiled ruefully and shook her head. "One of the funniest things is, and I say that not meaning funny, but in recent months people in the White House have called my friends and said, 'Why do you listen to Martha Mitchell? She's crazy as a loon. Don't print anything about her.'"

"I want to ask Martha," said Miss Angelo. "Did you enjoy living in the spotlight? Are you happy you had those years as a public figure?"

"I don't think I've had time to get around to that,

Bonnie," said Martha Mitchell. "There've been too many hurts to really analyze the situation."

Friday, after her last show, I sat down with Martha Mitchell in the *Panorama* offices at WTTG. A staff member came in to tell her that they had gotten hundreds of phone calls praising her performance. "Isn't that great?" she said. "With all the hell I've been through, to hear a little praise. I've gone through all this by myself, as you know. This has been an extremely trying period for me, from the standpoint of Martha. I've been fighting a one-man battle, and I haven't just been fighting City Hall—I've been fighting the federal government. You must realize that everything that's happened to me has been caused by the cover-up of Watergate. I was hidden, literally, for a long period of time, hidden by them, and also hidden by myself, because I had been so tremendously crushed. When you believe as I believed, and worked as hard as I worked—and nobody in Washington worked as hard as Martha Mitchell—and then all of a sudden to have your world crushed in front of you, which happened to me in California. Why did people call her crazy? Why did people call her an alcoholic? Because they were trying to shut Martha Mitchell up, and they didn't know how to do it.

"I lived for my family. We were the tightest-knit little family you've ever seen. They used to say we had a perfect marriage, a perfect love affair. We did. Every day he used to tell me I was the most wonderful woman in the world. And John always had so much confidence in me. I don't feel I'm a deserted woman. This is not a normal marital breakup. It's much more intricate. Because a man doesn't change in twenty-four hours from thinking his wife is the most wonderful person in the world."

And so Martha Mitchell went off to her hotel. She was spending the weekend in Washington and planned to attend the Counter-Gridiron party. "The busy person is the happy person," she said as she left. Oh, sure. And maybe the crazy person is the happy person, too. But Martha Mitchell is neither busy nor crazy nor happy. There is not much call for yesterday's celebrities. There is probably a lesson in this, something about crazy ladies, or crying wolf, or maybe something about Richard Nixon—but I don't know what it is. To some extent Martha Mitchell got what she deserved. But still . . .

April, 1974

Conundrum

As I suppose everyone knows by now, James Morris was four years old and sitting under the piano listening to his mother play Sibelius when he was seized with the irreversible conviction that he ought to have been born a girl. By the age of nine, he was praying nightly for the miracle. "Let me be a girl. Amen." He went on to the army, became a journalist, climbed Mount Everest with Sir Edmund Hillary, won awards for his books, and had four children with a wife who knew that all he really wanted was a sex change. Almost two years ago, he went off to a clinic in Casablanca that had dirty floors, shaved off his pubic hair, "and went to say goodbye to myself in the mirror. We would never meet again, and I wanted to give that other self a long last look in the eye and a wink of luck." The wink of luck did that other self no good at all: the next morning, it was lopped off, and James Morris woke up to find himself as much a woman as hormones and surgery could make him. He promptly sold his dinner jacket and changed his name.

This entire mess could doubtless have been avoided had James Morris been born an Orthodox Jew (in which case he could have adopted the standard Jewish prayer thanking God for *not* making him a woman) or had he gone to see a good Freudian analyst, who might have realized that any young boy sitting under a piano was probably looking up his mother's skirt. But no such luck. James Morris has become Jan Morris, an Englishwoman who wears sweater sets and pearls, blushes frequently, bursts into tears at the littlest things, and loves having a gossip with someone named Mrs. Weatherby. Mrs. Weatherby, Morris writes, "really is concerned . . . about my migraine yesterday; and when I examine myself I find that I am no less genuinely distressed to hear that Amanda missed the school outing because of her ankle."

Conundrum is Jan Morris's book about her experience, and I read it with a great deal of interest, largely because I always wanted to be a girl, too. I, too, felt that I was born into the wrong body, a body that refused, in spite of every imprecation and exercise I could manage, to become anything but the boyish, lean thing it was. I, too, grew up wishing for protectors, strangers to carry my bags, truck drivers to whistle out windows. I wanted more than anything to be something I will never be— feminine, and feminine in the worst way. Submissive. Dependent. Soft-spoken. Coquettish. I was no good at all at any of it, no good at being a girl; on the other hand, I am not half-bad at being a woman. In contrast, Jan Morris is perfectly awful at being a woman; what she has become instead is exactly what James Morris wanted to become those many years ago. A girl. And worse, a forty-seven-year-old girl. And worst of all, a forty-seven-year-old *Cosmopolitan* girl. To wit:

"So I well understand what Kipling had in mind, about sisters under the skin. Over coffee a lady from Montreal effuses about Bath—'I don't know if you've done any traveling yourself' (not too much, I demurely lie) 'but I do feel it's important, don't you, to see how other people really live.' I bump into Jane W—— in the street, and she tells me about Archie's latest excess— 'Honestly, Jan, you don't know how lucky you are.' I buy some typing paper—'How lovely to be able to write, you make me feel a proper dunce'—and walking home again to start work on a new chapter, find that workmen are in the flat, taking down a picture-rail. One of them has knocked my little red horse off the mantelpiece, chipping its enameled rump. I restrain my annoyance, summon a fairly frosty smile, and make them all cups of tea, but I am thinking to myself, as they sheepishly help themselves to sugar, a harsh feminist thought. It would be a man, I think. Well it would, wouldn't it?"

It is a truism of the women's movement that the exaggerated concepts of femininity and masculinity have done their fair share to make a great many people unhappy, but nowhere is this more evident than in Jan Morris's mawkish and embarrassing book. I first read of Morris in a Sunday *New York Times Magazine* article that brought dignity and real sensitivity to Morris's obsession. But Morris's own sensibility is so giddy and relentlessly cheerful that her book has almost no dignity at all. What she has done in it is to retrace his/her life (I am going to go crazy from the pronouns and adjectives here) by applying sentimental gender judgments to everything. Oxford is wonderful because it is feminine. Venice is sublime because it is feminine. Statesmen are dreadful because they are masculine. "Even more than now," Morris writes of his years as a foreign correspondent, "the world of affairs was dominated by men. It was like stepping from cheap theater into reality, to pass from the ludicrous goings-on of minister's office or ambassador's study into the private house behind, where women were to be found doing real things, like bringing up children, painting pictures, or writing home."

And as for sex—but let Morris tell you about men and women and sex. "You are doubtless wondering, especially if you are male, what about sex? . . . One of the genuine and recurrent surprises of my life concerns the importance to men of physical sex. . . . For me the actual performance of the sexual act seemed of secondary importance and interest. I suspect this is true for most women. . . . In the ordinary course of events [the sex act] struck me as slightly distasteful, and I could imagine it only as part of some grand act, a declaration of absolute interdependence, or even a sacrifice."

Over the years, Morris saw a number of doctors, several of whom suggested he try homosexuality. (He had tried it several times before, but found it aesthetically unpleasant.) A meeting was arranged with the owner of a London art gallery. "We had a difficult lunch together," Morris writes, "and he made eyes at the wine waiter over the fruit salad." The remark is interesting, not just because of its hostility toward homosexuals but also because Jan Morris now makes exactly those same sorts of eyes at wine waiters—on page 150 of her book, in fact.

As James turns into a hermaphrodite and then into Jan, the prose in the book, which is cloying enough to begin with, turns into a kind of overembellished, simile-laden verbiage that makes the style of Victorian women novelists seem spare. Exclamation points and italicized words appear with increasing frequency. Everything blushes. James Morris blushes. His "small breasts blossomed like blushes." He starts talking to the flowers and wishing them a Happy Easter. He becomes even more devoted to animals. He is able for the first time ("the scales dropped from my eyes") to look out a plane window and see things on the ground below not as cars and homes seen at a distance but "Lo! . . . as dolls' houses and dinky toys." Shortly before the operation, he and his wife, Elizabeth, whose understanding defies understanding, take a trip, both as women, through Oregon. "How merrily we traveled!" Morris writes. "What fun the Oregonians gave us! How cheerfully we swapped badinage with boatmen and lumberjacks, flirtatious garage hands and hospitable trappers! I never felt so liberated, or more myself, nor was I ever more fond of Elizabeth. 'Come on in, girls,' the motel men would say, and childish though I expect it sounds to you, silly in itself, perhaps a little pathetic, possibly grotesque, still if they had touched me with an accolade of nobility, or clad me ceremonially in crimson, I could not have been more flattered." The only thing Morris neglects to write into this passage is a little face with a smile on it.

Morris is infuriatingly vague about the reactions of her children (she blandly insists they adjusted perfectly) and of Elizabeth (she says they are still the closest of friends). "I am not the first," Morris writes, "to discover that one recipe for an idyllic marriage is a blend of affection, physical potency and sexual incongruity." (Idyllic marriage? Where your husband becomes a lady? I suppose we owe this to creeping Harold-and-Vitaism; still, it is one of the more ridiculous trends of recent years to confuse great friendships with great marriages; great marriages are when you have it all.) As for her new sex life, Jan Morris lyrically trills that her sexuality is now unbounded. But how?

Unfortunately, she is a good deal more explicit about the details of what she refers to as "truly the symptoms of womanhood." "The more I was treated as a woman, the more woman I became," she writes. "I adapted willy-nilly. If I was assumed to be incompetent at reversing cars, or opening bottles, oddly, incompetent I found myself becoming. If a case was thought too heavy for me, inexplicably I found it so myself. . . . I discovered that even now men prefer women to be less informed, less able, less talkative, and certainly less self-centered than they are themselves; so I generally obliged them. . . . I did not particularly want to be good at reversing cars, and did not in the least mind being patronized by illiterate garage-men, if it meant they were going to give me some extra trading stamps. . . . And when the news agent seems to look at me with approval, or the man in the milk-cart smiles, I feel absurdly elated, as though I have been given a good review in the Sunday *Times*. I know it is nonsense, but I cannot help it."

The truth, of course, is that Jan Morris does not know it is nonsense. She thinks that is what it is about. And I wonder about all this, wonder how anyone in this day and age can think that this is what being a woman is about. And as I wonder, I find myself thinking a harsh feminist thought. It would be a man, I think. Well, it would, wouldn't it?

June, 1974

Acknowledgments

I want to thank Susan Edmiston, Rosalind Krauss, Mary Ann Madden, and Jennifer Rogers for the number of times they stayed on the telephone trying to help me figure out what on earth I was getting at; Martha Duffy for suggesting Josie's title; Betty Suyker for her efforts in the opposite direction; the editors of *Esquire* and *New York* magazines for their encouragement and suggestions; my agent Lynn Nesbit; and, most of all, Lee Eisenberg at *Esquire* for being the best magazine editor I have ever worked with.

I would also like to have thanked Josie Davis.

Scribble Scribble

Scribble Scribble

Dorothy Schiff and the New York Post

I feel bad about what I'm going to do here. What I'm going to do here is write something about Dorothy Schiff, and the reason I feel bad about it is that a few months ago, I managed to patch things up with her and now I'm going to blow it. She had been irritated with me for several years because I told the story about her and Otto Preminger's sauna on the radio, but we managed to get through a pleasant dinner recently, which made me happy—not because I care whether or not Dorothy Schiff is irritated with me but simply because I have a book coming out this summer, and if she were speaking to me, I might have a shot at some publicity in the *New York Post*. Ah, well. It's not easy being a media columnist. The publicity I had in mind, actually, was this little feature the *Post* runs on Saturdays called "At Home With," where semi-famous people tell their favorite recipes. Mine is beef borscht.

Dorothy Schiff is the publisher, editor and owner of the *New York Post*, America's largest-selling afternoon newspaper. I used to work there. The *Post* is a tabloid that has a smaller news hole than the New York *Daily News*—five front pages, various parts of which are often rented out to Chock full o' Nuts and Lüchow's. It also has a center magazine section containing mostly *Washington Post* columnists, a first-rate sports section and drama critic, and Rose Franzblau, Earl Wilson and Dear Abby. It takes about eleven minutes to read the *Post*, and there are more than half a million New Yorkers like me who spend twenty cents six days a week to kill eleven minutes reading it. It is probably safe to say that fewer and fewer young people read the *Post*, and that fewer and fewer young people understand why anyone does. It is a terrible newspaper.

The reason it is, of course, is Dorothy Schiff. A great deal has been written about Mrs. Schiff in various places over the past years, and some of it—I'm thinking here of Gail Sheehy's article in *New York* at the end of 1973—has captured perfectly her coquettish giddiness, her penchant for trivia and her affection for gossip. It is taken for granted in these articles that Dolly Schiff is a very powerful woman—she is in fact very powerful for a woman and not particularly powerful for a newspaper publisher. What is rarely discussed is her product. In Sheehy's article, I suppose this was partly because Mrs. Schiff had manuscript approval, and partly because the publisher of *New York*, like so many other men Mrs. Schiff toys with, thinks that someday he will buy the *New York Post* from her. But it is a major omission: There is no other big-city newspaper in America that so perfectly reflects the attitudes and weaknesses of its owner. Dorothy Schiff has a right to run her paper any way she likes. She owns it. But it seems never to have crossed her mind that she might have a public obligation to produce a good newspaper. Gail Sheehy quite cleverly compared her with Scheherazade, but it would be more apt,

I think, to compare her with Marie Antoinette. As in let them read schlock.

In 1963, when I went to work there as a reporter, the *New York Post* was located in a building on West Street, near the Battery. The first day I went there, I thought I had gotten out of the elevator in the fire exit. The hallway leading to the city room was black. Absolutely black. The smell of urine came wafting out of the men's room in the middle of the long hallway between the elevator and the city room. The glass door to the city room was filmed with dust, and written on it, with a finger, was the word "Philthy." The door was cleaned four years later, but the word remained; it had managed to erode itself onto the glass. Then, through the door, was the city room. Rows of desks jammed up against one another, headset phones, manual typewriters, stacks of copy paper, cigarette butts all over the floor—all of it pretty routine for a city room, albeit a city room of the 1920s. The problem was the equipment. The staff of the *Post* was small, but it was too large for the city room and for the number of chairs and desks and telephones in it. If you arrived at the *Post* five minutes late, there were no chairs left. You would go hunt one up elsewhere on the floor, drag it to an empty space, and then set off to find a phone. You cannot be a newspaper reporter without a phone. The phones at the *Post* were the old-fashioned headset type, with an earpiece-mouthpiece part that connected to a wire headpiece. Usually you could find the earpiece-mouthpiece part, but only occasionally was there a headpiece to go with it, which meant that you spent the day with your head cocked at a seventy-degree angle trying to balance this tiny phone against your shoulder as you typed. If you managed to assemble a complete telephone in the morning, it was necessary to lock it in your desk during lunch, or else it would end up on someone else's head for the afternoon. The trouble with that was that half the staff did not have desks, much less desk drawers to lock anything in.

None of this was supposed to matter. This was the newspaper business. You want air conditioning, go work at a newsmagazine. You want clean toilets, go work in advertising. Besides, there was still a real element of excitement to working at the *New York Post* in 1963. The paper had been a good paper once, when James Wechsler was the editor, and for a while it was possible to believe that it would be again. Mrs. Schiff had kicked Wechsler upstairs, had changed the focus of the paper from hard-hitting, investigative and left-wing to frothy, gossipy and women-oriented, but we all thought that would change eventually. At some point in the next few years, several New York papers would shut down. None of us really thought the *Post* would. "The most depressing thing about the *Post*," a reporter who once worked there used to say, "is that it will never shut down." When the other papers folded, the *Post* would have to get better. It would have to absorb the superior financial-page reporters from the other afternoon papers, the superior columnists from the *Herald Tribune*. It would have to run two more pages of news, enlarge its Washington bureau, beef up its foreign coverage, hire more staff, pay them better, stop skimping on expense accounts. Why I believed this I don't know, but I believed it for years. The managing editor, Al Davis, who once dumped four gallons of ice water on my head in an attempt to tell me how he felt about the fact that I was leaving the *Post* for a while to go live in Europe, was fired in 1965, and we all had several months of euphoria thinking his replacement would make a difference. Blair Clark, the former CBS newsman and thread millionaire, came in as Mrs. Schiff's assistant—he too thought he would be able to buy the *Post* from her—and we all thought he would make a difference. The *Trib* folded, and the *Journal*, and the *World Journal Tribune*, and we all thought that would make a difference. Nothing made a difference.

I first met Mrs. Schiff a few weeks after I started working at the *Post*. I was summoned to lunch in her office, a privilege very few other reporters were granted in those days, and the reason for it had mainly to do with the fact that my parents were friends of her daughter, and I suspect she felt safe with me, thought I was of her class or some such. "You're so lucky to be working," she said to me at that meeting. "When I was your age, I never did anything but go to lunch." Mrs. Schiff's custom during these lunch meetings—perhaps as a consequence of spending so much of her youth in expensive restaurants at midday—was to serve a sandwich from the fly-strewn luncheonette on the ground floor of the *Post* building. A roast beef sandwich. Everyone who had lunch with her got a roast beef sandwich. Lyndon Johnson, Bobby Kennedy and me, to name a few. She thought it was very amusing of her, and I suppose it was. She would sit on one of her couches, looking wonderful-for-her-age—she is seventy-two now, and she still looks wonderful-for-her-age—and talk to whoever was on the other couch. There was, as far as I could tell, almost no way to have an actual conversation with her. She dominated, tantalized, sprinkled in little tidbits, skipped on to another topic. Once, I remember, she told me apropos of nothing that President Johnson had been up to see her the week before.

"Do you know what he told me?" she said.

"No," I said.

"He told me that Lady Bird fell down on the floor in a dead faint the other day, with her eyes bulging out of her head."

"Yes?" I said, thinking the story must go on to make a point, to relate to whatever we'd just been talking about. But that was it.

In the course of that first meeting, I asked Mrs. Schiff a question, and her answer to it probably sums her up better than anything else she ever said to me. The newspaper strike was still on—she had walked out of the Publishers' Association a few weeks before and had resumed publication—and I was immensely curious about what went on during labor negotiations. I didn't know if the antagonists were rude or polite to one another. I didn't know if they said things like "I'll give you Mesopotamia if you'll give me Abyssinia." I asked her what it had been like. She thought for a moment and then answered. "Twenty-eight men," she said. "All on my side." She paused. "Well," she said, "I just ran out of things to wear."

That was Mrs. Schiff on the 114-day newspaper strike. She took everything personally, and at the most skittishly feminine personal level. There was always debate over what made her change her endorsement from Averell Harriman to Nelson Rockefeller in the 1958 gubernatorial election, but the only explanation I ever heard that made any sense was that a few days before the election, she went to a Harriman dinner and was left off the dais. She was obsessed with personal details, particu-

larly with the medical histories of famous persons and
the family lives of Jews who intermarried. I once spent
two days on the telephone trying to check out a story she
heard about Madame Nhu and a nervous breakdown ten
years before, and I was constantly being ordered to call
back people I had written profiles on in order to insert
information about whether they were raising their children as Jews or Episcopalians or whatever.

Every little whim she had was catered to. Her yellow
onionskin memos would come down from the fifteenth
floor, and her editors, who operated under the delusion
that their balls were in escrow, would dispatch reporters.
In 1965, during the New York water shortage, she sent
the one about Otto and the sauna. "Otto Preminger has
added two floors to his house under my bedroom window," she wrote. "One, I understand, is for a movie projec-
tion room and the other, a sauna bath. Frequently, I hear
water running for hours on end, from the direction of
the Preminger house. It would be interesting to find out
if a substantial amount of water is or is not required by
such luxuries. Please investigate." The memo was given
to me, and I spent the next day writing and then rewriting a memo to Mrs. Schiff explaining that saunas did
not use running water. This did not satisfy her. So Joe
Kahn, the *Post*'s only investigative reporter, was sent up
to Lexington Avenue and Sixty-second Street to find the
source of the sound of running water. He found nothing.

Ultimately, I discovered what union negotiations were
like. I became a member of the grievance committee and
the contract committee, and the head of the plant and
safety committee. About the plant and safety committee—I was also the only member of it, and I think it is

accurate to say that everyone at the *Post* thought I was crazy even to care. It wasn't precisely a matter of caring, though. I was physically revolted by the conditions at the newspaper, none of which had changed at all since I began there. The entrance to the lobby was still black, Philthy and the dust were still on the door, and there was a slowly accumulating layer of soot all over the city room. Then there were the bathrooms. They were cleaned only once a day and had overflowing wastebaskets and toilets. The men's room in the entrance hall still had no door, and there was something wrong with the urinals. In the summertime, it was especially unpleasant to walk past it.

I first began to bring up my complaints about plant conditions to management in the grievance committee. Mrs. Schiff was not present. I asked that the hallway be painted. I asked for a snap lock on the men's room door. I asked for more chairs and phones in the city room. I asked if it were possible to hire a few more maintenance people—there was one poor man whose job consisted of cleaning all the bathrooms and of sweeping out the city room each day. Nothing happened. About a year after I began to complain, I was summoned to lunch again by Mrs. Schiff because of a memorandum I had written about Betty Friedan. I asked her about the possibility of cleaning the city room and repainting the entrance, and she looked at me as if the idea had never occurred to her. (The next week, the hallway was in fact painted and the city room cleaned for the first time in four years.) Then I mentioned the bathrooms, which she referred to for the rest of the conversation as the commodes. She listened to me—as just about everyone did—as if I were addled, and then said that she didn't really see the point of keeping the commodes clean because her employees were the kind of people who were incapable of not dirtying them up. I tried to explain to her that if the plant were clean, her employees would not be careless about dirtying it. I suggested that she had exactly the same sort of people working for her as there were at the *Daily News*, and the bathrooms at the *Daily News* looked fine. I don't think she understood a word I said.

One more thing about that lunch. We were talking about Betty Friedan. I had written a memo about an article she had written for the magazine section of the Sunday *Herald Tribune*; I thought we could develop a series about women in New York from it. The memo had been sent up to Mrs. Schiff, who wanted to talk about it. It turned out that she was upset with Betty Friedan and seemed to think that *The Feminine Mystique* had caused her daughter, a Beverly Hills housewife, to leave her household and spend a lot of money becoming a California politician. Mrs. Schiff thought I wanted to write a put-down of Mrs. Friedan—which was fine with her. I explained that that wasn't what I had in mind at all; I agreed with Betty Friedan, I said. "For example," I said, reaching for something I hoped Mrs. Schiff would understand, "Betty Friedan writes that housewives with nothing else to do often put a great deal of nagging pressure on their husbands to earn more money so they can buy bigger cars and houses."

Mrs. Schiff thought it over. "Yes," she said. "I've often thought that was why the men around here ask for raises as much as they do."

Top pay for reporters at that time was around ten thousand dollars a year. Mrs. Schiff had no idea that it took more than that to raise a family. She had no idea how the people who worked for her lived. She did not know that one hundred dollars was not a generous Christmas bonus. She did not even have a kind of noblesse oblige. She just sat up there serving roast beef sandwiches and being silly.

Jack Newfield, another *New York Post* alumnus, wrote an article about the paper in 1969 for *Harper's*, and in it he quoted Blair Clark, who was then assistant publisher of the *Post* for a brief interlude. "Dolly's problem," said Clark, "is that her formative experience was the brutal competitive situation the *Post* used to be in. She doesn't know how to make it a class newspaper." In the lean years, she survived by cutting overhead, keeping the staff small, cutting down on out-of-town assignments, paying her employees as little as possible. And all this still goes on, not just because she still thinks she is in a competitive situation but also because she survived, and she did it her way. She did it by being stingy, and she did it by being frothy and giddy; she was vindicated and she sees no reason to do things differently.

The last time I saw her, she mentioned that she had heard the things I said about her on the radio. "Nora," she said to me, "you know perfectly well you learned a great deal at the *Post*." But of course I did. I even loved working there. But that's not the point. The point is the product.

Nora Ephron's Beef Borscht

Put 3 pounds of beef chuck cut for stew and a couple of soupbones into a large pot. Add 2 onions, quartered, and 6 cups beef broth and bring to a boil, simmering 15 minutes and skimming off the scum. Add 2 cups tomato juice, the juice from a 1-pound can of julienne beets, salt, pepper, the juice of 1 lemon, 1 tablespoon cider vinegar, 2 tablespoons brown sugar, and bring to a boil. Then simmer slowly for 2½ hours until the beef is tender. Add the beets left over from the beet juice, and another can of beets and juice. Serve with huge amounts of sour cream, chopped dill, boiled potatoes and pumpernickel bread. Serves six.

April, 1975

People *Magazine*

The people over at *People* get all riled up if anyone suggests that *People* is a direct descendant of anything at all. You do not even have to suggest that it is; the first words anyone over there says, *insists*, really, is that *People* is *not* a spin-off of the *Time* "People" section (which they are right about), and that it is *not* a reincarnation of *Life* (which they are, at least in part, wrong about). *People*, they tell you, is an original thing. Distinctive. Different. Unto itself. They make it sound a lot like a cigarette.

People was introduced by Time Inc. a year ago, and at last reports it was selling 1,250,000 copies a week, all of them on newsstands. It is the first national weekly that has been launched since *Sports Illustrated* in 1954, and it will probably lose some three million dollars in its first year, a sum that fazes no one at Time Inc., since it is right on target. *Sports Illustrated* lost twenty-six million in the ten years before it turned the corner, and *People* is expected to lose considerably less and turn the corner considerably quicker. There is probably something to be said for all this—something about how healthy it is for the magazine business that a thing like this is happening, a new magazine with good prospects and no nudity that interests over a million readers a week—but I'm not sure that I am the person who is going to say it. *People* makes me grouchy, and I have been trying for months to figure out why. I do read it. I read it in the exact way its editors intend me to—straight through without stopping. I buy it in airline terminals, and I find that if I start reading it at the moment I am seated on the Eastern shuttle, it lasts until shortly before takeoff. This means that its time span is approximately five minutes longer than the *New York Post* on a day with a good Rose Franzblau column, and five minutes less than *Rona Barrett's Gossip*, which in any case is not available at the Eastern shuttle terminal in La Guardia Airport.

My problem with the magazine is not that I think it is harmful or dangerous or anything of the sort. It's almost not worth getting upset about. It's a potato chip. A snack. Empty calories. Which would be fine, really— I like potato chips. But they make you feel lousy afterward too.

People is a product of something called the Magazine Development Group at Time Inc., which has been laboring for several years to come up with new magazines and has brought forth *Money* and two rejected dummy magazines, one on photography, the other on show business. The approach this group takes is a unique one in today's magazine business: Most magazines tend to be about a sensibility rather than a subject, and tend to be dominated not by a group but by one editor and his or her concept of what that sensibility is. In any event, the idea for *People*—which was a simple, five-word idea: let's-call-a-magazine-*People*—started kicking around the halls of Time Inc. a couple of years ago. Some people, mainly Clare Boothe Luce, think it originated with Clare Boothe Luce; others seem to lean toward a great-idea-whose-time-has-come theory, not unlike the Big Bang, and they say that if anyone thought of it at all (which they are not sure of), it was Andrew Heiskell, Time Inc.'s chairman of the board. But the credit probably belongs, in some transcendental way, to Kierkegaard, who in 1846 said that in time, all anyone would be interested in was gossip.

From the beginning, *People* was conceived as an inexpensive magazine—cheap to produce and cheap to buy. There would be a small staff. Low overhead. Stringers. No color photographs except for the cover. It was intended to be sold only on newsstands—thus eliminating the escalating cost of mailing the magazine to subscribers and mailing the subscribers reminders to renew their subscriptions. It was clear that the magazine would have to have a very strong appeal for women; an increasing proportion of newsstands in this country are in supermarkets. Its direct competitor for rack space at the check-out counter was the *National Enquirer.* A pilot issue of the magazine, with Richard Burton and Elizabeth Taylor on the cover, was produced in August, 1973, and test-marketed in seven cities, and it is the pride of the Time Inc. marketing department that this was done in the exact way Procter & Gamble introduces a new toilet paper. When Malcolm B. Ochs, marketing director of the Magazine Development Group at Time Inc., speaks about *People*, he talks about selling "packaged goods" and "one million units a week" and "perishable products." This sort of talk is not really surprising—I have spent enough time around magazine salesmen to know

they would all be more comfortable selling tomatoes—
but it is nonetheless a depressing development.

The second major decision that was arrived at early
on was to keep the stories short. "We always want to
leave people wishing for more," says Richard B. Stolley,
People's managing editor. This is a perfectly valid editorial slogan, but what Stolley does not seem willing to
admit is the reason for it, which is that *People* is essentially a magazine for people who don't like to read. The
people at *People* seem to believe that people who read
People have the shortest attention spans in the world.
Time and *Life* started out this way too, but both of them
managed to rise above their original intentions.

The incarnation of *Life* that *People* most resembles
is not the early era, where photographs dominated, nor
even the middle-to-late period, when the photography
and journalism struck a nice balance, but the last des-
perate days, when Ralph Graves was trying to save
the magazine from what turned out to be its inevitable death. This is not the time to go into Graves's most
serious and abhorrent editorial decision, which was to
eliminate the *Life* Great Dinners series; what I want
to talk about instead is his decision to shorten the articles. There are people over at the Time-Life Building,
defenders of Graves, who insist he did this for reasons of
economy—there was no room for long pieces in a magazine that was losing advertising and therefore editorial
pages—but Graves himself refuses to be so defended. He
claims he shortened the articles because he believes in
short articles. And the result, in the case of *Life*, was a
magazine that did nothing terribly well.

People has this exact quality—and I'm not exactly
sure why. I have nothing against short articles, and no

desire to read more than 1500 words or so on most of the personalities *People* profiles. In fact, in the case of a number of those personalities—and here the name of Telly Savalas springs instantly to mind—a caption would suffice. I have no quarrel with the writing in the magazine, which is slick and perfectly competent. I wouldn't mind if *People* were just a picture magazine, if I could at least see the pictures; there is an indefinable something in its art direction that makes the magazine look remarkably like the centerfold of the *Daily News*. And I wouldn't even mind if it were a fan magazine for grownups—if it delivered the goods. But the real problem is that when I finish reading *People*, I always feel that I have just spent four days in Los Angeles. *Women's Wear Daily* at least makes me feel dirty; *People* makes me feel that I haven't read or learned or seen anything at all. I don't think this is what Richard Stolley means when he says he wants to leave his readers wanting more: I tend to be left feeling that I haven't gotten anything in the first place. And even this feeling is hard to pinpoint; I am looking at a recent issue of *People*, with Hugh Hefner on the cover, and I can't really say I didn't learn anything in it: On page 6 it says that Hefner told his unauthorized biographer that he once had a homosexual experience. I didn't actually know that before reading *People*, but somehow it doesn't surprise me.

Worst of all—yes, there is a worst of all—I end up feeling glutted with celebrity. I stopped reading movie magazines in the beauty parlor a couple of years ago because I could not accommodate any more information about something called the Lennon Sisters. I had got to the point where I thought I knew what celebrity was—celebrity was anyone I would stand up in a restaurant and stare at. I had whittled the list down to Marlon Brando, Mary Tyler Moore and Angelo "Gyp" DeCarlo, and I was fairly happy. Now I am confronted with *People*, and the plain fact is that a celebrity is anyone *People* writes about; I know the magazine is filling some nameless, bottomless pit of need for gossip and names, but I haven't got room in my life for so many lights.

People's only serious financial difficulty at this point is in attracting advertisers, and one of the reasons the people at *People* think they are having trouble doing so is that their advertisers don't know who the *People* reader is. Time Inc. has issued a demographic survey which shows that *People*'s readers are upscale, whatever that means, and that 48 percent of them have been to college. I never believe these surveys—*Playboy* and *Penthouse* have them, and theirs show that their readers are mainly interested in the fine fiction; in any case, I suspect that *People*'s real problem with advertisers is not that they don't know who's reading the magazine, but that they know exactly who's reading it. In one recent issue there are three liquor ads—for Seagram's Seven Crown, Jim Beam and a bottled cocktail called the Brass Monkey, all of them brands bought predominantly by the blue-collar middle class. It's logical that these brands would buy space in *People*—liquor companies can't advertise on television. But any product that could would probably do better to reach nonreaders through the mass-market women's magazines, which at least sit around all month, or on television itself.

"The human element really is being neglected in national reporting," says Richard Stolley. "The better newspapers and magazines deal more and more with events and issues and debates. The human beings caught up in them simply get squelched. If we can bring a human being out of a massive event, then we've done what I want to do." I don't really object to this philosophy—I'm not sure that I agree with it, but I don't object to it. But it seems a shame that so much of the reporting of the so-called human element in *People* is aimed at the lowest common denominator of the also-so-called human element, that all this coverage of humanity has to be at the expense of the issues and events and ideas involved. It seems even sadder that there seems to be no stopping it. *People* is the future, and it works, and that makes me grouchiest of all.

March, 1975

The Palm Beach
Social Pictorial

I am sitting here thinking a mundane thought, which is that one picture is worth a thousand words. The reason I am sitting here thinking this is that I am looking at one picture, a picture of someone named Mignon Roscher Gardner on the cover of the *Palm Beach Social Pictorial*, and I cannot think how to describe it to you, how to convey the feeling I get from looking at this picture and in fact every other full-color picture that has ever appeared on the cover of this publication.

The *Palm Beach Social Pictorial* appears weekly throughout the winter season in Palm Beach and I get it in the mail because a friend of mine named Liz Smith writes a column in it and has it sent to me. There are several dozen of us on Liz Smith's list, and I think it is safe to say that we all believe that the *Palm Beach Social Pictorial* is the most wonderful publication in America. Beyond that, each of us is very nearly obsessed with the people in it. My particular obsession is Mignon Roscher Gardner, but from time to time I am unfaithful to her, and I get involved instead with the life of Anky

Von Boythan Revson Johnson, who seems to live in a turban, or Mrs. Woolworth Donahue, who apparently never goes anywhere without her two Great Danes nuzzling her lap. One friend of mine is so taken with Helene (Mrs. Roy) Tuchbreiter and her goo-goo-googly eyes that he once made an entire collage of pictures of her face.

Mignon Roscher Gardner, who happens to be a painter of indeterminate age and platinum-blond hair, has appeared on the cover of the *Pictorial* twice in the last year, both times decked in ostrich feathers. Anyone who appears on the cover of the *Pictorial* pays a nominal sum to do so; Mrs. Gardner's appearances usually coincide with an opening of her paintings in Palm Beach, although the last one merely coincided with the completion of her portrait of Dr. Josephine E. Raeppel, librarian emeritus of Albright College in Reading, Pennsylvania. Most of the painters whose work appears on the cover of the *Pictorial* are referred to as "famed, international" painters, but Mrs. Gardner is a local, and the furthest the *Pictorial* will go in the famed-international department is to call her prominent. "Prominent artist-aviatrix," for example—that's what they called her last February, when she appeared on the cover in her hair and turquoise ostrich feathers along with a painting from a new series she called "The Cosmobreds." The painting was of a naked young man on a flying black horse, and according to the *Pictorial*, it was a departure from her usual work in animals and sailboats and portraits because "Mignon wanted to combine her love for horses and for flying." In back of the painting of the Cosmobred and Mrs. Gardner herself are some curtains, and if you ask me, they're the highlight of the photograph. They are plain white curtains, but the valances are covered with chintz daisies, and the curtains are trimmed, but heavily trimmed, with yellow and green pompons, the kind drum majorettes trim their skirts and boots with.

Inside the *Palm Beach Social Pictorial* are advertisements ("Dress up your diamond bracelet"), columns and pictures. The pictures show the people of Palm Beach eating lunch, wearing diamonds in the daytime, eating dinner, attending charity functions, and wearing party clothes. Most of the people are old, except that some of the women have young husbands. It is apparently all right to have a young husband if you are an old woman in Palm Beach, but not vice versa; in fact, the vice versa is one of the few things the columnists in the *Social Pictorial* get really upset about. Here, for instance, is columnist Doris Lilly writing about the guests at a recent party she attended: "Bill Carter (now U.N. ambassador to U.N.I.C.E.F.) proved he really does love children by bringing his latest airline hostess." And here from another columnist, Maria Durell Stone, is another guest list: "Then there were the Enrique Rousseaus, she's Lilly Pulitzer, and even Lilly's ex, Peter, was there with, well, as someone said, 'I don't think it's his daughter but she just might be.'" Every so often, the *Pictorial* prints pictures of people they describe as members of Palm Beach's Younger Set; they all look to be in their mid-forties.

There are two types of columnists who write for the *Pictorial*—locals, and correspondents from elsewhere. There are two advantages to being a correspondent from elsewhere: you don't have to spend the winter in Palm Beach, and you get a lofty title on the masthead. Wally Cedar, who writes from Beverly Hills and Acapulco, is the *Pictorial*'s International Editor, and Liz Smith, who writes from New York, is the National Editor. With one exception—and I'll get to her in a minute: she's Maria Durell Stone—the local columnists in the *Pictorial* have tended to be relentlessly cheerful women whose only quibbles about life in Palm Beach have to do with things like the inefficiency of the streetlights on Worth Avenue. Cicely Dawson, who owns the *Pictorial* along with her husband Ed, whom she always refers to as "our better half," writes a goings-on-about-town column in which she manages to summon unending enthusiasm and exclamation points for boutiques, galleries, parties, and new savings banks in town. "Congratulations to Nan and James Egan of the James Beauty Salon on their recent twenty-fifth anniversary," Dawson once wrote. "No client would guess from the cheerful attitude of this wonderful couple what hardship they have had these past few months. After an illness-free life, James was diagnosed as having chronic kidney failure last December. Oh that Palm Beach County had an Artificial Kidney Center! . . . because that's what James needs."

In all fairness, Mrs. Dawson is almost a grouch in comparison to Leone "Call Me the Pollyanna of Palm Beach" King, who until her retirement in 1973 could not find enough good things to say about the place. Where else, Mrs. King once asked in a long series of rhetorical questions, "could you find families offering living quarters to people of low incomes, without at least making some sort of charge? . . . Where could you find friends with splendid flower gardens leaving a message with their gardeners to send certain people bouquets during the winter while they are off on a trip around the world? Where could you find big bags of fruit from a Palm Beach orange grove on your doorstep at regular intervals? . . . Don't let fabulously rich people throw you. They are just the same as anyone else except they can do what they jolly well please when they jolly well please. They have likes and dislikes, aches and pains, problems. They are just people."

Maria Durell Stone has left the *Palm Beach Social Pictorial*—she has been stolen away by the West Palm Beach daily paper—but her two years on the weekly coincided, and not coincidentally either, with what I think of as the *Pictorial*'s Golden Era, so I cannot leave her out of this. Mrs. Stone is a Latin-looking lady with a tremendous amount of jet-black hair who is divorced from architect Edward Durell Stone and has taken not one but two of his names along with her. She began writing for the *Pictorial* three years ago, and no one writing in any of the Palm Beach publications comes near her gift for telling it like it is. "I've done nothing but praise the Poinciana Club since it opened," she wrote last year, "but being a critic means that every now and then one must speak the truth and I am sorry to say it, but Bavarian Night there was a disaster."

Mrs. Stone's main problem in life—and the theme of her column too—had to do with being a single woman in a place where there are few eligible men. There are a lot of us with this problem, God knows, but she managed to be more in touch with it than anyone I know. Not a column passed without a pointed remark to remind the reader that this Mrs. Stone was looking for a Roman spring. "I met Vassili Lambrinos this week and he's divine," she wrote one week. "Dorothy Dodson, petite, refreshing and vivacious, gave a luncheon for him and I got to know him better—unfortunately not as much as I would like to, but what's a poor bachelor girl to do?" Another week, Mrs. Stone went to a charity auction: "There were numerous items to bid on and I did covet that stateroom for two on the S.S. *France*, but as luck would have it, someone else got it. I wouldn't have known who to take with me anyway, so it's probably just as well." Age was no barrier: "One of the best things of the evening," she wrote of the Boys' Club Dinner, "was the Boys' Club Chorus, which consisted of adorable little boys of unfortunate circumstances who sang many lively numbers at the top of their divine adolescent voices. It was heartwarming to hear." Apparently, Mrs. Stone's subtlety was not lost on her readers: "Stanton Griffis, that amazing ex-ambassador who sat next to me at the Salvation Army luncheon the other day, told me that if I really wanted to get the right man, I should put an ad in my column saying, 'Wanted: Intelligent, handsome, lean, tall, romantic type with kindness and money.' Well, now that I've said it, let's see if my octogenarian friend is right."

From time to time, something sneaks into the *Pictorial* that has to do with the outside world, and when it does, it is usually in Liz Smith's column. Miss Smith writes for the publication as if she were addressing a group of—well, a group of people who winter in Palm Beach. She interrupts her column of easygoing gossip and quotes to bring her readers little chautauquas; last year's were about Richard Nixon ("Hope all you people who couldn't stomach poor old Hubert are happy these days," one of them concluded) and this year's are about oil and the Middle East. ("So here are the most fascinating and frightening statistics I've read recently, from *The New Republic*. You remember *The New Republic*— it's liberal, left, and riddled with integrity, but even so, don't ignore the statistics.")

The rich are different from you and me; we all know that even if some of the people in Palm Beach don't. But it is impossible to read the *Social Pictorial* without suspecting that the rich in Palm Beach are even more different. One of my friends tells me that Palm Beach used to be a rather nice place and that now it's become a parody of itself; I don't know if she's right, but if she is, the *Social Pictorial* reflects this perfectly. If there were more communities like it, I don't think I would find the *Palm Beach Social Pictorial* so amusing. But there aren't, so I do.

The *Palm Beach Social Pictorial*, P.O. Box 591, Palm Beach, Florida. By subscription $10 a year.

May, 1975

Brendan Gill and
The New Yorker

Brendan Gill's *Here at The New Yorker* was issued to coincide exactly with the fiftieth anniversary of *The New Yorker* magazine, and, as such, it became The Event of the anniversary, an occasion for critics to pat the magazine on the back and, in addition, to undo some of the devastation that was heaped on it and its editor, William Shawn, some ten years ago, when Tom Wolfe took them all on in the *Herald Tribune*'s *New York* magazine. *The New Yorker* has come through this round with garlands, and so has Gill's book. It is a charming book, the critics say.

The people who work at *The New Yorker* do not think Brendan Gill's book is charming, but they try to be nice about it. The ethic of Nice is, in its way, as much an editorial principle at *The New Yorker* as the ethic of Mean is at *New York* magazine, and you can see, when you bring up the subject of Gill's book, that the people who work with Gill really want to be polite about it. What they generally say is that they would not object so much if only Gill had presented it simply as a memoir, or if he had made it clear that he knew nothing whatever about *The New Yorker* after the death of Harold Ross, or if he had managed not to publish it at a time calculated to cash in on the anniversary. Any of these things would help, they say. Well, I don't know that any of this would help. *Here at The New Yorker* seems to me one of the most offensive books I have read in a long time.

Brendan Gill is now sixty and went to work at the magazine in 1938, and someone I know there suggested to me that he arrived too late to understand its early years, and too soon to understand the late ones. That is unfair: the explanation for Gill's insensitivity probably lies more in his character than in bad timing. Gill's character is the shall-I-compare-me-to-a-summer's-day variety: he is a joyous, happy man, he tells us, who has never suffered a day's pain in his life. Compared to other *New Yorker* writers, whom he describes as unsociable moles, he is uncommonly gregarious and fun-loving. He attends five or six parties a week. "I am acquainted with far more people out in the world than anyone else on *The New Yorker*," he writes. Life has been a lark. He was born into comparative wealth, went to Yale, made Skull and Bones (an achievement he mentions a half-dozen times), had a rich father to aid him in the purchases of his town houses and mansions and country homes, several of which are actually pictured in his book. The smug self-congratulation of all this extends to his professional achievements. "In sheer quantity of output—most trivial of measurements!—I am by now something of a nonpareil," he writes.

The book Gill has written is not really a book; it's a series of anecdotes star-dashed together at four hundred pages length, a sketchy memoir masquerading as history. The omissions in it are gigantic: there are bare mentions, captions really, of Lillian Ross, J. D. Salinger and Robert Benchley; on the other hand, there are oddly lengthy descriptions of pseudonymous minor writers and clerks who dressed badly, had oily hair, hung their wash in the men's room, committed suicide, or turned out to be homosexuals. The so-called younger writers at *The New Yorker* are virtually omitted. "I don't know the younger writers," Gill said recently, by way of explanation.

The people Gill does write about are a good deal less fortunate than the ones he omits. Part of the problem here is the form he has chosen; the anecdote is a particularly dehumanizing sort of descriptive narrative. But the main problem, once again, is Brendan Gill. Most of the people he writes about are, for the most part, people he clearly thinks of as friends. God help them. The stories he tells, stories he seems to mean to be charming and affectionate, are condescending, snobbish and mean. Here, to take one interesting and subtle example, is Gill on cartoonist Alan Dunn and his wife Mary Petty: "[They] were cherished by their friends like prizes that had been won in some incomparable secret lottery; none of these friends wanted to risk making the Dunns known to the world at large, and the Dunns were content within their small circle and with the superb consolation of their work." Wolcott Gibbs, the subject of a long section in the book, was a man who we discover married beneath himself not once but twice, was rude, would like to have been tapped for Skull and Bones, wore a brown fedora with a tuxedo, smoked and drank too much, and "had as many affairs as the next man." And what of Gibbs's work? Gill tells us Gibbs was bril-

liant at parody, "a form favored by writers of the second
or third rank," and then goes on to devote several pages
to an analysis of Gibbs's only play, *A Season in the Sun*,
which contained a character based on Harold Ross. The
play, Gill tells us, was a waste of Gibbs's talents and was
unfairly praised by the critics, who were fond of Gibbs.
Stanley Edgar Hyman, another writer who had the bad
luck to be Gill's friend, surfaces in his book to chase girls,
wear multicolored socks with sandals, and drink himself
into a stupor. He and his wife, writer Shirley Jackson,
attend an anniversary party at the Gills' country home.
"On a stretch of lawn between our house and the surrounding woods," Gill writes, "we had pitched an enormous white marquee; metal-lined boxes, ordinarily used
to hold potted flowers, were filled with ice and scores
of bottles of Piper-Heidsieck, and a very satisfactory
occasion it turned out to be. . . . Shirley was wearing a
shapeless, reddish coverall, which served to exaggerate
her size and not, as she must have hoped, to diminish it,
and with her sharp writer's eye she cannot have failed
to note that to many of the other guests she seemed an
apparition, impossible to account for in their world of
strict bodily discipline."

I feel squeamish even quoting all this; it seems to me
I am compounding Gill's cruelties by repeating them. I
want to make one more point, though, before moving on to
Shawn and Ross, and that is about Gill's prurience. Brendan Gill is uncommonly prurient, and his book is full of
leering references to women, sex and adultery. Gill notes
several times that he does not understand why his friends
persist in thinking of him as a Catholic when he is in fact
a *lapsed* Catholic; my guess is that they think of him this
way because he is as prurient in person as he is in print.

Brendan Gill's book is dedicated to William Shawn, who has been *The New Yorker*'s editor since 1952, and he provides a number of anecdotes about Shawn that are meant to be jolly. They mainly concern Shawn's fear of automatic elevators and his extreme discomfort about sexual references. I cannot imagine that a man who is constitutionally incapable of taking an automatic elevator finds anything but pain in the situation; that does not seem to have occurred to Gill. He has even less comprehension of what Shawn has done for the magazine: there is only one reference in his book to *The New Yorker*'s coverage of Vietnam and Watergate.

It is generally accepted over at *The New Yorker* that Gill's greatest sin is in not understanding Shawn. I'm not even sure he understands Shawn's predecessor, Harold Ross. He paints him as a buffoon, a gat-toothed, ill-dressed social incompetent who made typographical errors and disdained Freud. All of this is doubtless true; but it is, like everything in Gill's book, only a small part of the picture. Shawn provided Gill with a seven-page essay on Ross that closes *Here at The New Yorker*. The essay tends to give Shawn's imprimatur to the book—it is said he regrets having done it. At the same time, though—and I have no idea whether it was intentional—Shawn's essay is a gentle but thorough rebuke to Gill: it has all the complexity and depth that Gill's book lacks. As Shawn writes of Ross: "He lent himself to anecdote. Because of this, and because his personal qualities were large in scale and included a formidable charm and magnetism, the serious and inspired work that he did as an editor tended at times to be lost sight of." The articles Ross published by Liebling, Mitchell, Bainbridge, McKelway, Hamburger . . . the list is endless, really, but the point is simply that *The New Yorker* has always published brilliant magazine writing; it has always been a serious publication—if not about its subjects, at least about its prose. Under Ross, the profiles had an edge and bite that have been sadly missing—and this is Shawn's weakness as an editor—in recent years. (In many ways, the war in Vietnam, and Shawn's decision to hammer at it, rescued the magazine from the blandness that still characterizes some of what it prints.)

Gill's *New Yorker*—under Shawn and Ross—is no more serious than Gill's view of life. It is a parody of *The New Yorker*, the Eustace Tilley stereotype, the frivolous, upper-class publication with a sensibility best described as Jaded Preppie, the old "Talk of the Town" column, we went to a party last night. Gill has written a history of the magazine to conform to his image of it. As he himself admits, albeit in another context: "I am always so ready to take a favorable view of my powers that even when I am caught out and made a fool of, I manage to twist this circumstance about until it becomes a proof of how exceptional I am. The ingenuities we practice in order to appear admirable to ourselves would suffice to invent the telephone twice over on a rainy summer morning."

June, 1975

Bob Haldeman and CBS

The decision by CBS to pay H. R. Haldeman at least fifty thousand dollars to appear in the *60 Minutes* time slot this spring is one that no one at the network—no one with any sense, that is—defends any longer. Dick Salant, the head of CBS News, has gotten to the point where he admits flat out that it was a mistake. The news personnel were appalled at the decision in the first place, and when the interview turned out as it did, they began walking around with a smug sense of vindication. The only person I spoke to at the network who was willing to defend the action was the man who negotiated it, Bill Leonard, the head of something called soft news; and even his defense lacks conviction. It was worth doing, Leonard says, because it raised the question of whether the networks should pay former public officials for interviews. It's a shame CBS could not have managed to raise this question without Haldeman's help; Gordon Liddy, to whom CBS paid fifteen thousand dollars earlier this year, ought to have been enough. At the same time, though, I think there is something to be said for the Haldeman transaction: it was worth every penny simply because of what it demonstrated about television.

Television news coverage has gotten away with a great deal in recent years—partly because of its coverage of the Vietnam war. Television showed us the war. It showed us the war in a way that was—if you chose to watch television, at least—unavoidable. You could not turn the page. You could not even switch channels: all you got was another network showing you the war. All of us who had worked side by side over the years with television reporters, who had watched in dismay as the cameras moved in and the television reporter cornered the politician ("How do you feel about the vote, Senator?") or cornered the man on the stretcher being carried out of the burning building ("How do you feel about the fact that your legs were just blown off, sir?"), calmed down a bit during the war years. Television was showing us the war. But giving television points for that was a little like giving a hooker points for turning a trick; that, after all, is what television does: it shows things. And beyond that, television for the most part was showing us the war in much the same way it was showing us everything else. Simply, and in two-minute snippets. Bleeding babies and bleeding soldiers. Explosions. Helicopter insertions. GI's on stretchers being asked how they felt about the fact that their legs had just been blown off. We got very little from the Vietnamese: most Vietnamese do not speak English. We got very little about what the war was doing to Vietnam, about the corruption of the South Vietnamese government, its political prisoners, about the morale of ARVN, about the depth of racism among United States forces. There were exceptions to this, of course—documentaries, mostly, and here I think immediately of Robert Northshield's on mixed-race children in South Vietnam. But even documentaries were governed by the overriding fact of television: it is a performance medium. It must attract an audience. And the way to attract that audience, the people in television assumed, was to show the war in the most simple, sentimental way. Our boys. Dying children. And most recently, orphans. The condescension implicit in all this is obvious; what is not so obvious, I think, is the utter lack of thought among television people about how television *ought* to cover news.

I don't claim to know exactly how television ought to have handled H. R. Haldeman; what is clear, though, is that no one at the network ever considered doing anything but a traditional face-to-face interview. Haldeman approached Bill Leonard back in October, before the cover-up trial began. Through his lawyer, he submitted a handwritten outline for a book called *Inside the Nixon White House*, which an agent, Scott Meredith, had refused to handle. It is an astonishing document, amateurish and virtually puerile. "Richard Nixon led me," it begins, "into the four most satisfying, trying, productive, demanding, enjoyable, difficult, rewarding, challenging, stimulating—and truly whole—years of my life. . . . Nothing in the course of future events can change the facts or the goals, feelings and actions of those of us who proudly served a great man in a great time." The chapter outlines begin with short paragraphs of introductory remarks, followed by sections titled "Headlines," "Characters" and "Inside Stories." The introductory remarks to a chapter called "The Inner Circle" go like this: "Insightful anecdotes about the four key men—Kissinger, Connally, Mitchell and Ehrlichman—and other important men (Agnew, Rogers, Moynihan, Shultz and Burns) and groups of men and women (White House assistants, young staffers, Cabinet, Congress, personal friends and family) around the President, and their relations with Richard Nixon." The character list includes just about everyone who worked for Nixon, name after name, and the headlines, all properly capitalized, are: "Secret Nixon Plan To Make Connally VP"; "Martha Really Was the Reason Mitchell Quit"; "Kissinger's Salzburg Tantrum Was Just Latest in a Series."

Leonard and another CBS executive, Gordon Manning, went to Washington to discuss the proposal over dinner with Haldeman. "My conclusion," said Leonard, "was that there was a possibility it might be an interview of considerable lasting public value. I never did think he would say something on the air in terms of a holy confessional. He made that clear. But he ran the White House, and I thought if you could find out how he ran it . . ." Leonard paused. "Maybe I was a little naïve about that." The three men discussed where the interview was to be done, and who was to do it. (Leonard claims he thought of Mike Wallace from the first, which was logical: Wallace is a first-rate television interviewer, and he has always had good connections with the Nixon White House, which considered offering him Ron Ziegler's job in 1968.) All that remained to be worked out was the money. Haldeman's lawyer suggested a figure of either $150,000 or $200,000—Leonard, possibly from spending too much time around Haldeman, has suffered a memory loss about the exact figure. CBS said that was far too high. But they never attempted to call Haldeman's bluff by offering to put him on the air for nothing; they were, after all, doing him a favor. Instead, they settled on a price that was an incredible tactical error: CBS would pay Haldeman $25,000 *for each hour* of interview that was used. This was done, Salant says, to provide an incentive for Haldeman to be forthcoming, to be worth the money he was being paid. It did nothing of the kind. Haldeman managed to screw a television network in a way that eluded him in all his years of White House plotting against the media. (Haldeman also sold CBS twenty-five hours of home movies, of which the network used four minutes. Industry insiders suggest that Haldeman may have been paid additionally for the film.)

CBS never considered following Haldeman around for a couple of weeks with hand-held cameras in the hope that he might eventually reveal himself. They did not consider using Dan Rather, or any of the print journalists who knew enough about Watergate to interview Haldeman properly. They did not cut into the show some of the other television footage of Haldeman that was available, obtained at no cost, like the moment when he bared his teeth at the Ervin subcommittee; they did not contrast Haldeman's fuzzy, sugar-coated recollections with his remarks on the White House tapes. Instead, they sent in Wallace. Wallace does his homework. Wallace studies. Wallace was stuffed, like a Strasbourg goose, with papers and facts and questions and quotes. He spent fifty-five hours in preliminary talks with Haldeman—a period of time so long as to make me suspect he left the fight in the locker room—and when he sat down to tape, for over six hours, he found out firsthand why H. R. Haldeman used to be called the Berlin Wall. Haldeman gave a brilliant performance: he played the part of a vibrant football player who had been taken out of the game by a fluke, a minor muscle spasm no one could cure. I said only a paragraph ago that Wallace is a first-rate television interviewer; that is what he is, and that is all he is. He too gave a performance. He gave us a bit of obsequiousness, and he gave us a lot of exasperated sighs. And two hours of sweet talk and exasperation did not make up for the fact that Wallace just did not know enough to follow through. Time after time, Haldeman made remarks that were not supported by the facts, and time after time, Wallace blew it.

When Haldeman insisted that many of the excesses of the campaign were the fault of the Committee to Re-Elect the President, not the White House, Wallace failed to point out that there was no real difference between the two, that Haldeman in fact controlled the CREEP secret fund. When Haldeman claimed that Woodward and Bernstein had admitted in their book they were wrong about him, Wallace did not correct him; what Woodward and Bernstein actually wrote was that they were wrong in saying that Hugh Sloan had named Haldeman before the grand jury as one of the men who controlled the fund. When Haldeman made what was the only potential news of the interview, by admitting that he occasionally chose not to carry out Nixon's orders, Wallace did not press him for an example not already publicly known; more important, he neglected to ask Haldeman how, in view of this, he could base his defense at the cover-up trial on the claim that he was just following orders. Haldeman's outline had made the CBS people believe that he would be anecdotal and gossipy about the so-called inner circle. But all Wallace got from him were the headlines of his book. Secret Nixon Plan To Make Connally VP. Martha Really Was the Reason Mitchell Quit. Kissinger's Salzburg Tantrum Was Just Latest in a Series. Wallace prodded Haldeman for embellishment, but to no avail.

Back in the days when it was still defending its

decision, CBS claimed that it was paying not for hard news but for memoirs. Solzhenitsyn, Eisenhower, Lyndon Johnson and Walter Lippmann were also paid under this guideline. The other networks were swift—and hypocritical—in denouncing CBS. NBC, which paid Marina Oswald, Sirhan Sirhan, the Fischer quints, and recently negotiated a roundabout deal with John Dean, said through News President Richard C. Wald that they would never have done it. ABC, having paid Lieutenant William Calley indirectly for an interview, said through its News President William Sheehan: "A news maker should not be paid for an interview." CBS continued to insist for a time that it paid only for memoirs; in fact, the network paid Dispatch News Service and Seymour Hersh ten thousand dollars for an interview with Private Paul Meadlo on the My Lai massacre.

A few days after the second Haldeman interview appeared on the air, New York's WNET did a *Behind the Lines* show on the whole business, and on it, CBS's Bill Leonard asked a question. "If we could forget just a moment whether he was paid or not," Leonard asked, "was it in the nature of a public service? Was it important or not important? Was it useful or not useful . . . ?" It is an interesting question—largely because it is totally invalid. There is no way to forget that Haldeman was paid. He was paid. The smell of money perfumed both hours. The shows were dominated by the fee, and Haldeman's responses were dictated by how far he thought he had to go to earn it. And all in all, the entire episode has made me change my point of view on checkbook journalism. I used to think it was a mistake to pay anyone for a story. I used to think it made it impossible for serious journalists to cover events. I used to think it would mean that news stories would begin to go to the highest bidder. Now I think the networks should pay everyone. Hard news sources, soft news sources, everyone. It will serve to remind us that, at this point at least, there is no reason to confuse television news with journalism.

July, 1975

The Making of Theodore H. White

He was alone, as always.

A man who finishes a book is always alone when he finishes it, and Theodore H. White was alone. It was a hot, muggy day in New York when he finished, or perhaps it was a cold, windy night; there is no way to be certain, although it is certain that Theodore H. White was certain of what the weather was like that day, or that night, because when Theodore H. White writes about things, he notices the weather, and he usually manages to get it into the first paragraph or first few pages of whatever he writes. "Hyannis Port sparkled in the sun that day, as did all New England" (*The Making of the President 1960*). "It was hot; the sun was blinding; there would be a moment of cool shade ahead under the overpass they were approaching" (*The Making of the President 1964*). "Thursday had been a cold day of drizzling rain in Manhattan, where Richard Nixon lived" (*The Making of the President 1968*). "I could see the fan of yellow water below shortly before the plane dipped into the overcast" (*The Making of the President 1972*). And now Theodore H. White looked at the opening line of his new book, *Breach of Faith*: "Wednesday dawned with an overcast in Washington—hot, sticky, threatening to rain—July 24th, 1974." It had worked before and it would work again.

White flicked a cigarette ash from his forty-sixth Marlboro of the day and took the last sheet of one hundred percent rag Strathmore parchment typing paper from his twenty-two-year-old IBM Executive typewriter. It was the 19,246,753rd piece of typing paper he had typed in his sixty years. He was tired. He was old and tired. He was also short. But mainly he was tired. He was tired of writing the same book over and over again. He was tired of being taken in, taken in by John F. Kennedy, Lyndon Johnson, Robert Kennedy, General Westmoreland, Richard Nixon, tired of being taken in by every major politician in the last sixteen years. He was tired of being hornswoggled by winners. He was tired of being made to look like an ass, tired of having to apologize in each successive book for the mistakes he had made in the one before. He was tired of being imitated by other journalists, and he was tired of rewriting their work, which had surpassed his own. He was tired of things going wrong, tired of being in the wrong place at the wrong time; the night of the Saturday Night Massacre, for example, he found himself not in the Oval Office but on vacation in the South of France, where he was reduced to hearing the news from his hotel maid. He was tired of describing the people he was writing about as tired.

We must understand how Theodore H. White got to be that way, how he got to be so old and so tired. We must understand how this man grew to have a respect and awe for the institutions of American government that was so overweening as to blind him to the weak-

nesses of the men who ran them. We must understand
how he came to believe that all men in power—even
base men—were essentially noble, and when they failed
to be noble, it had merely to do with flaws, flaws that
grew out of a massive confluence of forces, forces like
PR, the burgeoning bureaucracy, television, manipulation and California. We must understand his associates,
good men, tired men but good men, men he lunched with
every week, men who worked at newsmagazines which
had long since stopped printing run-on sentences with
subordinate clauses attached to the end. And to understand what has happened to Theodore H. White, which
is the story of this column, one would have to go back to
earlier years, to the place where it all started.

Time magazine.

That was where it all started. At *Time* magazine.
Not everything started at *Time* magazine—Theodore
H. White developed his infuriating style of repeating
phrases over and over again later in his life, after he
had left *Time* magazine—but that is where most of it
started. It was at *Time* magazine that White picked up
the two overriding devices of newsmagazine writing.
The first was a passion for tidbits, for small details, for
color. President Kennedy liked to eat tomato soup with
sour cream in it for lunch. Adlai Stevenson sunned himself in blue sneakers and blue shorts. Hubert Humphrey
ate cheese sandwiches whenever he was in the midst of
a crisis.

The second was omniscience, the omniscience that
results when a writer has had a week, or a month, or
a year to let events sift out, the kind of omniscience, in
short, that owes so much to hindsight.

Until 1959, when Theodore H. White began work

on the four-hundred-one-page, blue-bound *Making of the President 1960*, no reporter had written a book on a political campaign using these two devices. White did, and his book changed the way political campaigns were covered. He wrote the 1960 campaign as a national pageant, a novelistic struggle for power between two men. He wrote about what they wore and what they ate and what they said behind the scenes. He went to meetings other reporters did not even ask to attend; the participants at the meetings paid scant attention to him. And then, of course, the book was published, became a best seller, and everything began to change.

Change.

Change begins slowly, as it always does, and when it began, White was slow to notice it. He covered the 1964 campaign as he had covered the one before; he did not see that all the detail and color and tidbits and dialogue made no difference in that election; the political process was not working in the neat way it had worked four years before, with hard-fought primaries and nationally televised debates and a cliff-hanger vote; the 1964 election was over before it even began. Then he came to 1968, and the change, mounting like an invisible landslide, intensified, owing to a massive confluence of factors. The first was the national press, which began to out-report him. The second was White himself. He no longer went to meetings where he was ignored; he was, after all, Theodore H. White, historian to American Presidential elections. Had he been a student of physics and the Heisenberg uncertainty principle, instead of a student of history and all the Cicero he could cram into his books, he might have understood what was happening. But he did not. The change, the invisible landslide of change, eluded him. He wrote a book about a new Nixon, an easier, more relaxed, more affable Nixon. He missed the point. He missed the point about Vietnam; he missed the point about the demonstrations. Larry O'Brien used to be important; now it was these kids; who the hell were these kids to come along and take politics away from Theodore H. White? He missed the point about the Nixon campaign too. And so, in 1969, came the first great humiliation. A young man named Joe McGinniss, a young man who had gone to low- and mid-level meetings of the Nixon campaign, where the participants had paid him scant attention, produced the campaign book of the year, *The Selling of the President*, and even knocked off Theodore H. White's title in the process. Then, before he knew it, it was 1972, another campaign, another election, and White went through it, like so many other reporters, ignoring Watergate; months later, as he was finishing the 1972 book, he was forced to deal with the escalating scandal; he stuck it in, a paragraph here, a paragraph there, a chapter to wrap it all up, all this sticking out like sore thumbs throughout the manuscript. That year, the best book on the campaign was written not by White but by Timothy Crouse, who had stayed at the fringes, reporting on the press. To make matters worse, Crouse's book, *The Boys on the Bus*, included a long, not entirely flattering section on Theodore H. White, a section in which White complained, almost bitterly, about the turn things had taken. He spoke of the night McGovern won the nomination in Miami:

"It's appalling what we've done to these guys," he told Crouse. "McGovern was like a fish in a goldfish bowl. There were three different network crews at different times. The still photographers kept coming in in groups of five. And there were at least six writers sitting in the corner—I don't even know their names. We're all sitting there watching him work on his acceptance speech, poor bastard. He tries to go into the bedroom with Fred Dutton to go over the list of Vice-Presidents, which would later turn out to be the fuck-up of the century, of course, and all of us are observing him, taking notes like mad, getting all the little details. Which I think I invented as a method of reporting and which I now sincerely regret. If you write about this, say that I sincerely regret it. Who gives a fuck if the guy had milk and Total for breakfast?"

White sat in the Harvard chair given to him by the Harvard Alumni Association and looked with irritation at his new manuscript, *Breach of Faith*. Here it was 1975 and he had a new book coming out. What in Christ was he doing with a book coming out in 1975? He wasn't supposed to have to write the next one until 1977. Theodore H. White shook his close-cropped, black-haired head. It was these damned politicians. He'd spent the best years of his life trying to train these assholes, and they couldn't even stay in office the full four years.

White stared at the title. Breach of faith. The new book's thesis was that Richard Nixon had breached the faith of the American people in the Presidency; that was what had caused him to be driven from office. But deep down, Theodore H. White knew that the faith Nixon had breached had been his, Theodore H. White's. White was the only American left who still believed in the institution of the Presidency. Theodore H. White was depressed. Any day now, he might have to start work on the next book, on *The Making of the President 1976*, and where would he ever find a candidate who measured up to his own feelings about the United States and its institutions? The questions lay in his brain cells, growing like an invisible landslide, and suddenly Theodore H. White had the answer. He would have to run for President. That was the only way. That was the only way to be sure that the political processes would function the way he believed they ought to. That was the only way he could get all those behind-the-scenes meetings to function properly. That was the only way he could get all those other reporters out of his story. White realized that something very important was happening. And so he did what he always does when he realizes something very important is happening: he called the weather bureau.

It was forty-nine degrees and raining in Central Park.

August, 1975

Richard Collin and the Spaghetti Recipe

It is generally agreed among the people who have any perspective on it at all—and there are only a handful who do—that the entire civic scandal of Richard Collin and the mysterious spaghetti sauce recipe could only have happened in New Orleans—which was, in fact, where it did happen—and for fairly obvious reasons. For one thing, New Orleans is one of the two most ingrown, self-obsessed little cities in the United States. (The other is San Francisco.) For another, people in New Orleans really care about food, care about it passionately, can spend hours arguing over whether Antoine's is better than Galatoire's or the other way around. What sets the people of New Orleans apart from the people of San Francisco in this respect is that in New Orleans, there is basically nothing to do but eat and then argue about it.

All of which should have made Richard Collin a welcome addition to the New Orleans food scene. Richard Collin is a restaurant critic. He is New Orleans's first and only serious restaurant critic. A professor of American history at the University of New Orleans, Collin, forty-three, began his career in food in 1970 as the author of *The New Orleans Underground Gourmet* (Simon and Schuster). A few months after its publication he was hired by the *New Orleans States-Item* to write a weekly restaurant column. In it, Collin employs an extremely elaborate system of stars and dots and parentheses and *X*'s which takes over five column-inches of space to explain each week. In addition, he uses an expression he coined to describe things he particularly loves; he calls them platonic dishes. "This is my own personal accolade," Collin once explained. "The term is derived from Plato's *Republic*. It simply means the best imaginable realization of a particular dish." Collin's style of criticism can best be described as hyperbolic; it can also be described as self-important and long-winded. But he works hard, and his guidebook is considered as reliable as any city restaurant guide in the country.

In New Orleans, however, the question of whether Collin is reliable is not the point. The point is that he is critical—and in public. Arguing privately about the merits of various restaurants is one thing, but criticizing them publicly runs completely counter to the local spirit of boosterism. To make matters worse, Collin is not even from New Orleans; he is from Philadelphia and he is seen as an outsider who has stumbled onto a gold mine at the expense of local merchants. So when the episode of the spaghetti sauce recipe and the two thousand dollars surfaced a few months ago, the city fathers fell upon it as an excuse to ask the *States-Item* to investigate Collin. But I'm getting ahead of the story.

The position of restaurant critic is a new slot at most newspapers; nonetheless, the job has a tradition and a set of ethics. The classic American restaurant critic is rarely photographed, makes reservations under a pseudonym, cannot accept free meals, and never reveals his identity to a proprietor. Some restaurant critics have gone to extraordinary lengths to preserve their anonymity; last year, for example, Jack Shelton of *San Francisco* magazine was subpoenaed to testify in a local trial, and he appeared wearing a mask.

Prior to the publication of his book, Richard Collin followed traditional practices; in any case, it would have done him no good to reveal himself, since his name meant nothing. But the success of the book, the newspaper column (which ran a sketch of Collin alongside his by-line) and subsequent public appearances made Collin's face and name well-known. By 1973, when the revised edition of *The Underground Gourmet* was published, Collin had moved into a slightly revisionist phase of behavior. He continued to pay for his meals, but he admitted that from time to time a restaurateur managed to force a free one on him. He continued to reserve under a pseudonym, but it became increasingly difficult to keep from being recognized. He began to metamorphose into a role he thought of as kindly godfather, but which might more correctly be defined as participatory journalist. He became a close friend of Warren Le Ruth, whose restaurant, Le Ruth's, received Collin's highest rating: four stars and ten platonic dishes. He gave advice to owners and to chefs. He seemed to regard himself as an impresario who was going to bring to New Orleans cuisine the acclaim it deserved. "I frequently introduce myself *after* the check has been paid," he wrote, "especially in smaller restaurants that are doing well and that deserve to be encouraged. I also notify restaurants in advance when a favorable review is to appear in the Saturday paper so that the restaurant does not run out of food by six or

seven in the evening, as has happened when the pend-
ing review was kept a secret. For this edition I have not
been quite as anonymous as I was for the first edition.
Many restaurateurs saw me on television or met me at
speaking engagements around town. However, known or
unknown, distant or friendly, I have continued to base
my evaluations solely on the genuine merits of the food
restaurants serve. I enjoy being a restaurant critic too
much to allow my integrity to be compromised."

The trouble began in April, 1973, with what
looked—to Richard Collin, at least—like a pure case
of civic duty. Turci's Original Italian Restaurant was
about to close. Turci's was a typical grubby neighborhood restaurant on Poydras Street in downtown New
Orleans; it had sluggish service but a platonic spaghetti
sauce. It also had a platonic veal parmigiana, but the
important thing was the spaghetti sauce: it had a rich,
tomatoey, almost burned flavor, and it was packed with
meatballs, mushrooms and chicken. Collin had given the
restaurant three stars and, with his customary enthusiasm, announced that Turci's cooking was "unsurpassed
in New Orleans or in Italy itself." But times got hard
for Turci's, the neighborhood changed, and Rose Turci
Serwich, the daughter of the original owners, decided
she would have to shut down. Collin heard the news
and wrote a column suggesting that someone raise the
money to move Turci's to a better location and save the
restaurant.

A New Orleans businessman named Joe Bernstein
read the article. Along with two partners, he had just
bought a building on Magazine Street and was looking for a ground-floor tenant. Bernstein called one of
his partners, Ben C. Toledano, who occasionally wrote

book reviews for the *States-Item* and knew Collin; Toledano called Collin and asked him to serve as interme-
diary in arranging the purchase of Turci's. "It was an
uncomfortable position," Collin recalled recently, "but it
was part of my responsibility to the community at large."
Collin went ahead and arranged for Turci's to sell its
name and good will for a reported ten thousand dollars
and for Mrs. Serwich to sign an employment contract.
A year later, the new Turci's opened. It was beautiful.
It was crowded. It was fashionable. And it was terrible.
Everyone knew it—Joe Bernstein knew it and Mrs. Serwich knew it. Both of them were on the phone to Richard Collin to complain about restaurant personnel. Mrs.
Serwich hated the chef. Mrs. Serwich had objections to
the manager. Joe Bernstein was going crazy because of
the tension between Mrs. Serwich and the chef and Mrs.
Serwich and the manager. But most of all, there was the
problem of the spaghetti sauce. "I couldn't go to a cocktail
party or go out on the street without someone telling me
the sauce just wasn't the same," Joe Bernstein recalled.
"I became frantic." The problem with the spaghetti sauce
was really a very simple one: there was no recipe for
it, and there never had been. The old Turci's spaghetti
sauce had been a concoction made of tomato paste and
leftovers. The new Turci's had no leftovers, owing to a
streamlined kitchen and cost accounting; the new chef
had no idea what to do under the circumstances. In the
midst of all this, Richard Collin dropped in to Turci's for
dinner.

The next day, he called Bernstein and told him to
come by his house immediately. Bernstein arrived
within a few minutes, and the first thing Collin asked
him to do was to sign a release absolving Collin of any

responsibility for what he was about to say. Bernstein signed and Collin began talking. He told Bernstein to fix the spaghetti sauce, eliminate the crab claws from the menu, and do something about the chef, who, Collin said, was "a Massachusetts Greek who didn't know from Turci's." If Bernstein failed to make improvements, Collin said he would be forced to give the restaurant a bad review—which he had in fact already written, and he read a few sample sentences from a piece of paper: "Frankly, we would all have been better off last year had the real Turci's been allowed to die a natural though unwelcome death. . . . It seems to me that in the move uptown what the new Turci's has proven is that one can turn a silk purse into a sow's ear. Requiescat." Within a few days, the chef quit—Bernstein says it had nothing to do with Collin's ultimatum—and Collin returned to the restaurant for a review. He gave the new Turci's three stars. "Try finding the likes of Turci's even in Italy," he wrote. "The new Turci's has the setting this marvelous restaurant has always deserved—a splendid place in which to serve its grand food. . . ."

At this point, we must pause to introduce a new character in this drama, a person Collin refers to as "my own favorite platonic dish." Rima Drell Reck Collin is a professor of comparative literature at the University of New Orleans, an editor of *The Southern Review*, and, according to her husband, "the most creative and gifted cook in the world now." She had just finished writing a New Orleans cookbook with her husband and was planning to open a food consulting firm in partnership with Warren Le Ruth of four-star, ten-platonic-dish fame. "The firm," says Collin, "was an attempt to get her out from being Mrs. Underground Gourmet. She's got enor-

mous talent, but in this town she is still Mrs. Underground Gourmet."

One day a few weeks after the good review appeared,
Joe Bernstein visited Richard and Rima Collin to talk
about the restaurant. He was still concerned about its
inconsistency, particularly when it came to the spaghetti
sauce. One thing led to another, and before the session
was up, Bernstein had hired Mrs. Collin's firm to fix the
sauce. Bernstein paid her two thousand dollars for two
months' work—after which time she and Le Ruth, who
had not been able to implement a new recipe, fought
with each other and dissolved the partnership. The next
month, Mrs. Collin sent Bernstein another bill, which
Bernstein refused to pay. There was considerable shouting on Bernstein's part and considerable crying on Mrs.
Collin's part. According to Bernstein, Mrs. Collin threatened his bookkeeper and said that if he did not pay up,
the restaurant would be hurt. Bernstein did not pay.

It was at this point, Richard Collin says, that he
realized for the first time that he was in a spot. "I was
in a very bad situation," he said. "It was okay as far as
helping the restaurant and shaking out the sauce—that
struck me as a civic restoration—but once a falling-out
occurred, I knew that anytime I changed the rating it
would look suspect." In January, 1975, just before the
Super Bowl, Collin nonetheless printed a revised set
of ratings for New Orleans restaurants. Turci's was
stripped down to an altogether new category—a star
within parentheses, meaning "some good food but not a
recommended restaurant." What intrigued the owners
of Turci's about this new rating was that Collin had not
eaten in Turci's at any time since his original review had
appeared.

A month later, *Figaro*, a small New Orleans weekly newspaper (in which, in keeping with the tenor of this saga, Joe Bernstein's children own a minority interest), broke the story. *Figaro*'s editor, James Glassman, quoted Bernstein and Collin on the Turci's episode, and also quoted Chris Ansel, the owner of Christian's Restaurant, who said that Collin told him to fire his chef and cut down on the salt; when the chef failed to do so, Collin stripped Ansel of his stars and eleven platonic dishes. The *Figaro* article caused a sensation. The New Orleans Restaurant Association wrote the *States-Item* demanding that Collin be investigated. The Louisiana chefs association seconded the motion. A group of local restaurateurs tried to pressure the National Restaurant Association to drop Collin from a panel discussion at the association's annual convention. There were television debates. There was an acrimonious press conference. Mrs. Galatoire of Galatoire's accused Collin of not ordering a dish he subsequently reviewed. The New Orleans *Times-Picayune*—which has an active rivalry with the *States-Item* although both are owned by the Newhouse chain—unleashed its food writer to attack Collin.

Eventually, of course, the furor died down. The editor of the *States-Item* admitted that Collin had been "indiscreet" and that some of his behavior bordered on "a conflict of interest." The *Times-Picayune* food writer announced that he would write a rival restaurant guide in which no restaurant would receive an unfavorable rating. Bernstein, not having managed to formulate the spaghetti sauce, moved on to specialize in canneloni. The people of New Orleans settled down to dinner. And Richard Collin learned a lesson. Not the exact lesson he might have—about the function of a critic, for example, or about the limits of critical involvement, or about the ethics of critical behavior—but he did learn something. "I learned," he said, "that restaurants have a limited life-span, and there's no point in trying to save them."

September, 1975

How to Write a Newsmagazine Cover Story

You Too Can Be a Writer

You can learn, in your spare time, to write articles for publication, and if you master the art, you can be paid to do it on a full-time basis.

Of course, there are all sorts of writers. There are reporters, for example. Reporters have to learn how to uncover FACTS. This is very difficult to learn in your spare time. There are also serious journalists. But serious journalists have TALENT. There is no way to learn to have talent. There are also fiction writers. But fiction writers need IMAGINATION. Either you have imagination or you don't. You can't pick it up in a manual.

But there is one kind of writer you can learn to be and you will not need FACTS, TALENT or IMAGINATION. You can become a newsmagazine cover story writer. Just master the six rules enumerated below and you will know all you need to about how to write a newsmagazine cover story—or at least the kind of newsmagazine cover story dealing with life style, soft news, and cultural figures.

RULE ONE:
*Find a subject too much has
already been written about.*

To do this, read with care the following: *Women's Wear
Daily, Vogue,* Joyce Haber's column, Suzy's column,
the "Arts and Leisure" section of the Sunday *New York
Times, Rolling Stone* and the movie grosses in *Variety.*

Any name mentioned more than four or five hundred
times in the last year is a suitable subject for a newsmagazine cover.

RULE TWO:
Exaggerate the significance of the cover subject.

Study the following examples to see how this is done by
the experts:

"Today, a few weeks shy of twenty-six, Liza has
evolved in her own right into a new Miss Show Biz, a
dazzlingly assured and completely rounded performer.
The Justice Department should investigate her. She is a
mini-conglomerate, an entertainment monopoly" (*Time*
on Liza Minnelli, February 28, 1972).

"At thirty-five, Coppola stands alone as a multiple
movie talent: a director who can make the blockbuster
success and the brilliant, 'personal' film" (*Newsweek* on
Francis Ford Coppola, November 25, 1974).

"Finally, the film confirms that Robert Altman, the
director of *Nashville,* is doing more original, serious—
yet entertaining—work than anyone else in American
movies" (*Newsweek* on *Nashville* and Robert Altman,
June 30, 1975).

"At twenty-nine, salty Lauren Hutton is America's

most celebrated model of the moment—and the highest-paid in history, as well. . . . Her extraordinarily expressive face and throwaway sex appeal, captured in the strong, spirited photographs of Richard Avedon, have made Hutton a permanent fixture in the pages of *Vogue* and at least a passing fancy in five movies. And in contrast to the exotic stone-faced beauties of the 1960s, her natural gap-toothed, all-American good looks epitomize the thoroughly capable, canny, contemporary woman of the Seventies" (*Newsweek* on Lauren Hutton, August 26, 1974).

"Margaux is the American Sex Dream incarnate, a prairie Valkyrie, six feet tall and one hundred thirty-eight pounds. . . . Effortlessly, Margaux stands out in a gallery of fresh young faces, newcomers who are making their names in modeling, movies, ballet and in the exacting art of simply living well. They add up to an exhilarating crop of new beauties who light up the landscape in the U.S. and abroad" (*Time* on Margaux Hemingway and the New Beauties, June 16, 1975).

RULE THREE:
Find people who know the subject
personally and whose careers are bound up
with the subject's. Get these people to comment
on the subject's significance.

"Add to all this her beliefs in the trendy cults of mysticism and metaphysics and she becomes thoroughly modern Marisa, aptly crowned by the *International Herald Tribune*'s society chronicler Hebe Dorsey as 'the girl who has everything plus'" (*Newsweek* on Marisa Berenson, August 27, 1973).

" 'This event is the biggest thing of its kind in the history of show business,' modestly declared David Geffen, the thirty-year-old human dynamo, 'Record Executive of the Year,' chairman of the board of Elektra/Asylum Records, who just pulled off one of the great coups in the music business—signing Dylan away from Columbia Records" (*Newsweek* on Bob Dylan's concert tour, January 14, 1974).

"This is Roy Halston Frowick . . . known simply as Halston—the premier fashion designer of all America. . . . Halston's creative strength derives from personally dressing the most famous and fashionable women in the world, and while his name is not yet a household word, his impact on fashion trend setters is considerable. 'Halston is the hottest American designer of the moment,' says James Brady, the former publisher of *Women's Wear Daily* and now publisher of *Harper's Bazaar.* Fashion consultant Eleanor Lambert goes even further. 'Along with Yves St. Laurent,' says Miss Lambert, 'Halston is the most influential designer—not only in America, but in the world'" (*Newsweek* on Halston, August 21, 1972).

RULE FOUR:
Try, insofar as it is possible, to imitate the style of press releases.

"On the one hand she is very American, with deep roots in the South and an almost apple-pie adolescence (from cheerleader to campus queen). There is about her a touching innocence, openness, expansiveness and vulnerability. But at the same time she is no bright-eyed square. She breathes sophistication, elegance, grace, passion, experience. Dunaway has become more than a star—she is a style and a symbol" (*Newsweek* on Faye Dunaway, March 4, 1968).

"She is the rural neophyte waiting in a subway, a free spirit drinking Greek wine in the moonlight, an organic Earth Mother dispensing fresh bread and herb tea, and the reticent feminist who by trial and error has charted the male as well as the female ego" (*Time* on Joni Mitchell, December 16, 1974).

"There are many things gorgeous about Robert Redford. The shell, to begin with, is resplendent. The head is classically shaped, the features chiseled to an all-American handsomeness just rugged enough to avoid prettiness, the complexion weather-burnished to a reddish-gold, the body athletically muscled, the aura best described by one female fan who says: 'He gives you the feeling that even his sweat would smell good'" (*Newsweek* on Robert Redford, February 4, 1974).

RULE FIVE:
*Use statistics wherever possible.
Better yet, use statistics so mind boggling
that no reader will bother to do simple
arithmetic to determine their impossibility.*

One example will suffice here:

"[There are] one hundred million dogs and cats in the U.S. . . . Each day across the nation, dogs deposit an estimated four million tons of feces" (*Time* on the American Pet, December 23, 1974).

RULE SIX:
Study the examples.

Read more newsmagazine cover stories.

Learn to use adjectives like "brilliant," "gorgeous," "original," "serious" and "dazzling" with devil-may-care abandon.

Learn to use clichés with devil-may-care abandon.

Master this technique and you too will be able to get a job writing back-of-the-book cover stories at a newsmagazine. You too will be able to take a subject, any subject, and hype it to the point where it bears no resemblance to reality. Whomever you write about will never be able to live up to what you write about him, but never mind. The important thing is that people will talk about YOUR STORY. They will talk about it for years. They will say how strange it was that the career of whomever you wrote about seemed somehow to slip after the cover *you wrote* appeared. They will allude ominously to the Newsmagazine Cover Curse. But you will know better.

So begin now, before it's too late. If it doesn't work out, you can always go work at a fan magazine.

October, 1975

The Boston Photographs

"I made all kinds of pictures because I thought it would be a good rescue shot over the ladder . . . never dreamed it would be anything else. . . . I kept having to move around because of the light set. The sky was bright and they were in deep shadow. I was making pictures with a motor drive and he, the fire fighter, was reaching up and, I don't know, everything started falling. I followed the girl down taking pictures . . . I made three or four frames. I realized what was going on and I completely turned around, because I didn't want to see her hit."

You probably saw the photographs. In most newspapers, there were three of them. The first showed some people on a fire escape—a fireman, a woman and a child. The fireman had a nice strong jaw and looked very brave. The woman was holding the child. Smoke was pouring from the building behind them. A rescue ladder was approaching, just a few feet away, and the fireman had one arm around the woman and one arm reaching out toward the ladder. The second picture showed the fire escape slipping off the building. The child had fallen on the escape and seemed about to slide off the edge. The woman was grasping desperately at the legs of the fireman, who had managed to grab the ladder. The third picture showed the woman and child in midair, falling to the ground. Their arms and legs were outstretched, horribly distended. A potted plant was falling too. The caption said that the woman, Diana Bryant, nineteen, died in the fall. The child landed on the woman's body and lived.

The pictures were taken by Stanley Forman, thirty, of the *Boston Herald American*. He used a motor-driven Nikon F set at 1/250, f 5.6–8. Because of the motor, the camera can click off three frames a second. More than four hundred newspapers in the United States alone carried the photographs; the tear sheets from overseas are still coming in. The *New York Times* ran them on the first page of its second section; a paper in south Georgia gave them nineteen columns; the *Chicago Tribune*, the *Washington Post* and the *Washington Star* filled almost half their front pages, the *Star* under a somewhat redundant headline that read: SENSATIONAL PHOTOS OF RESCUE ATTEMPT THAT FAILED.

The photographs are indeed sensational. They are pictures of death in action, of that split second when luck runs out, and it is impossible to look at them without feeling their extraordinary impact and remembering, in an almost subconscious way, the morbid fantasy of falling, falling off a building, falling to one's death. Beyond that, the pictures are classics, old-fashioned but perfect examples of photojournalism at its most spectacular. They're throwbacks, really, fire pictures, 1930s tabloid shots; at the same time they're technically superb and thoroughly modern—the sequence could not have been taken at all until the development of the motor-driven camera some sixteen years ago.

Most newspaper editors anticipate some reader reaction to photographs like Forman's; even so, the response around the country was enormous, and almost all of it was negative. I have read hundreds of the letters that were printed in letters-to-the-editor sections, and they repeat the same points. "Invading the privacy of death." "Cheap sensationalism." "I thought I was reading the *National Enquirer.*" "Assigning the agony of a human being in terror of imminent death to the status of a sideshow act." "A tawdry way to sell newspapers." The *Seattle Times* received sixty letters and calls; its managing editor even got a couple of them at home. A reader wrote the *Philadelphia Inquirer:* "*Jaws* and *Towering Inferno* are playing downtown; don't take business away from people who pay good money to advertise in your own paper." Another reader wrote the *Chicago Sun-Times*: "I shall try to hide my disappointment that Miss Bryant wasn't wearing a skirt when she fell to her death. You could have had some award-winning photographs of her underpants as her skirt billowed over her head, you voyeurs." Several newspaper editors wrote columns defending the pictures: Thomas Keevil of the *Costa Mesa* (California) *Daily Pilot* printed a ballot for readers to vote on whether they would have printed the pictures; Marshall L. Stone of Maine's *Bangor Daily News*, which refused to print the famous assassination picture of the Vietcong prisoner in Saigon, claimed that the Boston pictures showed the dangers of fire escapes and raised questions about slumlords. (The burning building was a five-story brick apartment house on Marlborough Street in the Back Bay section of Boston.)

For the last five years, the *Washington Post* has employed various journalists as ombudsmen, whose job is to monitor the paper on behalf of the public. The *Post*'s current ombudsman is Charles Seib, former managing editor of the *Washington Star*; the day the Boston photographs appeared, the paper received over seventy calls in protest. As Seib later wrote in a column about the pictures, it was "the largest reaction to a published item that I have experienced in eight months as the *Post*'s ombudsman. . . .

"In the *Post*'s newsroom, on the other hand, I found no doubts, no second thoughts . . . the question was not whether they should be printed but how they should be displayed. When I talked to editors . . . they used words like 'interesting' and 'riveting' and 'gripping' to describe them. The pictures told something about life in the ghetto, they said (although the neighborhood where the tragedy occurred is not a ghetto, I am told). They dramatized the need to check on the safety of fire escapes. They dramatically conveyed something that had happened, and that is the business we're in. They were news. . . .

"Was publication of that [third] picture a bow to the same taste for the morbidly sensational that makes gold mines of disaster movies? Most papers will not print the picture of a dead body except in the most unusual circumstances. Does the fact that the final picture was taken a millisecond before the young woman died make a difference? Most papers will not print a picture of a bare female breast. Is that a more inappropriate subject for display than the picture of a human being's last agonized instant of life?" Seib offered no answers to the questions he raised, but he went on to say that although as an editor he would probably have run the pictures, as a reader he was revolted by them.

In conclusion, Seib wrote: "Any editor who decided to

print those pictures without giving at least a moment's thought to what purpose they served and what their effect was likely to be on the reader should ask another question: Have I become so preoccupied with manufacturing a product according to professional traditions and standards that I have forgotten about the consumer, the reader?"

It should be clear that the phone calls and letters and Seib's own reaction were occasioned by one factor alone: the death of the woman. Obviously, had she survived the fall, no one would have protested; the pictures would have had a completely different impact. Equally obviously, had the child died as well—or instead—Seib would undoubtedly have received ten times the phone calls he did. In each case, the pictures would have been exactly the same—only the captions, and thus the responses, would have been different.

But the questions Seib raises are worth discussing—though not exactly for the reasons he mentions. For it may be that the real lesson of the Boston photographs is not the danger that editors will be forgetful of reader reaction, but that they will continue to censor pictures of death precisely because of that reaction. The protests Seib fielded were really a variation on an old theme—and we saw plenty of it during the Nixon-Agnew years—the "Why doesn't the press print the good news?" argument. In this case, of course, the objections were all dressed up and cleverly disguised as righteous indignation about the privacy of death. This is a form of puritanism that is often justifiable; just as often it is merely puritanical.

Seib takes it for granted that the widespread though fairly recent newspaper policy against printing pictures of dead bodies is a sound one; I don't know that it makes any sense at all. I recognize that printing pictures of corpses raises all sorts of problems about taste and titillation and sensationalism; the fact is, however, that people die. Death happens to be one of life's main events. And it is irresponsible—and more than that, inaccurate—for newspapers to fail to show it, or to show it only when an astonishing set of photos comes in over the Associated Press wire. Most papers covering fatal automobile accidents will print pictures of mangled cars. But the significance of fatal automobile accidents is not that a great deal of steel is twisted but that people die. Why not show it? That's what accidents are about. Throughout the Vietnam war, editors were reluctant to print atrocity pictures. Why *not* print them? That's what that war was about. Murder victims are almost never photographed; they are granted their privacy. But their relatives are relentlessly pictured on their way in and out of hospitals and morgues and funerals.

I'm not advocating that newspapers print these things in order to teach their readers a lesson. The *Post* editors justified their printing of the Boston pictures with several arguments in that direction; every one of them is irrelevant. The pictures don't show anything about slum life; the incident could have happened anywhere, and it did. It is extremely unlikely that anyone who saw them rushed out and had his fire escape strengthened. And the pictures were not news—at least they were not national news. It is not news in Washington, or New York, or Los Angeles that a woman was killed in a Boston fire. The only newsworthy thing about the pictures is that they were taken. They deserve to be printed because they are great pictures, breathtaking pictures of something that happened. That they disturb readers is exactly as it should be: that's why photojournalism is often more powerful than written journalism.

November, 1975

Barney Collier's Book

Barney Collier has written a book about Washington journalists, and the thing the Washington journalists in the book said to me when I called them up to say I was writing a column about it was: Don't; don't write anything about it; you'll just give the book publicity and end up selling copies of it. This is interesting, since it implies that these journalists believe that all publicity is good publicity, and if they believed that, none of them would be half as upset about the book as they are.

Nonetheless, it's a tricky problem.

Collier's book is called *Hope and Fear in Washington (The Early Seventies): The Story of the Washington Press Corps*. The Dial Press is publishing it, and I'll get to them in a minute. The author, who is thirty-seven, was a reporter for the *New York Herald Tribune* and later for the *New York Times*. He left the *Times* in 1969 under murky circumstances—he was not fired, but it is clear that he was in some way made to feel that his presence in the newsroom was no longer desirable. A few years later, he published an article in the *New York Times Magazine* on columnist Joseph Alsop; subsequently, he was given $7,500 and a contract from the David McKay Company to write a book on Washington journalists. Because he was an old colleague, or a friend of a friend, the journalists he wanted to see gave him interviews; most reporters believe they have that obligation to other reporters. Because he was clearly down-and-out, they usually paid for lunch. Because he seemed a little strange—he did not take notes, and he asked odd questions like "What do you think of sex?" and "What is your definition of intelligence?" and "How much money do you make?"—most of them eventually stopped returning his phone calls. As Sally Quinn said to him at one point: "I get terrible vibes from you, and I don't know why."

Collier turned the book in to David McKay about two years ago, and it was rejected. His editor had expected a serious book on journalists and journalism; what Collier delivered, in the opinion of the publisher, was self-indulgent, inaccurate, impressionistic and libelous. "We felt," said a spokesman for McKay, "that it would have been immoral to publish it." The book was sent around to a number of other publishers—Collier claims that seventeen or eighteen of them turned it down, though his agent says that is a slight exaggeration. Finally, it came to rest at Dial, which paid ten thousand dollars for it. Dial felt the book would be controversial, and that it would sell. (I am continually fascinated at the difficulty intelligent people have in distinguishing what is controversial from what is merely offensive.) This faith was bolstered when material from the book on Sander Vanocur appeared in *[MORE]*, the journalism review, and received more mail in protest than anything *[MORE]* had ever printed.

In his introduction to the book, Collier writes: "One of the ideas behind this book is that in order to more nearly understand the news from Washington you must more nearly understand the life of the person who tells you what the news may be." This is a valid proposition, and it might have made for a good book. It helps to know, for example, that Melvin Laird leaks to Evans and Novak when you read an Evans and Novak column saying that Gerald Ford is considering appointing Melvin Laird Vice-President. This sort of thing is not in Collier's book. Instead, the reader learns that Bob Novak has just given up smoking, and that Rowland Evans won't let Barney Collier see his tax return. (It's unfortunate that Evans did not: Collier might have discovered, in looking at it, how to spell Evans's first name.) Collier treats his subjects as celebrities. He writes about their marriages, hints leeringly at their infidelities, twists the quotes, jumbles the facts, misspells the names. He makes fun of what they order for lunch, how they eat it, and even that they paid his check. Nothing is off the record. "People tell you something and expect you to take care of them," Collier says. "They assume that off the record is everything you as a pal would leave out. It's a permeating thing in Washington." It is indeed permeating—and it's relevant when reporters end up taking care of someone like Henry Kissinger. But here it's ridiculous. Anyone who has ever done interviews knows how easy it is to make an interview subject sound foolish by quoting his casual conversation with a waiter, or by asking him asinine questions.

And that, of course, is precisely Collier's aim: to make his subjects look foolish. They have succeeded and he has failed; Collier's bitterness at the injustice of it all permeates everything he writes. It makes for an incredibly ugly book, which is in no way redeemed by the fact that Collier is open about his own life—his first marriage, his decision to give up his sons for adoption, his trials at the *Times*, and his travels in and out of sanity. The crack-up is one thing when Scott Fitzgerald writes it, and quite another when Barney Collier does.

But I wanted to write about Collier's book because it raises a couple of interesting questions. The first is about its publisher, and what I think of as the lie-down-with-dogs-get-up-with-fleas syndrome. The Dial Press sent Collier's book out with six jacket and publicity quotes. Two of them—from Sydney Gruson and Richard Goodwin—are accurate. Two others—from David Halberstam and Theodore H. White—were lifted from their letters to *[MORE]* objecting to the Vanocur piece; they were used without permission and referred only to the piece; Halberstam's quote is completely out of context. I spoke to Donna Schrader, publicity director at Dial, and Joyce Engelson, Collier's editor, and neither of them saw anything wrong with using the quotes.

Then there are quotes from Art Buchwald (". . . I came out good, but you better make sure the hood of your car is locked after the other people in the book read it!") and Helen Thomas ("I love it. I found myself going through all the emotions with it. I cried one minute and laughed the next. It's thrilling. It's spine-tingling. You got the people . . . just right . . . they all revealed themselves. It's really the anatomy of the press corps"). I called Buchwald and asked if he had given Collier that quote. "I didn't say that," Buchwald said. "He asked me for a quote, and I said, 'Weird.' 'That's it?' he said. 'That's it,' I said. 'Weird. W-e-i-r-d.' It's outrageous he's using something I didn't say."

I then called Helen Thomas, who had no idea she

was being quoted at all. "I thought I was just talking to Barney," she said. "He gave me the book, and then he called to ask my opinion of it. I haven't really read it— I just went through it in a cursory fashion. If I wanted to put something in writing I would have done it myself. I didn't realize it was going to be used in that form. Life is difficult, to put it mildly."

"The first person I gave the manuscript to was Art Buchwald," Collier said when I asked him about all this. "I told him I needed a quote and that I didn't care if he liked it or hated it, but he could only read the book if he gave me a quote. My wife and I went to pick up the manuscript a couple of days later and I asked him if he would give me a quote. 'No,' he said, 'I'd like to get out of it. I don't want to be known as a collaborator.' 'Art,' I said, 'you made a promise.' 'Will you settle for one word?' he said. 'What's the word?' I said. 'Weird,' he said. We got up to go, and as we went out the door, he pointed to our car. 'That's a nice car,' he said. 'I came out good, but you better make sure the hood of your car is locked after the other people in the book read it.'"

"Did you ask him if you could use that quote?" I asked.

"Nope," said Collier. "He said I could use a quote, and he didn't make a beginning or an end to it."

Collier went on: "The second person I brought it to was Helen Thomas. I called her up afterward, and she said these things. She didn't put a beginning or an end on it, and she said I could quote her."

Collier sent both quotes off to Dial. Neither his editor nor the publicity director called Buchwald or Thomas to confirm the quotes; in fact, they seemed rather surprised when I suggested they might have done so. "I haven't followed this step by step," said Schrader. "I haven't looked at the material. We have six authors out on tour."

"This is the kind of book that obviously creates a sort of fuss," said Engelson. "The point of the book is that these people are public figures. A lot of the negative reaction to it came because of the article in [MORE], and a lot of that was people objecting to it because Sander Vanocur's wife was dying. It's certainly not Barney's responsibility that his wife, I forget her name, was dying. The timing had nothing to do with Barney. Mr. Buchwald is another set of fish. One day he says he said it. One day he says he didn't."

"What about the Helen Thomas quote?" I asked.

"I have it in writing from Helen Thomas," said Engelson.

"I don't think you do."

"I'm sure we do."

"I don't think so."

"Then Barney got it from her," said Engelson. "I don't see why she should object, anyway. It's a beautiful portrait of Helen Thomas."

I realized, as I read Collier's book, that I would not have been nearly as offended by it if it had been about movie stars—and that brings me to the second question it raises, about journalists and celebrity. In the past few years, journalists have indeed become celebrities; meanwhile, as if nothing had changed, they continue to parrot the old rule: "I'm a journalist, and I feel I have an obligation to give interviews to other journalists since I ask for them myself." Journalists may in fact have an obligation to help other journalists, particularly on substantive points, but they are under no obligation to promote themselves. And if they are going to—if they are going to behave like movie stars—eventually someone is going to come along and make fools of them. In some terrible way, the profession deserves the Collier book; it's the inevitable outcome of this daisy chain, this circle jerk of media interviewing media.

The logical ending for this column, I suppose, is for me to stop writing a media column. I'm part of the daisy chain. I stole one of the best lines in this column from Marty Nolan of the *Boston Globe*. I couldn't write this without the cooperation of other journalists. I really ought to give it up. I'm not going to, not yet.

But it's a tricky problem.

January, 1976

The Assassination Reporters

Hugh Aynesworth and Bob Dudney work in a little office just off the city room of the *Dallas Times Herald*, and things were running fairly normally there the day I dropped in to see them. A woman had just telephoned to say that she knew for a fact that Jack Ruby's brain had been controlled by a television station near the Dallas airport. The day before, a little man in high-topped sneakers had come by, whispered about some inside information he claimed to have, and finally confided that the Jews had killed President Kennedy.

Dudney, twenty-five, was in the eighth grade when John F. Kennedy was shot. He is new to the assassination beat, and he is still a little amazed by the people he meets on it. But Aynesworth, forty-four, has been covering the story on and off since November 22, 1963, and nothing fazes him anymore. "In 1963 only the most brazen kooks came out," he says, "but by the time Jim Garrison started in in 1966 and 1967, even the timid ones were getting into it. People want to be involved in this. I've heard five or six people confess that they were part of a conspiracy to kill Kennedy—only it turns out they were in jail, or in a loony bin in Atlanta, at the time.

There were about five hundred people in Dealey Plaza that day. In twenty years, there'll be ten thousand."

The day of the assassination, Aynesworth was working as science and aviation editor of the *Dallas Morning News*, and he decided to walk over and have a look at the President's motorcade. He was standing catty-corner to the School Book Depository when he heard three shots. "I thought the first one was a motorcycle backfiring," he says, "but by the time I heard the second, I knew what it was. People started reacting in a very violent way. They threw their children down and started screaming. There was one big black woman who had been thrilled to death because she was wearing a pink dress the same color as Jackie Kennedy's. She threw up within five seconds of the shots."

After a while, Aynesworth saw a group of people running toward the Depository building. "On the fifth floor we saw three black guys pointing up to the sixth-floor window. There were FBI cars and a radio car. And then a funny thing happened. This shows what bad luck can do for you. There was a long-time police reporter for the *Dallas News* there named Jim Ewell. The FBI was working up floor by floor in the Depository building, and here comes a call over the radio: 'This is a citizen, an officer's been shot.' It was on Tenth Street, three or four miles away. I said to Ewell, 'You stay here, I'll go after that one.' He stayed, and of course he saw no one. I ran off with two TV guys and a Channel Eight news car, and we go to the Tippit killing. Then a call came in that there was something going on at the Texas Theater. I got there, and there was Jim Ewell, and I said, 'Jim, you take the upstairs and I'll take the downstairs.' Turned out Oswald was downstairs. I just got there in time. Oswald came up with his fist, which had a gun in it, and slugged McDonald, and the other cop jumped him from the back.

"Within a few minutes of that, I got a tip from someone at the police station about the two addresses in Oswald's wallet. We went tearing over to the Elsbeth address, where he wasn't living—I burst in on some wino and his girl shacked up together. Then we went to 1026 Beckley, where he actually lived. We were twenty minutes behind the FBI. There was that little old room, it couldn't have been more than eight by ten. The only thing they left in it was a banana peel.

"On Sunday morning, Jim Ewell had the assignment at the jail, but he got a flat tire on the way. I went over just to see what was going on and saw Ruby kill Oswald. It was pure luck that I saw it and he missed it all. He feels snakebit, I'm sure."

Today Jim Ewell is still a police reporter in Dallas, and Hugh Aynesworth—well, Aynesworth is still a reporter too, but he is also an odd sort of footnote to the assassination, the journalist who has spent more time on the story than any other. He is a walking compendium of names of FBI agents, New Orleans informers, assistant district attorneys, bus drivers and cabbies. He was the first reporter to print Oswald's diary and he sat shivah with Jack Ruby's family.

Aynesworth became so emotionally involved in the Clay Shaw trial that one of his dreams influenced the outcome of the case. "Suddenly one night I awakened out of a nightmare," he told James Kirkwood, author of *American Grotesque*. He had dreamed that District Attorney James Garrison produced a surprise witness who came in "and sat down and captivated the jury, win-

ning the case hands down." He was so shaken by the
dream that he wrote a letter to Shaw's lawyer, urging
him to hire a private detective to investigate one of Garrison's witnesses, a dapper man named Charles Spiesel
who claimed he had heard Shaw discuss the possibility of assassinating Kennedy. The detective discovered
that Spiesel had filed a sixteen-million-dollar lawsuit
charging the New York police and a psychiatrist with
hypnotizing him and preventing him from having normal sexual relations; the information was crucial in dis-
crediting Spiesel's testimony.

In some way, of course, Aynesworth is probably as
addled about the assassination as some of the genuinely crazy people who come to see him. Unlike them,
though—and unlike most of the buffs—he continues to
believe that John F. Kennedy was killed by Lee Harvey
Oswald, acting alone. "I sort of feel like a damn fool,"
he says. "There's nobody on earth who'd rather prove a
conspiracy than me. I'd love to write it—if there was any
damn thing that made me believe it." It's an odd position: investigative reporters try to bring conspiracies to
light; Aynesworth has spent much of his time knocking
them down.

"Let me tell you how the story about Oswald's being
an FBI informer got started," he said. "There was a
note in Oswald's papers with the name James Hosty
on it. Hosty was an FBI agent, and in the beginning we
thought Oswald was some kind of a spy or paid informer.
I worked the FBI stuff, and we'd run down everything
you could imagine. I even got Hosty's phone records.
I called the phone company and I just asked, 'How do
you get phone records if you've moved?' I never actually said I was Hosty—she just assumed I was, and she

sent them. Anyway, we couldn't put it together except for these interviews where Hosty had come to see Marina. And that's where Lonnie Hudkins came along.

"Lonnie Hudkins was on the *Houston Post*, and he'd been sent to Dallas to work on the story. He called me up all the time, he would bug me and give me all these tips that were nothing. I just didn't want him bugging me anymore. So one day he called up and said, 'You hear anything about this FBI link with Oswald?' I'd just about had it. I said to him, 'You got his payroll number, don't you?' 'Yeah, yeah,' said Lonnie. I reached over on my desk, and there was a Telex number on a telegram, S. 172 I think it was, and I told it to Lonnie. 'Yeah, yeah,' he said, 'that's it. That's the same one I've got.' Lonnie could see the moon coming out at high noon." The number eventually became part of the lore of the assassination.

Aynesworth stayed on the *News* until 1966, did some work for *Life*, and was on the staff of *Newsweek* from 1967 to 1974. The story would die down for a while and then crop up again. "Something was always coming up," he said. "*Look* magazine bought the Manchester book, so *Life* felt it had to have something to counteract it. They put an investigative team on it, and in 1966 they were digging around. They moved to New Orleans and worked with Garrison, did a lot of investigation for him. Jack Fincher, the San Francisco bureau chief, comes up with a little fag from New Orleans, a short-order cook who told him a story about Oswald and Ruby being seen in New Orleans as lovers, and then at the YMCA in Dallas. He wove a great tale. Fincher didn't know enough to know whether it was good, so they told him in New York to run it by Dallas and see what Hugh thinks.

"We got a motel room at the Executive Inn out by

the airport, and we taped this story, and he really had it down. There was no way I could break him. I was beginning to wonder myself. He was going on and on, he'd seen them swimming, hugging and kissing, and he said they'd even tried to entice him. Finally, I looked at him and said, 'Wasn't that a terrible scar on Ruby's leg, that shark bite? Which leg was it on, anyway?' He said, 'It was the right leg.' He took a pause. 'No,' he said, 'it was the left leg. I remember now.' I said, 'You little son of a bitch, he didn't have a scar on his leg.' He started crying. I felt sorry for him—he'd been promised a good bit of money for his story."

Last year, after working a spell as a private investigator, Aynesworth joined the *Times Herald* and began working with Dudney. They make an interesting pair: Aynesworth is stocky and square, Dudney is lean and long-haired; Aynesworth is disorganized, Dudney is a compulsive file keeper; Aynesworth works the phone, Dudney writes. The *Times Herald*, under the by-line of its publisher Tom Johnson, broke the story last fall of the threatening letter Oswald wrote to the FBI prior to the assassination; Aynesworth and Dudney did much of the legwork and wrote the backup stories. Their biggest story, both agree, was a non-story that took them weeks to put together. An FBI clerk named William Walter, who was working in the New Orleans office in 1963, told them that five days before the assassination he saw a Teletype saying there would be an assassination attempt in Dallas and that no one had done anything about it.

"When we first talked to him on the phone," Dudney said, "we were both extremely excited. The guy was very convincing."

"We interviewed him twenty-some times," said Aynes-worth, "and we talked to everybody who ever knew him."

"We got red flags everywhere," said Dudney.

"We gave him a polygraph," said Aynesworth, "and he didn't pass it."

"We never could get the one bit of information that proved it or disproved it," said Dudney.

"When we were three weeks into it," Aynesworth said, "CBS got onto it. Dan Rather called and asked me what I thought. I said, 'I'm ninety percent sure he's lying, but I'm not sure.' They did some film with him, chartered a plane to get it out, and once again Dan and I were back and forth on the phone. I gave him the results of the polygraph—with Walter's permission. Finally, CBS went with it—but in a very positive manner. So we came back with a detailed, massive study. Knocking these stories down is no good—but you have to do it. There's a lack of willingness in this business to say that nothing is there. Especially after a few bucks have been spent."

There is a reason there are only a handful of report-ers working the Kennedy assassination—and that is that a lot of smart reporters have kept as far away from it as is possible. This is a story that begs for hundreds of investigators, subpoena power, forensics experts, grants of immunity; it's also a story that requires slogging through twenty-seven volumes of the Warren Commis-sion report and dozens of books on the assassination. A lot of people are dead. Some of the ones who are alive have changed their stories. The whole thing is a mess. And while it's not likely that Aynesworth and Dudney will get to the bottom of it—that would be a little like shooting a bear with a BB gun—it's nice to know they are still down there in Dallas plugging away.

"The other night I was at a party," Bob Dudney said, "and we were talking about certain great events that shaped the lives of people my age. The emergence of the Beatles and the Vietnam war were obvious influences. And I said that I thought the assassination of Kennedy was a big influence—and as soon as I said it I corrected myself. Oswald's death was more an influence than Kennedy's. Had he lived, so much more would have come out. His death left us a legacy of suspicion and doubt that's turned in on everybody. It's unusual. Such a neurotic little man, who was really such a loser, you know, and he's left a very profound influence. The country would have recovered from the death of John Kennedy, but it hasn't recovered yet from the death of Lee Harvey Oswald and probably never will."

February, 1976

The New Porn

Every so often, I manage to get through a day without reading the *New York Times*. This is an extremely risky thing to do—you never know whether the day you skip the *Times* will turn out to be the one day when some fascinating article will appear and leave you to spend the rest of your life explaining to friends who bring it up that you missed it. Fortunately, this rarely happens. But on Friday, November 14, 1975, I managed to miss the *New York Times*, and I learned my lesson.

That, as it happens, was the day the *Times* ran a page-one story by its food writer Craig Claiborne about a four-thousand-dollar meal he and his friend Pierre Franey ate at a Paris restaurant, and I think it is safe to say that no article the *Times* has printed in the last year has generated as much response. (The only recent exception that comes to mind is one that Charlotte Curtis wrote about cottage cheese.) In any case, a few days later, in desperation, I went back and read it. As you undoubtedly know, Claiborne had bid three hundred dollars in an auction for dinner for two at any restaurant in the world; because American Express was footing the bill, there was a stipulation that the restaurant be on the American Express card. Claiborne chose to dine at a chic spot on the Right Bank called Chez Denis, and there he and Franey managed to get through thirty-one courses and nine wines. Two things were immediately clear to me when I read the article: first, that the meal had been a real disappointment, though Craig only hinted at that with a few cutting remarks about the blandness of the sorrel soup and the nothingness of the sweetbread parfait; and second, that the *Times* had managed to give front-page play to a story that was essentially a gigantic publicity stunt for American Express. What good sports the people at American Express were about the entire episode! How jolly they were about paying the bill! "We were mildly astonished at first but now we're cheerful about it," a spokesman for the company said—and well he might have been. Four thousand dollars is a small price to pay for the amount of corporate good will the article generated—and that outraged me; I have dealt with the people at American Express about money on several occasions, and they have never been cheerful with *me*.

Because my outrage was confined to such a narrow part of the event, I was quite surprised a few days later when I began to read some of the letters the *Times* received about the dinner. There were eventually some five hundred in all, four to one against Claiborne, and the general tenor of them related to the total vulgarity of spending four thousand dollars on a dinner when millions were starving. Knee-jerk liberalism is apparently alive and well after all. There were references to Nero and Marie Antoinette, and there were also a few media-wise letter writers who chose to object not to the article itself but to the *Times*'s decision to run it on the front page. The *Times* printed a short and rather plain-tive reply from Claiborne, who said that he could not see how anyone could claim that the meal had "deprived one human being of one mouthful of food."

All of this raised some interesting questions. For openers, how much money did Claiborne have to spend to cross the line into wretched excess? Would five hundred dollars have done it? A thousand dollars? Had he spent two thousand dollars, would the *Times* have received only three hundred letters? Would the objections have been even more intense if he had spent the four thousand dollars but put the tab on his expense account? Then, too, there is the question of editorial play: how much difference would it have made if the *Times* had run the article inside the newspaper? These are obviously unanswerable, almost existential questions, and a bit frivolous to boot—but there is something more serious underlying this whole tempest.

Claiborne was clearly puzzled by the reaction to his piece. He had managed to commit a modern atrocity— even if he did rip off American Express, for which he is to be commended—and there is a good reason why it never crossed his mind that he was doing so: except for the price tag, what he did was no more vulgar and tasteless than what he and hundreds of other journalists do every day. Newspapers and magazines are glutted with recipes for truffle soufflés and nit-picking restaurant reviews and paeans to the joys of arugula. Which of us will ever forget the thrilling night that Gael Greene blew five hundred dollars on dinner at the Palace, or that spine-tingling afternoon when Craig and Pierre jumped into the car and drove all the way from East Hampton to Southampton just in time to find the only butcher on eastern Long Island with a pig's ear? Or was it pork fat for pâté? God knows what it was, but the point is that it should not have taken a four-thousand-dollar dinner at Chez Denis to remind the readers of the *Times* that Nero fiddled while Rome burned. All of this—let's face it—is pretty vulgar stuff. It's also fun to read. But when it's accompanied by a four-thousand-dollar price tag, it reminds people of something they should have known all along: it's not about food, it's about money. Craig Claiborne writes about consuming—which should not be confused with consumerism, or Ralph Nader, or anything of the sort. And in his way, he is representative of one of the major trends in publishing today; he is a purveyor of what I tend to think of as the new porn.

Before going further, I should define what I mean by porn in this context: it's anything people are ashamed of getting a kick out of. If you want to sell porn to a mass audience, you have to begin by packaging it in a way that's acceptable; you have to give people an excuse to buy it. *Playboy*'s Hugh Hefner was the first person in publishing to understand this; if he has done nothing else for American culture, he has given it two of the great lies of the twentieth century: "I buy it for the fiction" and "I buy it for the interview." Of late, Hefner has been hoist with his own petard. He has spent twenty years making the world safe for split beaver, and now he is surprised that magazines that print it are taking circulation away from his own.

The new porn has nothing to do with dirty pictures. It's simply about money. The new porn is the editorial basis for the rash of city and local magazines that have popped up around the country in the past ten years.

Some of these magazines are first-rate—I am particularly partial to *Texas Monthly*—but generally they are to the traditional shelter magazines what *Playboy* is to *Hustler*: they have taken food and home furnishings and plant care and surrounded them up with just enough political and sociological reporting to give their readers an excuse to buy them. People who would not be caught dead subscribing to *House & Garden* subscribe to *New York* magazine. But whatever the quality, the serious articles in *New York* have nothing whatever to do with what that magazine is about. That magazine is about buying plants, and buying chairs, and buying pastrami sandwiches, and buying wine, and buying ice cream. It is, in short, about buying. And let's give credit where credit is due: with the possible exception of the Neiman-Marcus catalog, which is probably the granddaddy of this entire trend, no one does buying better than *New York* magazine.

In fact, all the objections the *Times* readers made to Claiborne's article can be applied to any one of the city and local magazines. How can you write about the perfect ice cream cone or the perfect diet cola or the perfect philodendron when millions of people have never seen a freezer, suffer from sugar deficiencies, and have no home to put potted plants in? How can you publish a magazine whose motto is essentially "Let them eat cheesecake"? Well, you can. And thousands of people will buy it. But don't make the mistake of giving the game away by going too far. Five extra pages on how to survive in a thirty-thousand-dollar living room, one extra price tag on a true nonessential, and your readers will write in to accuse you of terminal decadence. And when this happens, what will be truly shocking will not be the accusation—which will be dead on—but the fact that it took them so long to get the point.

Terminal decadence.

Exactly.

March, 1976

Russell Baker

I have come to my devotion to the columns of Russell
Baker later than most of the people I know, and I'm not
sure whether this is because I am slow to catch on, or
because Russell Baker is even better than he used to
be. The answer, I suspect, is a little of both. In the last
year, Baker has moved from Washington to New York,
and the column he writes for the *New York Times* and
its news service has shifted away from politics and
toward urban life in general. I was about to go on to say
something or other about that, but I realize that I have
already begun to be unfair to Baker. Which is one of the
problems of writing about him: as soon as you start to
describe what he does, you do him an injustice. Urban
life indeed. Baker did a column the other day that began
with Franco dying and going straight to the New York
Department of Motor Vehicles; it was brilliant, and there
is no way to distill or describe it. You had to be there.
And in any case, when I went to interview Baker and
told him that column was a perfect description of urban
life in New York, he assured me it was about urban life
in Russia.

Baker is, of course, usually referred to as a humor

columnist and usually lumped together with Art Buchwald, and that, too, is unfair. He is to Buchwald what
Saul Steinberg is to Peter Arno: he tends to humor that
is abstract, almost flaky, off the wall, cerebral, a bit sur-
realistic. He almost never writes a column that is a long
joke; because of this, and because he builds on mood and
nuance, a neat paragraph summary of a typical Baker
column doesn't work at all. So I thought I would just go
see him and let him talk, and the hell with anyone who
wants a decent description of his writing. I should probably tell you that Baker is fifty, a tall, skinny man who
looks a little like a hayseed. He is extremely low-key, terribly nice, and often seems on the verge of being embar-
rassed, particularly by praise of any sort.

Q: *How did anyone at the* Times *know you
would write a funny column?*

BAKER: *Nobody knew what the column was
going to be. I didn't, the* Times *didn't. I was
in the* Times *Washington bureau, and I had
a reputation for being a "writer" in quotation
marks—the quotation marks implied that
there were reporters and then there were writers. I did a lot of feature-type stuff. There was
no expectation that the column was supposed
to be funny. I'd outlined what was essentially
an idea for a casual essay column, the sort of
thing* The New Yorker *had done in the late forties in "The Talk of the Town." The style would
be casual, monosyllabic, simple sentences,
small ideas. I did know at the outset that I was
interested in the ironies of the public condition.
I was fascinated by irony. But what you project*

*on a piece of paper and what finally emerges
are two wildly different things. When I sat
down to write, what came out was what was in
me. The first column ever printed was a spoof,
a send-up of a Jack Kennedy press conference.
Very quickly I began doing basic satires, traditional forms like dialogues, fantasies, hoaxes,
parodies, burlesques.*

Q: *Was it difficult?*

BAKER: *At the start, yes. I didn't know what it
was going to be. Now it has a rigid identity,
and there are days when it writes itself. When
you start a column, you're in a very creative
state; you're building a personality in a piece
of writing. It's a strange kind of business.
After a while the column becomes a tyrant.
You've created a personality that is one aspect
of yourself, and it insists on your being true
to it every time you sit down to write. As time
passes and you change, you may become bored
with that old personality. The problem then is
how you escape the tyranny of it. In a way, it's
always a struggle between you and this tyrant
you've created that is a piece of yourself. In the
last year I've gone back to the essay form and
abandoned the satirical form.*

Q: *Is that because of moving to New York?*

BAKER: *I'm not so aware of that. The change is
the subject matter. It's so easy to do Washington.
You have nothing but subject matter. But what
happens in New York? Who, after all, knows*

*who Abe Beame is, or Hugh Carey? I've had to
work a lot harder, to take special subject matter
and make it mean something to people outside
New York.*

Q: *Someone once said something to the effect
that he'd never known a writer who had a
happy childhood.*
BAKER: *I've had an unhappy life, thank God. I
suspect all childhoods are unhappy. My father
died when I was five—it's my first memory—
and I was lugged off from Virginia to New
Jersey to live with a brother of my mother. He
was the only member of the family who was
employed, and he was making thirty-five dollars a week. He was married to a lovely Irish-
woman who ran the household. My mother
had a job where she sewed smocks for twelve
dollars a week, and I was raised in a matriar-
chy. I was imbued with the business that you've
got to get ahead. I always had a job, an awful
job, usually selling* Saturday Evening Posts. *I
was just terrible at it. They'd open the door and
I'd say, "Well, I guess you don't want to buy a*
Saturday Evening Post," *and they'd slam the
door in my face.*

Q: *How did you get into journalism?*
BAKER: *I'd always been a drifter. When I was
at Johns Hopkins, I was the only guy on the
campus who didn't know what he wanted to be.
Everyone wanted to be a doctor or a scientist or
an engineer. It was very depressing. In a vague*

*way I wanted to be Ernest Hemingway—that
was in the days when he was still read. There
was a guy on the faculty who lectured on T. S.
Eliot and also wrote for the* Sun, *and he told
me about this job. I went to see the managing
editor, and he offered me a job, and I thought,
It's a good way to kill time until I get around
to writing a novel someone can publish. It was
1947 and I did police reporting at night. I
never went to the office, never wrote anything.
I drifted from police station to police station,
hung around hospitals listening to people die,
and phoned in police-blotter stuff. I did that
for two years. I was in love at the time; I was
leading this strange upside-down existence,
hanging out with raffish characters all night
and sleeping till one or two in the afternoon. I
kind of liked it. I was getting an education. But
after a year, I decided to go ahead and write a
novel. I spent a summer and wrote a ninety-
thousand-word novel in three months. You
know Capote's famous comment on Kerouac—
"That's not writing, it's typing." That's what the
novel was. I was a self-taught typist, and I was
combining the typing exercises with the writing
of a novel. It was very valuable to me later. I'm
a very fast typist.*

Q:　*And what happened to the novel?*
BAKER:　*Shipped it around a few places and
then I put it in the attic. It was about what it
was like to be twenty-three years old. I discovered then that the world I was living in was so*

*much more interesting than the world I was
capable of conceiving. I was hooked on journalism. That was the end of it. I never went back
to writing fiction.*

Q: *How did you get to the* Times?

BAKER: *The* Sun *sent me to London as its correspondent. I was twenty-seven, very young to
be in London, but very adventurous. Things
were very difficult in England then, and most
of the American reporters went to the PX for
food. I didn't. I lived like an Englishman off
the English economy, and I lost a lot of weight.
I was hungry all the time. I cut myself off from
the American community. Most of the reporters hung around the foreign office to get the
diplomatic poop. I felt the AP would provide
that. I went to Parliament and wrote about the
nature of British political debate. I wrote about
what Sunday afternoon was like, and British
eccentrics. I was really a kind of travel writer.
Everybody was writing about the British economy and taxes except me. So I began to attract
some attention. Scotty Reston was head of the*
Times *Washington bureau, and he wrote and
asked me to come work there. I said no. I was
happy—the* Sun *was about to bring me back to
be White House correspondent, and that was
my idea of paradise. I mean, what more was
there? I came back, and after two weeks I realized I had made the worst decision of my life.
I'd given up London for this pocket of tedium. I
was sitting in this awful lobby waiting for Jim*

*Hagerty to come out with a handout. At one
point I was vacationing in Denver—when you
covered Eisenhower you were always vacationing in Denver, writing stories on how many fish
he had caught that day, or what he'd said at
the first tee. Reston came through and offered
me the job again. So I came to the* Times *on the
condition I get off the White House. I went up
to the Hill for a while, and the following year I
was back at the White House. I got to Denver in
time to cover Eisenhower's first heart attack. I
handled the first Presidential bowel movement
in the history of the* New York Times.

Q: *I read somewhere that you eventually became
unhappy in the Washington bureau.*
BAKER: *I didn't have a period of unhappiness
where I was unhappy with the* Times. *I was
just at the end of my rope. It wasn't possible to
deal with Washington in a very sophisticated
way, and the* Times *was not a paper where
you could be very creative or innovative. For a
long time I was more than willing to trade all
that for the education. It was the best graduate school of political science in the world. If
you wanted to know what was going on in the
Senate, you went up there and Everett Dirksen
explained it to you. But I'd spent over seven
years doing it. I knew the personalities. I knew
what speeches they were going to make on any
issue. I became restless. It was really a matter
of discontent with myself—I knew the limita-
tions of the* Times. *Then the editor of the* Sun

offered me a column, a blank check, really,
any kind of column I wanted. I thought, Yeah,
that's what I want to do. It was a great out for
me. There was an intimation it would lead to a
bigger job at the Sun. *We shook hands on it. I*
told Reston I was leaving and he was appalled.
I was shocked that anybody cared. I went home
and that night Orvil Dryfoos, the publisher,
called and said, We're not going to let you leave
the Times, *and then they began making offers*
to me, and that's how the column began.

Q: *And why did you decide to move to New York?*
BAKER: *Basically it was because a pipe burst in*
my home in Washington on a Saturday morn-
ing. I was very depressed. I suddenly realized I
was going to have to put a lot more money into
this house, and I said, "Let's sell the son of a
bitch and get out of here."

April, 1976

My Cousin Arthur
Is Your Uncle Art

The other day, my sister Delia went up to the Bronx to buy a carpet from my cousin Arthur. I had last seen my cousin Arthur in 1963, when I went up to the Bronx to buy a carpet from my uncle Charlie, who is Cousin Arthur's father. Uncle Charlie and Cousin Arthur used to be in the carpet business together, but Cousin Arthur left the family business some years ago to go off on his own, largely because he did not get along with Cousin Norman, who was also in the family business and whom no one in the family gets along with except for Uncle Charlie, who gets along with everyone. Anyway, when my sister Delia came back from the Bronx, having bought a very nice carpet at a very good price, she called up.

"Guess who Cousin Arthur is?" she said.

"I give up," I said.

"Cousin Arthur is Uncle Art," she said.

Actually, as I later found out, Cousin Arthur is Uncle Art only some of the time; the rest of the time a person named Jeremiah Morris is Uncle Art, and that is part of the problem. Still, Cousin Arthur is Uncle Art more than Jeremiah Morris is Uncle Art, and if you don't know who Uncle Art is, that's either because you haven't had to buy a discount carpet in New York lately, or because you're not in the carpet business. Uncle Art is to the carpet business what Frank Perdue is to the chicken business: in short, he has his own commercial.

"My name is Art Ephron," read the first of Cousin Arthur's Uncle Art advertisements, which ran, along with a large picture of Cousin Arthur himself, in the New York *Daily News* in 1972, "and I've been in the carpet business for, oh, longer than I care to remember. And every few weeks it seemed one of my relatives would say, 'Uncle Art, I was wondering, well, uh, maybe you could get us a break on some carpet. You know, something *nice.* Cheap.' So, one night, I was thinking. If I could do this for my relatives, why not for everybody?" The ad went on at some length, spelling out the special things about Cousin Arthur's Redi-Cut Carpets outlets (coffee, no pushy salesmen, a money-back guarantee, free rug cutting), and it ended with what has become the chain's slogan: "It's like having an uncle in the carpet business."

I was so stunned to discover that one of those people you see pitching their products on late-night television was a relative of mine that I promptly went up to the Bronx to see Cousin Arthur for myself. I found him on Webster Avenue, at one of his stores, and he turned out to be an extremely affable man. He was also, incidentally, the largest Ephron I have ever met (he is six feet tall and weighs two hundred ten pounds) and the only member of the family I know of who has a beard (although I haven't seen my cousin Erwin lately, and for all I know he may have one too). In any event, we went out to lunch and he told me about his advertising campaign.

"I started this company in 1971," Cousin Arthur began. "I'd been living in Detroit, working in the carpet business, and I felt that carpet retailing was ripe for a plain, pipe-rack approach, sort of like Robert Hall. I'd had a run with regular carpet retailing. I'd worked for Korvettes. . . ."

"Is it true," I asked, "that E. J. Korvettes stands for Eight Jewish Korean War Veterans?"

"It's a base canard," said Cousin Arthur. "The 'E' is for Eugene Ferkauf, the 'J' is for Joe Zwillenberg, and Korvette is the name of a subchaser in World War Two. To get back to what I was saying, I thought there was room for a no-frills approach to carpet retailing with remnants, so I called my friend Lenny, and he found a location in Mount Vernon, and we opened up. We hired a small ad agency in Scarsdale, and they came up with an ad that read: 'Redi-Cut Carpets, a nice place to buy.' We stayed with them for about a year. The business was growing, but we weren't getting results from the ads. I'm a great advertising critic, but I can't create an ad from scratch. So I called Cousin Mike and asked him what to do." Cousin Michael Ephron is media director of Scali, McCabe, Sloves, the agency that created the Frank Perdue ad; he and Cousin Arthur had recently become friends on account of a carpet Michael needed for his den. "Michael didn't want the account for his agency," Arthur went on. "Big agencies hate handling retail ads. The detail work is incredible." Michael suggested that Arthur and his partner Len Stanger go see a small creative agency called Kurtz & Symon. "They made a presentation," said Arthur, "and we got married."

Kurtz & Symon went to work and came up with the Uncle Art ads; in addition, the agency had Uncle buttons printed for all the salesmen at Redi-Cut. Even Cousin Arthur's wife, Hazel, got a button that said Uncle Hazel.

The ads worked. Pictures of Cousin Arthur as Uncle Art filled New York and Westchester County papers. Business got better. More branches were opened. And Kurtz & Symon began to press Cousin Arthur to take his advertising campaign to television. At the time, a man named Jerry Rosenberg, proprietor of J.G.E. Enterprises, a discount appliance store in Queens, had become a household word in New York because of his commercial, delivered in an unrelenting Brooklyn accent, that began: "So what's the story, Jerry?" It was logical for Cousin Arthur to go on television too. But it didn't work out that way.

"I got scared," said Cousin Arthur. "I'm no actor. I'm impatient. I'd gotten really annoyed with the amount of time it took just to do the print ads. They were doing these photo sessions of me where they roped off half the Mount Vernon store for two and a half hours just to take a picture. I was losing business. I was going crazy. And I didn't think I'd be any good on television. Lenny could have done it. Lenny's a real ham. Maybe the campaign should have been Uncle Len. But I didn't think I could do it. Suppose I blew it? So I said, Let's get a professional guy. They got an actor named Jeremiah Morris. Jerry's about five inches shorter than me, ten years older, he's bald and has no beard. Outside of that, he looks exactly like me."

Kurtz & Symon brought Morris and a toupee and a false beard up to the store to shoot the commercials. "I'm Uncle Art from Redi-Cut Carpets," Morris began, and Cousin Arthur became upset. He began to complain to both Don Kurtz and Jim Symon. "He kept trying to change the actor's performance," said Jim Symon, whom I spoke to about all this. "Most of his complaints had to do with the fact that he, Arthur, was more handsome than the actor, and that he, Arthur, was taller. Then we showed him the ad when it was done and he complained some more. He said the actor was playing it too much like Jerry of J.G.E. By that time there was so much money committed to the ad it had to be run. It was an academic discussion."

A few weeks later, in the fall of 1973, the commercials went on the air. Cousin Arthur would sit in front of his television set, switching from one non-network channel to the next, watching Jeremiah Morris come on as Uncle Art six times a night. "I would look and listen and I would sort of resent the fact that he really didn't look or sound like me. It really began to bother me." Every so often, he would make his wife, Uncle Hazel, sit through yet another viewing of the commercial. "After it was over, I'd ask her, 'Do I really sound like that? Do I really look like that?' She'd say no. But everyone else thought I did. I began getting calls from people I'd known for years. 'I saw you on TV last night,' they'd say. No one ever said to me, 'Hey, that wasn't you.' Tell me. You've seen the commercial. Does that look like me? Does that sound like me?"

In fact, it doesn't. But in any case, the commercials worked. Soon there were four of them on television, and soon Cousin Arthur and his partner Lenny owned eight carpet outlets. Cousin Arthur could hardly complain. Or could he?

"There's something I think I should tell you," he said, lowering his voice so that no one in the Red Coach Grill at the Cross County Shopping Center could hear. "I think I'm getting a divorce from Kurtz and Symon."

"What?" I said.

"I'm thinking of dropping them and going absolutely gigantically big into radio."

"Why?"

"I spend thirty percent of my budget on agency fees," said Cousin Arthur. "On radio you spend nothing. The radio station writes the ad for you. And my selling will be done by disk jockeys like Bob Grant, William B. Williams and Julius LaRosa."

"But what will happen to Uncle Art?" I asked.

"That's a problem," said Cousin Arthur. "We may be at the crossroads for Uncle Art."

"Have you talked to Cousin Michael about all of this?" I asked.

"No," said Cousin Arthur.

"I think you should," I said. "I think what all this is really about is that you wish you'd done the commercial yourself."

"I do wish I'd done it," said Cousin Arthur. "I can't get angry at anyone about it, though. I could have done it. It was my fault I didn't. But you want to know a thing I really regret? I had a chance to be head of a giant record company once. That I really regret. For five hundred dollars I could have owned twenty-five percent of Elektra Records. You know why I didn't?"

"Why?"

"My father talked me out of it."

That didn't surprise me. Thirty years ago Cousin Arthur's father, who you may recall is my uncle Charlie, told my parents it was a good thing they were selling their house on Turtle Bay in Manhattan, because the United Nations was being built and property values in the neighborhood were going to drop.

Cousin Arthur shook his head. "I should have done

the ad," he said. "It would have been a thrill to see myself on television. Let's be honest about it. Everyone wants to be recognized."

"But you *are* recognized," I said.

"Only by family and friends," said Cousin Arthur.

"That's not true," I said. "My sister Delia's cabdriver recognized you."

"What did he say?" said Cousin Arthur.

"He said, 'Isn't that guy on TV?'"

"That's what I mean," said Cousin Arthur. "That's not really being recognized."

May, 1976

Daniel Schorr

At the CBS Washington bureau, they are trying to keep straight faces over what has happened to Daniel Schorr, but it's not easy. Schorr is not a popular man, and there are a lot of people who are thrilled that he has been caught committing the journalistic sins of coyness, egomania and self-service. These sins are, of course, common to all journalists, which is no excuse for getting caught at them. Nonetheless, his colleagues might have gritted their teeth and supported Schorr but for one thing: he panicked and attempted to shift the blame for what he had done, tried to implicate one of his co-workers in the deed, and that gave everyone the excuse they needed to abandon him entirely.

The issue of character probably should not intrude on a First Amendment case, but when it comes to Dan Schorr it's difficult to leave it out. Schorr insists that his problem ought to be shared by the journalistic community, that we must all hang together or we will most assuredly hang separately. As he put it recently: "It serves CBS, and it serves me, and it serves you—because whatever happens to me will someday happen to you—that we preserve a united front now. I really feel a little bit like the alliance in World War Two, where De Gaulle and Stalin and Roosevelt and Churchill sit down and say, You know, we're going to have some problems, but let's lick the Nazis first. . . ." This is an extremely peculiar metaphor, but the part that interests me is not the equation of Nazis with the House of Representatives but the phrase "whatever happens to me will someday happen to you." It is quite probable that what happened to Dan Schorr happened to him precisely because he was Dan Schorr. There are elements of the story, in fact, that are reminiscent of *Appointment in Samarra*, or any novel the theme of which is that a man's character is his fate (or, put another way, that the chickens always come home to roost). The plot is a simple one: a reporter whose obsession with scoops occasionally leads him to make mistakes develops an obsession about a secret document and makes several terrible blunders that lead to his downfall. What happened to Dan Schorr is a real tragedy, but only because he did so much of it himself.

To recapitulate: Schorr, fifty-nine, a CBS reporter since 1953, managed to make a Xerox of the Pike Committee report on the CIA a few days before it was scheduled to be released. He broadcast several stories based on it. Then, a few days later, on January 29, the House of Representatives voted not to release the report. Schorr discovered he was the sole possessor of it, and set about getting it published, preferably in a paperback edition for which he would write an introduction. He asked his boss, CBS News head Richard Salant, whether any of CBS's publishing subsidiaries were interested and sent Salant a Xerox of the report. After a few days, Schorr realized that CBS was dragging its feet, so he contacted the Reporters Committee for Freedom of the Press.

The committee put him in touch with its lawyer, Peter Tufo, who was also a board member of New York Magazine Company, which owns *The Village Voice*. Tufo and Schorr's business agent, Dick Leibner, struck out at two paperback houses—neither of CBS's publishing subsidiaries was contacted by them or Salant—and Tufo then made a deal with *New York* editor Clay Felker to publish the report. Felker agreed to make a voluntary contribution to the Reporters Committee, which he subsequently failed to do. In any case, the Reporters Committee had reversed ground and said it would not accept payment.

Schorr, meanwhile, had lost control. The report was about to be published in *The Village Voice*, which had recently printed an uncomplimentary article about Schorr. For that reason, and to protect his source and himself, Schorr decided to abandon the idea of doing an introduction. "Once you start down a certain line," Schorr said later, "the steps by which one thing leads to another come very swiftly, and suddenly you're totally wrapped up in it. You want *your* copy published and not somebody else's. You find yourself saying, 'By God, I don't care if this appears in *Pravda* as long as it appears.' In the end you're amazed at how far you've come from what you originally wanted to do."

But what did Schorr originally want to do? These days, he says that his sole concern was getting the report out in public. "I had to consider whether I was going to cast the final decisive vote to suppress that report. . . . I would have been the one who prevented the American people from seeing a report that had been paid for with four hundred fifty thousand of their tax dollars." But that is only part of the story: Schorr was also concerned with getting the credit for his scoop. And he got his wish.

On Wednesday, February 11, the report appeared in *The Village Voice*, with an introduction by *New York* writer Aaron Latham. On Thursday, February 12, Laurence Stern of the *Washington Post* published an article linking the report to Schorr. The *New York Times* denounced Schorr in an editorial, the House Committee on Ethics announced it would investigate him, and CBS suspended Schorr from his reporting duties.

The story so far is an exercise in bad judgment and bad form—neither of which ought to have cost Schorr the support of his colleagues. But it gets worse.

On January 29, the night the House voted to suppress the report, Schorr was at a reception at the Israeli embassy, where he saw his friend Harry Rosenfeld, the *Washington Post* national editor. Rosenfeld, whose paper had not been able to obtain access to the report, good-naturedly approached Schorr, grabbed him by the lapels and said, "I want that report." A conversation ensued. Schorr volunteered to write a series of articles for the *Post* based on the report. Rosenfeld said he was not interested, that he wanted his own reporters to see it. Schorr said he wanted the *Post* to print the entire text. Rosenfeld said he could make no such guarantee. Schorr said he could not do anything without consulting CBS. "Of course," said Rosenfeld. "The question is, are you through with it?" If Schorr and CBS were, said Rosenfeld, he would be glad to pay the cost of Xeroxing.

The next morning, Schorr saw *Washington Post* reporter Walter Pincus and told him that Rosenfeld had offered him money for the Pike report. Pincus reported the conversation to Rosenfeld, who had already talked with two other *Post* editors, who thought any sort of arrangement with Schorr was a bad idea. He called

Schorr and withdrew the request for the report; he also told Schorr he was outraged at what Schorr had told Pincus. "Schorr is a fucking liar," Rosenfeld said later. "We don't pay for news." For his part, Schorr claims he misunderstood Rosenfeld. "Somehow money was mentioned," he says. "Harry says he was only talking about the cost of Xeroxing the report. I don't know what that is supposed to mean. I had a Xerox machine and he has a Xerox machine."

The day *The Village Voice* appeared, Laurence Stern of the *Post* called Schorr and asked if he was the source of the report. Schorr was unprepared for the call. On the record, he denied that he had any connection with the *Voice*. Off the record, he conceded that he did have a copy of the report and had tried to get it published through the Reporters Committee, but he continued to deny responsibility for the *Voice* leak. "The last thought I would have would be Clay Felker," he said. Stern had independent confirmation that Schorr had provided the report to the *Voice* and went with his story. A few days later, though, when he was going through his notes of his telephone conversation with Schorr, he noticed a remark of Schorr's he had not paid much attention to at the time: "I thought I had the only copy," Schorr had told Stern, "but someone must have stolen it from under me."

The "someone" Daniel Schorr was trying to implicate at that shabby point was Lesley Stahl, a CBS reporter who is one of several CBS employees (along with Eric Sevareid, Phil Jones and Dan Rather) who do not get along with Schorr. The morning *The Village Voice* appeared, Schorr took it into the office of Washington bureau chief Sandy Socolow. This is Schorr's version of the story:

"*The Village Voice* came in on Wednesday. So I go into Sandy Socolow's office with it. I'm still in this funny in-between stage. How do I tell CBS about my partners? How do I tell the *Washington Post* about my involvement? So here you have a day when CBS does not know it's me who's done this, and there is the Aaron Latham by-line. You have to understand that Aaron Latham is a boyfriend of Lesley Stahl's; he's a familiar figure around the office. Sandy looks at the by-line and says, 'Are you thinking what I'm thinking?' I shrugged. I did not say to him, 'You're off on a wrong tangent.' I did not at this point disabuse him. Then I heard Sandy asking one of the producers if he had been in the office when the thing was Xeroxed. I could see him formulating a theory that Lesley or Aaron had gotten hold of it in that way. None of this was said explicitly. The point is that there were a couple of hours when I did not dispel the suspicion. I couldn't have without saying it was me." Schorr paused.

"I think I went further," he said. "I had lunch with a junior Cronkite producer that day. 'What do you think of this report?' I said. I kind of led him to think that Lesley had something to do with it. I realized later in the afternoon that I was playing games for no reason at all. I went to Sandy and said, 'Before you start any investigation of the Xeroxing, I know Lesley had nothing to do with it.' I don't want to pretend I did anything particularly smart or wise. But if all this is blown up into a theory that I planned to blame Lesley or Aaron, it's just not true."

Sandy Socolow says that Schorr's version is "a fucking rearrangement of what happened of the worst sort. It is just an absolute rewrite of history. He came into my office that morning with *The Village Voice*. I had no reason to believe he was the source of the *Voice* story—he had hated the piece the *Voice* ran about him, and he'd stopped speaking to the woman who wrote it. He came in, and these aren't specific quotes, but he said to me, Shouldn't we check where Lesley and/or Aaron were while the Xeroxing was going on. The next morning the *Washington Post* article appeared, and Dan came in again and said, You have no reason to suspect Lesley or Aaron, and you can disregard everything I said to you yesterday." Don Bowers, the producer Schorr lunched with, called Lesley Stahl a few days later and told her that Schorr had flatly accused her of stealing the report from him. (Stahl consulted a lawyer about the possibility of a slander suit.)

There are a number of interesting peripheral issues here—the question of whether Schorr broke the ground rules in Xeroxing the report, the question of whether CBS or Schorr owned the report, the question of whether Peter Tufo informed Schorr of his conflict of interest—and I'm sorry I don't have the space to go into them. In any case, whether he had a right to or not, Schorr went ahead and bargained away a copy of the Pike report he had obtained as a CBS employee; that is the situation we're stuck with. I don't think CBS had the right to suspend him because he is the subject of an inquiry; they may have had the right to suspend him for not fully informing his employer that he intended to act as an agent for the report.

And so Dan Schorr is in what he calls "the full-time martyr business." He sees his lawyer, he speaks to college audiences, he picks up awards from the American Civil Liberties Union. And underneath it all, underneath this squalid episode, there is one thing that is crystal clear, and that is the legal question: whether the House of Representatives, having passed a resolution prohibiting publication of one of its reports, can then hold a citizen in contempt for causing that report to be published. The answer, for anyone who believes in the First Amendment, is that it cannot. It is impossible not to be angry with Dan Schorr for having made it so difficult for the rest of us to march in his parade.

June, 1976

Upstairs, Downstairs

My friend Kenny does not feel as bad about the death of Hazel as I do. My friend Ann has been upset about it for days. My friend Martha is actually glad Hazel is dead. I cried when Hazel died, but only for a few seconds, partly because I wasn't at all surprised. About three months ago, someone told me she was going to die, and since then I have watched every show expecting it to be her last. Once she stuck her head into a dumbwaiter to get some food for James, who had finally recovered enough from his war injuries to have an appetite, and I was certain the dumbwaiter was going to crash onto her head and kill her instantly. Another time, when she and Lord Bellamy went to fetch James from a hospital in France (and Hazel and Georgina had a fight over whether he should be moved), I was sure the ambulance would crash on the way back. Hazel lived on, though, show after show, until there came the thirteenth episode. As soon as they mentioned the plague, I knew that would be it. It was. The particular plague Hazel died of was the Spanish influenza, which, according to Alistair Cooke, was the last true pandemic. I was sorry that Alistair Cooke had so much more to say about the plague than he did about the death of Hazel, but perhaps he has become wary of commenting on the show itself after everyone (including me) took offense at some of the things he had to say about George Sand.

Of course, Hazel should never have married James Bellamy in the first place. James is a big baby. Hazel should have married Lord Bellamy, which was impossible since Lady Marjorie had just gone down on the *Titanic.* Or she should have run off with the upwardly mobile air ace, which was impossible since he was killed on the very next show after she met him, along with Rose's fiancé, Gregory. (I never laid eyes on Gregory, but Kenny tells me he was a very interesting man, a natural radical, who met Rose by sitting on her cake.) Hazel's finest moment was the show when she met the ace, and they went dancing, and she wore a dress with tiny, delicate beaded straps, and turned out to have the most beautiful back I have ever seen. But other than her back, and her fling with the ace, and her occasional success in telling Hudson off, and her premature death, Hazel left something to be desired. Not as far as Ann is concerned, but certainly as far as Martha is concerned. "Let's face it," said Martha. "Hazel was a pill." In fairness, we might all be pills if we had had to spend our lives sitting on a chesterfield couch pouring tea, but that's no excuse, I suppose. Hazel *was* a pill (though not nearly as terrible a pill as Abigail Adams and her entire family), and she really ought to have married an older man who wanted nothing more than to go to bed early. Still, James had no cause to treat her so badly. Kenny is the only person I know who has a kind word to say for James, and here it is: "Somewhere there must be something good about him that we'll find out about eventually." Actually,

James did have a couple of good weeks there, when he returned from the front to report the army was dropping like flies, but I am told by a reliable source that his behavior was derivative of Siegfried Sassoon, and in any case, he shortly thereafter reverted to type. The worst James ever treated Hazel—aside from when she was sick and dying of the plague and he was playing rummy with his father's new fiancée, the Scottish widow—was when she had her miscarriage, and he totally ignored her, and went off dancing with Cousin Georgina.

Which brings us to Cousin Georgina. Martha doesn't much like Georgina either. This puzzles me. I can understand not liking Hazel and liking Georgina, or not liking Georgina and liking Hazel, but not liking both of them? Georgina was a true ninny when she arrived in the Bellamy household, and she hung around with Daisy, who is the most unrelenting ninny in television history. (For example, when Rose found out that Gregory had left her twelve hundred pounds, Daisy said: "Some people have all the luck." I rest my case.) But Georgina has become a wonderful nurse, and I'm proud of her. Also, her face is even more beautiful than Hazel's back. As for the burning question preoccupying us all—will Georgina marry James now that Hazel is dead?—I say no. (Martha says yes.) Georgina sees through James. I know it. I see her marrying the one-armed officer she went off to Paris with, if only because she is the only person on the show saintly enough to marry a man with one arm. Ann, on the other hand, does not trust Georgina as far as she can spit. "I know she was a great nurse," says Ann, "but she reminds me of those bitchy women you went to college with who were great biology students. She has no heart." There is indeed some recent evidence pointing to Georgina's heartlessness: when Hazel died, she went off to a party. But the war was over, and who could blame her? I was far more shocked at the la-di-da way Lord Bellamy behaved; he got off an Alistair Cooke-like remark about the plague itself, and that was that. Only Rose was magnificent about it. Ann thinks the reason everyone (except Rose) behaved so unemotionally about Hazel's death was that she was a petit bourgeois and they had never accepted her. I disagree. I think it's possible that the same person who tipped me off about Hazel's death tipped off the Bellamy household, and they just weren't all that surprised when it finally happened.

Even Martha loves Rose. Rose reminds me, in some metaphysical way, of Loretta Haggers. She is so good, so honest, so pure, so straight and so plucky. Kenny worries that Rose is going to leave the show now that she has come into all this money, but I say she'll never leave: the actress who plays Rose created the show itself, so she'll never be got rid of. I sometimes wonder how they do get rid of people at that show. They sank Lady Marjorie, I read somewhere, because the actress playing her wanted to take a vacation in Europe. But what about Hazel? Did they know all along? Did they hire her in the beginning and say, "Look here, Hazel, we'll carry you through World War One, but then you're through"? Or did they hire her planning to use her straight through the Depression? Did she do something to antagonize them? Did she know she was going to die, and if so, when?

We all know that Mrs. Bridges and Hudson are going to get married at the end of the next batch of episodes, which have already been shown in England. The reason we all know this is that the information was mentioned in the obituary of the actress who played Mrs. Bridges, who died of the flu in real life in Essex a couple of weeks before Hazel died of the flu on television in America. Was this planned too? Did they say to her, "Well, Mrs. Bridges, we'll give you a nice fat part for the entire series and marry you off to the butler in the end, but shortly thereafter you'll have to die"? I wonder. I also wonder how I'm going to feel about Mrs. Bridges and Hudson getting married. There's something a little too neat about it. Besides, Mrs. Bridges is a much better person than Hudson, who has become a mealy-mouthed hypocrite as well as a staunch defender of the British class system. All this would probably be all right and deliciously in character except that it is beginning to look as if Hudson is going to personify, in microcosm, the entire rise of Fascism in Europe. Ann is more concerned on this point than I am.

As for Edward and Daisy, they talk a lot about leaving the Bellamy household, but it is Kenny's theory that they are beginning to sound more and more like the three sisters and Moscow. Which is a shame, because I wish they would leave.

Here are some things we all agree on:

We are all terribly worried that Rose will never find a man.

We all miss Lady Marjorie a lot more than the Bellamys do, and are extremely apprehensive about meeting the Scottish widow's children.

We all think the best show of the year was the one with the scene in the train station with the dying and wounded soldiers. The second-best show was the one in which Gregory and the ace died.

We would all like to know some of the technical details of the show—how the writers are picked, how much of the plot is planned ahead of time—but it is too dangerous to find out. Someone, in the course of giving out the information, might let slip a crucial turn of the plot. We would all rather die than know what is going to happen.

Mostly, we all wish *Upstairs, Downstairs* would last forever.

July, 1976

Porter Goes to the Convention

Porter checked into his hotel on Sunday night and went to Madison Square Garden to pick up his credentials. He wasn't sure what he was going to need them for, since his story had fallen through. Porter was a reporter for the *Tulark Morning Herald* of Tulark, Idaho, and his editor had sent him to the Democratic convention to cover the mayor of Tulark, J. Neal Dudley, who was a delegate. "Just follow him around," said the editor. Porter had had big plans. He would follow Dudley to the Empire State Building and the Statue of Liberty. He would follow him into a taxi and they would have a funny experience with a New York cabdriver. He would follow him to Eighth Avenue, where J. Neal Dudley would be mugged while Porter looked on helplessly, taking notes. He would follow him to dinner at Windows on the World, where with any luck Dudley would be thrown out for wearing a leisure suit.

Porter had begun by following Dudley to the Boise airport and onto the plane to New York. After a couple of drinks, he asked Dudley what he planned to do at the convention.

"Fuck my eyes out," said Dudley, "and if I catch you within twenty feet of my room I'll kill you."

"I'm supposed to follow you around," said Porter.

"Make it up," said J. Neal Dudley.

Dudley got into a cab at Kennedy airport and vanished. Porter got onto the bus and rode to his hotel. It occurred to him that if he could just find J. Neal Dudley fucking his eyes out, he could bring down the administration of Tulark, Idaho, such as it was.

On the other hand, Porter had read enough articles in journalism reviews to realize that he would have to find J. Neal Dudley in flagrante with a secretary who could not take shorthand and who had been flown into town on a ticket paid for with the proceeds from a secret sale of Tulark municipal bonds. Otherwise, his editor would refuse to print the story on the grounds that it was an invasion of J. Neal Dudley's privacy and a sure-fire way for the paper to lose the advertising from J. Neal Dudley's appliance dealership.

Porter decided to forget it. He would make the story up. He could always talk to enough delegates to put something together about what J. Neal Dudley would have done at the convention had he actually attended it.

So after getting his credentials, Porter set out to find a delegate. He went to the Statler Hilton lobby and spotted a large man wearing a ridiculous hat. Porter approached him.

"Porter of the *Tulark Morning Herald*," he said.

"Ken Franklin of *Newsday*," said the man in the hat. "Can I interview you?"

"I beg your pardon?" said Porter.

Franklin explained that he was the media reporter for *Newsday* and he just wanted to ask Porter the questions he'd been asking other reporters.

"Sure," said Porter. "Shoot."

"What are you planning to write about?" asked Franklin.

"I don't know," said Porter.

"That's what they all say," said Franklin. "There are twice as many media people here as delegates, and there's no story."

"There's no story?" said Porter.

"That's what they all say," said Franklin.

"What else do they all say?" said Porter.

"They all say that because there's no news story, there are no feature stories either."

"What about the hookers?" said Porter.

"All the hookers are taken," said Franklin. "The *New York Post* signed them all to exclusive contracts last week."

Porter bought himself a beer in the bar and looked around. He spotted a man wearing delegate's credentials and went over to him.

"Porter of the *Tulark Morning Herald*," he said.

"Suzanne Cox of the *Chicago Tribune*," said the woman sitting next to the delegate. "Get lost. This one's mine for the week."

"Could I ask *you* a question?" Porter said to Suzanne Cox.

"No, you can't," said a small boy next to Miss Cox.

"Who are you?" asked Porter.

"Brian Finley," said the boy. "I'm a reporter from *Children's Express*, and *I'm* covering *her*."

"Who's covering you?" asked Porter.

"Scotty Reston," said Brian Finley, "but he's gone to the men's room."

"I see," said Porter and went back to the bar.

"Jarvis of *Time* magazine," said a voice behind him. He turned around. Jarvis of *Time* magazine was very pretty. She was also a media reporter.

"Porter of the *Tulark Morning Herald*," Porter said. "I don't know what I'm writing about. There's no story. Because there's no news story, there are no feature stories either."

"What about the hookers?" said Jarvis.

"The hookers are taken," said Porter.

"Oh, God," said Jarvis. "I wonder if my writer knows that."

"Your writer?" said Porter, but Jarvis had rushed out of the bar.

Monday night Porter got a floor pass and watched Sally Quinn and Ben Bradlee being photographed. Then he joined a large crowd that was watching in disbelief as Evans and Novak had a conversation with each other. In the distance, Porter could hear Barbara Jordan speaking, but just barely. He wished he had stayed in his room and watched the convention on television. When the session ended, he bumped into Ken Franklin from *Newsday*.

"What are you writing about?" asked Franklin.

"I don't know," said Porter.

"Nobody's saying that today," said Franklin. "Today people have figured out what they're doing."

"Not me," said Porter.

Franklin took Porter to the *Rolling Stone* party that night. When they arrived, several hundred people on the street were pushing up against the door to the party, and several dozen police were trying to hold them back.

"Who's that with Seymour Hersh?" someone asked.

"Paul Newman," someone answered.

Porter managed to push his way up to the front door, but it was locked. Every so often, a man would appear at the door and point out someone in the crowd and the police would scoop up the someone and get him through the door. Porter squeezed in with Walter Cronkite's entourage, but once inside he found that the only topic of conversation was what was going on outside. A large group of people upstairs were watching a television monitor showing pictures of the scene on the street, and another large group of people were watching themselves on a public-access television channel.

"Porter of the *Tulark Morning Herald*!" a voice shouted.

Porter looked around. It was Jarvis of *Time* magazine.

"What are you doing?" she said.

"Leaving," he said. "Do you want to come?"

"Yes," said Jarvis.

Later, in Porter's hotel room, Jarvis began to undress. "I hope this is off the record," she said.

"Likewise," said Porter.

At that moment, the phone rang.

"Porter of the *Tulark Morning Herald*," said Porter.

"This is the New York City police," said a man on the phone. "We picked up a naked man dancing on Thirty-sixth Street. He says he's the mayor of Tulark, Idaho. Your name was in his pocket."

"Is he with his secretary?" asked Porter.

"Yes," said the policeman.

"Was she flown here on city money?" asked Porter.

"Yes," said the policeman.

"Can she take shorthand?"

"No," said the policeman.

"I'll be right there," said Porter. He put down the phone and started to dress. "I'm sorry, Jarvis," he said. "I have to go out to become a media star."

"That's all right," said Jarvis. "I can wait."

October, 1976

Gentlemen's Agreement

Esquire *refused to run this column. It was printed in* [MORE], *the journalism review.*

In November, 1975, *Esquire* magazine published an article by a young writer named Bo Burlingham. It was called "The Other Tricky Dick," and it was a long reporting piece, ten thousand words or so, on Richard Goodwin, author, speechwriter to Presidents, and then-fiancé of Lyndon Johnson's biographer Doris Kearns. I was the editor on the piece. Burlingham portrayed Goodwin as an ambitious, crafty manipulator, a brilliant man who loved to outsmart his friends and associates to further his career. The article was carefully reported, the facts in it checked by the magazine's research department, and *Esquire*'s lawyer and managing editor grilled Burlingham on his sources for the article. All of us on the editorial side of the magazine believe that Burlingham's article was solid. Which does not explain how it came to pass that a few weeks ago, Esquire, Inc., decided to pay Goodwin $12,500 and to print the apologetic column about the article which appears in the November issue.

Magazines settle libel suits out of court all the time, of

course. Not all magazines—*The New Yorker* has a strict policy against it; but many other magazines believe that it is cheaper to settle than to pay the high costs of litigation. At *Playboy*, I'm told, they say that they have never lost a libel case; the reason is that the magazine settles before it gets to court. All of this is a fairly well-kept secret in the magazine business; in fact, one of the arguments put to me against my writing this column was that if it becomes known that *Esquire* settles out of court, every joker whose name is mentioned in the magazine might end up suing. I rather doubt that will happen—but in any case, my concern is not with future nuisance suits, merely with this one.

The trouble with Goodwin began in August, 1975, before Burlingham's article even appeared in the magazine. Doris Kearns, who is now Goodwin's wife, came to New York to see me and Don Erickson, editor of *Esquire*. She asked us to kill the article. She said that Goodwin had become so nervous about what it might contain that he had taken to his bed on Cape Cod and had been there for two weeks. At that point, the article was on the presses and could not have been killed if Richard Goodwin dropped dead. We told her this. Then, a few days before publication, a telegram arrived—I can't remember whether it was from Goodwin or from a friend of Goodwin—putting the magazine on some sort of legal notice. A rumor came floating through that Goodwin had hired President Nixon's former lawyer James St. Clair and was planning to sue *Esquire* for libel. Then nothing for a while.

In the early months of 1976—I'm sorry to be so fuzzy about dates, but I didn't know what was going on—a man named Arnold Hyatt telephoned the president of

Esquire, Inc., A. L. Blinder. Hyatt, a Boston shoe manufacturer and contributor to Democratic campaigns,
knew both Blinder and Goodwin, and he apparently
suggested the two men get together and work this thing
out like gentlemen. A couple of points about Abe Blinder.
The first is that a few years ago, he and the rest of the
magazine's management were slightly traumatized by
the result of a lawsuit William F. Buckley filed against
Esquire over an article by Gore Vidal. *Esquire*'s lawyers
wanted to fight the suit; they were certain it would be
dismissed in a summary judgment. But it wasn't, and
the ultimate cost to the company, including the even-
tual out-of-court settlement, was in the neighborhood
of $350,000. A second point is that Blinder takes pride
in the fact that he rarely interferes in the magazine's
editorial matters. When I interviewed him about the
Goodwin matter, he told me that he probably would not
allow this column to be printed in the magazine—but he
added that he had vetoed only one other article in his
thirty-three-year history at *Esquire*. "It was about Morris Lapidus, the architect of the Fontainebleau Hotel," he
said, "and it was very negative, very uncomplimentary.
The Tisch brothers are good friends of mine, and they
called and told me it would be bad for the hotel business
if we printed it."

After Hyatt's call, Blinder spoke to Goodwin and
arranged a lunch for himself, Goodwin, Kearns and
Arnold Gingrich, the editor in chief and founder of
Esquire. Goodwin arrived at the lunch with a set of
papers containing a legal complaint and an itemization
of grievances against the article. Blinder told Goodwin he
had three alternatives: he could write a letter to the editor, he could sue, or he could forget it. Goodwin said that

a letter to the editor would simply be his word against Burlingham's. But he indicated that he would be willing to work something out short of a lawsuit. At this point, Arnold Gingrich made a suggestion. He wrote a monthly column in which he often commented on articles in the magazine, and he might be able to write something that would reflect Goodwin's version of events. A token payment of one thousand dollars was mentioned, and everyone went home. A few weeks later, Goodwin met with Gingrich to draft the column. The next day, Gingrich was hospitalized with lung cancer; he died in July.

While Gingrich was ill, the column that appears in this issue was written by Don Erickson, now editor in chief of the magazine. In it, Gingrich relates that after reading Burlingham's article, which portrayed Goodwin as a Sammy Glick, he was surprised to meet Goodwin and find no trace at all of the ruthlessness Burlingham alluded to. Burlingham's portrait, said Gingrich, "is sufficiently at odds with the man himself that an appraisal is in order. . . . The piece made him out to be a guy who didn't pay his debts. But what we didn't say was that he had never had his credit withdrawn anywhere and that, with his holdings in Maine, he has assets several times his liabilities. And we made him out to be a man who goes around scaring people, including women, with guns. We didn't report that his gun hobby has never gone further than shooting at small birds and clay pigeons. He never owned a handgun, he told me. The one we reported on turned out to be a toy belonging to his son, he said. We implied that he had a streak of kleptomania and produced an incident that didn't prove it."

As it continues, the column is extremely clever. It is framed as one man's opinion, not as a formal apology, so there was no need for the magazine to show it to the author or editor involved. It is full of "he said" and "he told me," so that nothing is actually denied; still, the impression is that there was somehow faulty, incomplete or inaccurate reporting. Gingrich claims to be speaking as an editor in disagreement with the other editors of the magazine, but this is not really accurate. Gingrich was not just the founder of the magazine but its guiding spirit, and a reappraisal from him is considerably more loaded than a simple difference of opinion among equals.

But there's more to the story. Erickson's draft was sent to Goodwin for approval. Then, in June, *Esquire* received a letter from James St. Clair, who turned out to be Goodwin's lawyer after all, demanding sixteen thousand dollars for Goodwin to pay the legal fees entailed in reaching the settlement. This came as a surprise to the management. Blinder was under the impression that the token payment of one thousand dollars was agreed upon; he also believed that this was to have been a transaction among gentlemen, not lawyers. *Esquire*'s house counsel, Ron Diana, replied to St. Clair on July 7. He said the magazine was completely unwilling to pay such a high fee, particularly because it continued to believe in the accuracy of Burlingham's article; Diana instead offered five thousand dollars. Arnold Hyatt, the shoe man, then resurfaced. He called Blinder to say that Goodwin was shocked at the belligerent tone of Diana's letter; Goodwin, all injured innocence, could not understand how things had gotten so unpleasant. Blinder was apparently persuaded by the call, and the $12,500 fee was arrived at. Blinder then sent Hyatt a case of champagne.

Out-of-court settlements are extremely complicated,

or so I have found from talking to lawyers in the past couple of weeks. They're reached as a result of a combination of practical and ethical considerations. Generally speaking, though, if a magazine is willing to settle, the rule is this: if the magazine believes its article was right, it may settle for practical considerations and pay a token amount to avoid court costs. If the magazine is wrong, it may settle not only by paying off but also by printing a retraction, correction or apology. What is extremely rare—so rare that none of the lawyers I interviewed could recall a similar case—is for a magazine that believes it is right to pay off *and* print a retraction of sorts.

I can't quarrel with the financial settlement Goodwin got. I don't like it, but it's a business decision, I suppose. But Goodwin got the money *and* the apology. This is a tribute to him: he is as crafty and manipulative and brilliant as Bo Burlingham said he was. But it's a bad moment for this magazine. Abe Blinder told me that he had no problem with the settlement because: "There is no principle involved." I would like to state the principle involved. It's very simple. A magazine has an obligation to its writers and readers to stand by what it prints.

In any case, the Goodwin business is over. Bo Burlingham got $1,250 for his article and Dick Goodwin got $12,500 and an apology. There are all sorts of lessons to be drawn here, but the only one that seems to me at all worth mentioning is that I will henceforth try, when assigning articles on controversial subjects, to find writers who know the Tisch brothers.

In our conversation, Abe Blinder said that another reason he would probably not allow this column to run in *Esquire* was that Arnold Gingrich is dead and cannot defend himself. I am deeply sorry that Arnold is dead, for many reasons. For one thing, he was a man who could change his mind, and I like to think that by now he might have come around to Burlingham's way of seeing Dick Goodwin. For another, I think he meant it when he said what he did at the end of his monologue on Goodwin: "I've always said that this is a magazine of infinite surprises where people can say what they damn please, even to the extent of the editors disagreeing among themselves." If he were alive, I think that on those grounds he would have allowed me to print this column in the magazine: he would also have admitted that I outfoxed him just a little bit on that one small point.

One last thing. I speak only for myself, but I would like to apologize to Bo Burlingham.

November, 1976

Gourmet *Magazine*

I'm not sure you can make a generalization on this basis, which is the basis of twice, but here goes: whenever I get married, I start buying *Gourmet* magazine. I think of it as my own personal bride's disease. The first time I started buying it was in 1967, when everyone my age in New York City spent hours talking about things like where to buy the best pistachio nuts. Someone recently told me that his marriage broke up during that period on account of veal Orloff, and I knew exactly what he meant. Hostesses were always making dinners that made you feel guilty, meals that took days to prepare and contained endless numbers of courses requiring endless numbers of plates resulting in an endless series of guests rising to help clear. Every time the conversation veered away from the food, the hostess looked hurt.

I got very involved in this stuff. Once I served a six-course Chinese dinner to twelve people, none of whom I still speak to, although not because of the dinner. I also specialized in little Greek appetizers that involved a great deal of playing with rice, and I once produced something known as the Brazilian national dish. Then, one night at a dinner party, a man I know looked up from his chocolate mousse and said, "Is this Julia's?" and I knew it was time to get off.

I can date that moment almost precisely—it was in December, 1972—because that's when I stopped buying *Gourmet* the first time around. And I can date that last *Gourmet* precisely because I have never thrown out a copy of the magazine. At the end of each month, I place it on the top of the kitchen bookshelf, and there it lies, undisturbed, forever. I have never once looked at a copy of *Gourmet* after its month was up. But I keep them because you never know when you might need to. One of the tricky things about the recipes in *Gourmet* is that they often refer back to recipes in previous copies of the magazine: for example, once a year, usually in January, *Gourmet* prints the recipe for pâte brisée, and if you throw out your January issue, you're sunk for the year. All the tart recipes thereafter call for "one recipe pâte brisée (January, 1976)" and that's that. The same thing holds for chicken stock. I realize that I have begun to sound as if I actually use the recipes in *Gourmet*, so I must stop here and correct that impression. I don't. I also realize that I have begun to sound as if I actually read *Gourmet*, and I'd better correct that impression too. I don't actually read it. I sort of look at it in a fairly ritualistic manner.

The first thing I turn to in *Gourmet* is the centerfold. The centerfold of the magazine contains the *Gourmet* menu of the month, followed by four color pages of pictures, followed by the recipes. In December the menu is usually for Christmas dinner, in November for Thanksgiving, in July for the Fourth, and in April—when I bought my first *Gourmet* in four years owing to my marriage that month to a man with a Cuisinart Food

Processor—for Easter. The rest of the year there are fall luncheons and spring breakfasts, and so forth. But the point is not the menus but the pictures. The first picture each month is of the table of the month, and it is laid with the china and crystal and silver of the month. That most of the manufacturers of this china and crystal and silver advertise in *Gourmet* should not concern us now; that comes later in the ritual. The table and all the things on it look remarkably similar every issue: very formal, slightly stuffy, and extremely elegant in a cut-glass, old-moneyed way. The three pages of pictures that follow are of the food, which looks just as stuffy and formal and elegant as the table itself. It would never occur to anyone at *Gourmet* to take the kind of sleek, witty food photographs I associate with the *Life* "Great Dinners" series, or the crammed, decadent pictures the women's magazines specialize in. *Gourmet* gives you a full-page color picture of an incredibly serious rack of lamb persillé sitting on a somber Blue Canton platter by Mottahedeh Historic Charleston Reproductions sitting on a stiff eighteenth-century English mahogany table from Charles Deacon & Son—and it's no wonder I never cook anything from this magazine: the pictures are so reverent I almost feel I ought to pray to them.

After the centerfold I always turn to a section called "Sugar and Spice." This is the letters-to-the-editor department, and by all rights it should be called just plain "Sugar." I have never seen a letter in *Gourmet* that was remotely spicy, much less moderately critical. "I have culled so many fine recipes from your magazine that I feel it's time to do the sharing. . . ." "My husband and I have had many pleasant meals from recipes in *Gourmet* and we hope your readers will enjoy the following. . . ." Mrs. S. C. Rooney of Vancouver, B.C., writes to say that she and her husband leaf through *Gourmet* before every trip and would never have seen the Amalfi Drive but for the February, 1972, issue. "It is truly remarkable how you maintain such a high standard for every issue," she says. Almost every letter then goes on to present the writer's recipe—brownies Weinstein, piquant mushrooms Potthoff, golden marinade Wyeth, Parmesan puff Jupenlaz. "Sirs," writes Margy Newman of Beverly Hills, "recently I found myself with two ripe bananas, an upcoming weekend out of town, and an hour until dinnertime. With one eye on my food processor and the other on some prunes, I proceeded to invent Prune Banana Whip Newman." The recipe for one prune banana whip Newman (April, 1976) followed.

"You Asked For It" comes next. This is the section where readers write in for recipes from restaurants they have frequented and *Gourmet* provides them. I look at this section for two reasons: first, on the chance that someone has written in for the recipe for the tarte Tatin at Maxwell's Plum in New York, which I would like to know how to make, and second, for the puns. "Here is the scoop du jour," goes the introduction to peach ice cream Jordan Pond House. "We'd be berry happy," *Gourmet* writes in the course of delivering a recipe for blueberry blintzes. "Rather than waffling about, here is a recipe for chocolate waffles." "To satisfy your yen for tempura, here is Hibachi's shrimp tempura." I could go on, but I won't; I do want to mention, though, that the person who writes these also seems to write the headlines on the "Sugar and Spice" column—at least I think I detect the same fine hand in such headlines as "Curry Favor," "The Berry Best" and "Something Fishy."

I skip the travel pieces, many of which are written by ladies with three names. "If Provence did not exist, the poets would be forced to invent it, for it is a lyrical landscape and to know it is to be its loving captive for life." Like that. Then I skip the restaurant reviews. *Gourmet* never prints unfavorable restaurant reviews; in fact, one of its critics is so determined not to find fault anywhere that he recently blamed himself for a bad dish he was served at the Soho Charcuterie: "The potatoes that came with it (savoyarde?—hard to tell) were disappointingly nondescript and cold, but I seemed to be having bad luck with potatoes *wherever* I went." Then I skip the special features on eggplant and dill and the like, because I have to get on to the ads.

Gourmet carries advertisements for a wide array of upper-class consumer goods (Rolls-Royce, De Beers diamonds, Galliano, etc.); the thing is to compare these ads to the editorial content of the magazine. I start by checking out the *Gourmet* holiday of the month—in May, 1976, for example, it was Helsinki—and then I count the number of ads in the magazine for things Finnish. Then I like to check the restaurants reviewed in the front against the restaurant ads in the back. Then, of course, I compare the china, silver and crystal in the menu of the month against the china, silver and crystal ads. All this is quite satisfying and turns out about the way you might suspect.

After that, I am pretty much through looking at *Gourmet* magazine. And where has it gotten me, you may ask. I've been trying to figure that out myself. Last April, when I began my second round, I think I expected that this time I would get around to cooking something from it. Then May passed and I failed to make the rhubarb tart pictured in the centerfold and I gave up in the recipe department. At that point, it occurred to me that perhaps I bought *Gourmet* because I figured it was the closest I would ever get to being a gentile. But that's not it either. The real reason, I'm afraid, has simply to do with food and life, particularly married life. "Does everyone who gets married talk about furniture?" my friend Bud Trillin once asked. No. Only for a while. After that you talk about pistachio nuts.

December, 1976

The Detroit News

A few months ago, Seth Kantor went and laid an egg. Kantor works in Washington as an investigative reporter for the *Detroit News*, and in October, 1976, he broke a big one, a scoop on the Michigan Senate race, a front-page story that he clearly thinks ought to have earned him praise, if not prize nominations; instead, it got him nothing but criticism. Two columnists on his own paper attacked him. Mike Royko of the *Chicago Daily News* suggested that the *Detroit News* be awarded a large bronze laundry hamper for "the most initiative in poking around in somebody else's dirty underwear." Even Kantor's wife thought he went a little overboard.

Kantor's story said that Democrat Don Riegle, a Michigan congressman then running for the Senate, had had an affair in 1969 with a young woman who tape-recorded several of their conversations with his permission. (In 1969 Riegle was married to his first wife; he is now married to his second.) The *News* printed selected portions of the taped transcripts. Seth Kantor claims that the episode "tells you a lot about a man's judgment as well as his stability." A *News* editorial that endorsed Riegle's opponent Marvin Esch claimed that the story revealed Riegle's "arrogance, immaturity, cold-bloodedness and consuming political ambition."

The voters of Michigan apparently felt otherwise. The day Kantor's story appeared, Riegle had slipped to a bare 1 percent edge in the polls; on election day three weeks later he won the Senate seat by a 6 percent margin, and his staff considered sending the *News* a telegram reading: "Thanks. We couldn't have done it without you."

In the year or so since Fanne Foxe jumped into the Tidal Basin, journalists have begun to debate a number of extremely perplexing questions concerning the private lives of political figures. How much does the public have the right to know? How much does an editor have the right to determine what the public has a right to know? Where do you cross the line into invasion of privacy? Last summer, in the most successful book promotion stunt ever pulled off, Elizabeth Ray brought down Wayne Hays—but she was an editor's dream, the-mistress-on-the-payroll-who-can't-type. What about mistresses who *can* type? Editors justify printing just about anything about a politician on the grounds of character. Are those adequate grounds? These questions are worth thinking about, but they all assume that decisions on what to print will be made by responsible journalists. As it happens, that may not be the correct assumption in the case of the *Detroit News.*

The *News* is the largest afternoon newspaper in America (circulation 613,000), and until last year, when the *Detroit Free Press* overtook it, it was one of the few big-city afternoon papers that sold more copies than the local morning paper. The decline in *News* circulation is generally attributed to a number of factors: editorial lethargy, a rising number of white-collar workers within the city as well as overall population decline, and an increased antagonism toward the paper in Detroit's black community. On the editorial page, the *News* supports civil rights; but following the 1967 riots, publisher Peter Clark bricked up the first-floor windows of the *News* building; the paper also began printing a daily roundup of minor crimes, identifying suspects by race. In 1971, under a photograph, the *News* ran this caption: "Milton B. Allen, fifty-three, of Baltimore, isn't letting the fact that he's the city's first Negro state's attorney deter him from his crusade against narcotics, crime and corruption." Last year, Mike McCormick, news editor of the *News*, sent his staff a memo that leaked to Mayor Coleman Young, who attacked it in a widely reported speech. "We are aiming our product," McCormick wrote, "at the people who make more than $18,000 a year and are in the twenty-eight to forty group. Keep a lookout for and then play—well—the stories city desk develops and aims at this group. They should be obvious: they won't have a damn thing to do with Detroit and its internal problems."

Since 1959, the *News* has been run by Martin S. Hayden, a conservative who was one of the few editors of a major newspaper to oppose the printing of the Pentagon Papers. Hayden is the last of a breed—a power broker as well as an editor; one *News* political reporter recalls a recent Detroit mayoral campaign in which Hayden persuaded *both* candidates to run. In 1969, Hayden and publisher Clark were supporters of the missile program; during the ABM debate in Congress, Hayden sent a memo to the *News* Washington bureau that read: "The Washington staff should watch our editorial page, know our policy and help support it" by looking for "interpretative pieces and sidebars that help drive home the editorial point of view." Hayden insists he never asks reporters to slant the news, but several journalists who have been offered jobs in the Washington bureau got the impression that he expected them to investigate Democrats slightly more carefully than Republicans.

Now sixty-four, Hayden is retiring in June, and in the last year his power has become less than absolute. In 1975, a group of *News* employees met to discuss ways to improve the paper; they discovered that part of the problem was that the paper was perceived as stodgy and conservative. This group, which subsequently became known as the Kiddie Committee, set to work to hire younger reporters and columnists who were "with it" or "hip" or merely bearded. Meanwhile, publisher Clark offered a column to the *News*'s most outspoken critic, a local talk-show host named Lou Gordon. Gordon and the new columnists began to snipe regularly at each other and at the way the *News* handled various stories. Hayden was not amused. "It's too much of a discussion of the newspaper business," he says. "I've always disliked reporters who make themselves part of the story. It wasn't the way I was brought up." Hayden continues to keep a close eye on the Washington bureau, while the other editors deal directly with the local staff; as a result, the paper occasionally seems schizophrenic. During the Riegle-Esch campaign, for instance, two young local political reporters wrote a story saying that Republican Esch had lied about his role in passing a piece of legislation; twelve days later, John Peterson of the Washington bureau wrote a story saying that Esch's lie was only a *little* lie.

Seth Kantor reported directly to Martin Hayden on

all three stories he wrote about Don Riegle. The first, which ran in September, said that Riegle had signed his estranged wife's name to a tax rebate check in 1971 and then failed to give her half the refund. This was followed by a story quoting a Jack Anderson study that called Riegle one of the ten most unpopular members of Congress. Both stories were attacked by Riegle: the first was clearly a shabby episode in an acrimonious divorce, the second a harsh way of describing an unsurprising fact—congressmen who switch parties (as Riegle did, in 1973) are bound to be unpopular. Then Kantor got the tapes story.

In 1976, following the Elizabeth Ray revelations, a writer named Robin Moore (*The Green Berets*, *The Happy Hooker*) came to Washington to write a paperback about congressional sex. He was introduced to one Bette Jane Ackerman, who had had an affair with Riegle in 1969 while she was an unpaid staff worker in his office; during that period, she made some tapes of her conversations with him and supposedly replayed them like love letters while she was home sick. Eventually, the romance ended, Riegle divorced his wife and married another staff member. Last summer, Miss Ackerman accepted five hundred dollars from Robin Moore for her help as a go-between with other Washington women, and she played her tapes for New York *Daily News* reporter Joe Volz, who was then working with Moore. The tapes are predictably adolescent, childishly dirty and thoroughly egomaniacal. "I'll always love you," Riegle tells Miss Ackerman. "I—I—God, I feel such super love for you. By the way, the newsletter should start arriving."

Kantor got hold of a transcript of the tapes. He also obtained some love letters Riegle wrote to Miss Ackerman. And at some point, with editor Hayden's approval, he drew up and signed an agreement with Miss Ackerman's lawyer, David Taylor, pledging that he would not use her name in the stories. Kantor then flew to Detroit and went to confront Riegle with the story. Kantor's version will give you an idea of the tenor of the meeting:

"He agreed to meet me with a lawyer. They had a tape recorder. I had a tape recorder. I asked him about this relationship with this unpaid staff worker, taped with his knowledge, and I got a strong blast at both the *Detroit News* and at me. He said it was a well-known fact in Washington that I had been assigned by my editor to get him. I asked him who had told him that. He refused to tell me. He said I was absolutely the worst journalist in Washington. I said, Well, if I can't be the best, I'd just as soon be the worst. Well, he said, we all have to make a living."

Both Seth Kantor and Martin Hayden deny that anyone at the *News* was out to get Don Riegle—but somebody must have been; there's no other way to explain the decision to run the story Kantor turned in. Written in pulp-magazine style, it's loaded with phrases like "sex-tainted," "provocative brunet," "kiss-and-playback romance," "tell-tale tapes," "boudoir antics," and so forth. It refers to Miss Ackerman as "Dorothy"—allegedly her code name on the tapes—and fails to mention the fact that she was paid by Robin Moore. It also leaves out something that Kantor and Hayden knew—that Miss Ackerman had been what newspaper reporters call "close" with South Korean lobbyist Tongsun Park, as well as several other congressmen. The lead of the story says that Riegle once described the affair as "more important than 'a lousy subcommittee hearing.'" Later in the article, it becomes clear that Riegle used the expression in a casual, offhand way: "In one of their conversations, Riegle said he had to break away 'to go to a lousy subcommittee hearing now.'" Kantor added sanctimoniously: "It is in the subcommittees that Congress does its basic legislative work."

The article backfired totally, of course. *News* columnists Lou Gordon and Fred Girard wrote columns protesting it. The Associated Press and United Press International refused to run the story the day it broke. Says AP executive editor Louis Boccardi: "We try to make a decision like this based on whether there's some relevance to the individual's public responsibility, and we couldn't satisfy ourselves that was the case here." Within days, Riegle was the recipient of a wave of sympathy; he took the offensive, attacking the *News* and charging the paper with conspiring with his opponent to smear him.

Two weeks later, Saul Friedman of the *Detroit Free Press* wrote the other half of the story—he identified Miss Ackerman by name, linked her to Park, and revealed the financial details of her transaction with Moore. Which proved that in a healthy, competitive, two-newspaper town, the public is occasionally subjected to twice as much trash.

When I interviewed Martin Hayden in Detroit after the election, he did not believe he had made a mistake in running the Riegle story. "Seth said that all this information was coming out in Moore's book," said Hayden. "What if the book came out and people said, 'Did you know about this?'" Did Hayden ever consider not printing the transcript of the tapes? "Not after we had them. Without the tapes I don't know if there would have been any story. The question was of his judgment, not his sexual morality." Did he think the story was heavy-handed? "As a matter of fact, we went easy. Before we were through we became convinced this was not an isolated case." Did Hayden meet with Kantor or any *News* editors to discuss whether the story should be printed? "No. I handled it. Whatever blame there is is mine."

Should Hayden have printed the story? Probably not—the fact that it would eventually be printed in a quickie paperback is hardly justification. But if he decided to go ahead, he ought to have printed the whole story—including Miss Ackerman's name and details about her financial transactions concerning the tapes. In order to nail Riegle, the *News* gave up half the story.

Was the piece justified on the grounds that, finally, Riegle's character was revealed? No. Anyone who reads Riegle's book, *O Congress*, is perfectly able to perceive his "arrogance, immaturity, cold-bloodedness and consuming political ambition." Among other things.

Should Hayden have used the tapes? No. I can't make a rule about what constitutes an invasion of privacy, but I know one when I see one.

For some time after I came back from Detroit, I wondered what all this proved. Certainly it was clear that the voters of Michigan were more sophisticated than Seth Kantor and Martin S. Hayden, but that wasn't much of a point: so is my cat. Then, on November 7, Larry Flynt published a full-page advertisement in the *Washington Post* promising to pay $25,000 to any woman who would tell her story about sex with a congressman to *Hustler* magazine, and I looked for some way to tie that in, but I couldn't. I'm afraid, in fact, that I can't come up with a real point to any of this. Which may be the point. Nobody really cares. Newspaper editors have stumbled into a whole new area they're now allowed to publish stories about, and they're publishing ridiculous, irrelevant, hypocritical, ugly little articles that aren't dirty enough for *Hustler* or relevant enough for the papers that print them. "Maybe I'm on the wrong side of the pendulum swinging," Seth Kantor said to me. Maybe so.

February, 1977

The Ontario Bulletin

Two years ago, my husband bought a cooperative in the Ontario Apartments in Washington, D.C. The Ontario is an old building as Washington apartment buildings go, turn of the century, to be imprecise, and it has high ceilings, considerable woodwork, occasional marble and views of various capital sights. It also has the *Ontario Bulletin*. The *Ontario Bulletin* is a mimeographed news-letter that arrives every month or so in the mailbox. It is supplemented by numerous urgent memos and eleva-tor notices; many of these concern crime. The Ontario is located in what is charitably called a marginal neigh-borhood, and all of us who live there look for signs that it is on the verge of becoming less marginal. The fact that the local movie theater is switching from Spanish-language films to English-language films is considered a good sign. The current memo in the elevator is not: "During the past eight weeks, FIVE ONTARIO WOMEN HAVE HAD THEIR PURSES SNATCHED on the grounds or close by. Three of these events occurred this week." This memo, written by Sue Lindgren, chairperson, Security Committee, goes on to state: "Fortunately, none of the victims was seri-ously injured and no building keys were lost." We were all relieved to read this, though I suspect that Christine Turpin was primarily relieved to read the part about the keys. Mrs. Turpin was president of the Ontario during the crime wave of May, 1976, when she wrote a particularly fine example of what I think of as the Turpin School of memo writing:

"There have been *three purse snatchings* at the Ontario's front door in the last *two weeks* causing *lock changes twice* in the same period. All three incidents occurred in daylight hours; the three 'victims'—all women—were returning from grocery stores on Columbia Road. Two of the three had ignored repeated and publicized advice: DO NOT CARRY BUILDING KEYS IN YOUR POCKETBOOKS. They also ignored other personal safety precautions. Much as we sympathize with them over their frightening experience and over the loss of their personal belongings, the fact remains that had these 'victims' heeded the warnings, everyone at the Ontario would have been spared the inconvenience of a second lock/key change in two weeks as well as the expenditure of $250 for replacements."

As far as I can tell, several of the early warnings Mrs. Turpin refers to appeared in the *Ontario Bulletin*, but I can hardly blame the "victims" for not noticing them. Until recently, the *Ontario Bulletin* was written by Mildred A. Pappas, who appears to be as blithe and good-humored as Mrs. Turpin is the opposite. Here and there Mrs. Pappas tucks in a late-breaking crime story: "As we were going to press Security Chairman Sue Lindgren called to say that the cigarette machine in the basement had been vandalized and that both cigarettes and some change were missing. There were no known suspects at the time of the call." But Mrs. Pappas has a firm editorial philosophy which she expressed in the January, 1975,

Bulletin: "Both the trivial and the important are vital in portraying a clear picture of life in the Ontario—or anywhere else." And she has such a charming way with the trivial that her readers really ought to be forgiven their apparent tendency to skip over the important. In the February, 1975, *Bulletin*, for example, Mrs. Pappas does mention the business of not putting keys into pocketbooks, but that item pales next to the report on the revival of a limp African violet at the Houseplant Clinic, and it fades into insignificance next to the tantalizing mention of the removal of a hornets' nest from Elsie Carpenter's dining room window.

The information on the hornets' nest appeared in a regular feature of the *Bulletin* called "News and Notes," which includes birthdays, operations, recent houseguests and distinguished achievements of residents, as well as small bits of miscellaneous information like the announcement of the founding of the Ad Hoc Friends of the Pool Table Committee. Other regular sections of the publication are "The Travelers Return," a list of recent trips by residents; and "Committee Reports," summaries of the doings of the various building committees, of which there are nine. (This figure does not include the committee for the pool table, which has since disbanded, having successfully restored the table to use in the basement Green Room, which was recently and unaccountably painted yellow during the 1976 Painting Project.) The Ontario is surrounded by trees and gardens, so the *Bulletin* often mentions the planting of a new azalea or juniper tree, and it recently devoted an entire page to the final chapter of the eight-year controversy of the Great Red Oak, cut down on August 27, 1976, after the board of directors overruled what was known as the "wait and see" policy of the High Tree Subcommittee. Articles like these are often illustrated with simple drawings of birds and leaves. Occasionally, a photograph is used, but only on a major story like the flap over the water bill.

Ontario residents first learned of the water-bill flap in a July, 1975, *Bulletin* article headlined A SHOCKING BILL FOR A SHOCKING WASTE: "Chairman Chris Turpin has just announced that a staggering (and unbudgeted) $1,660.94 water bill for the last quarter has just been received, adding that the amount is more than *three* times the amount for the preceding quarter. A wrong billing? No. Uncommon usage for bad water, etc.? No. . . . The water company has advanced the opinion that only one malfunctioning toilet allowed to run continuously can be the cause. . . . The chairman stated that the board will decide on a method of payment of the unprecedented bill at its July meeting, the alternatives being (1) to find the resident or residents responsible and to bill accordingly, or (2) to specially assess *all* residents (owners and tenants alike) approximately $10 each to settle the bill."

For a month, we anxiously awaited word of what was up. Would ten dollars be added to the maintenance? Or would Chairman Turpin lead the Ad Hoc Committee on the Unprecedented Water Bill through each apartment in search of the hypothetical malfunctioning toilet? Finally, the July *Bulletin* appeared, with a terse report suggesting that the investigation was closing in: the prime suspect turned out to be not some irresponsible resident but the building's thirty-five-year-old water meter, which had just been removed for inspection by the water company. Meanwhile, Clarence K. Streit, a resident who was apparently unaware that human error was about to be ruled out, made a guest appearance in the *Bulletin* as the author of the Flask Water Dollar Saver. "It is quite practical," he wrote, "to save three pints of water every time one flushes a toilet. We have been doing it for a couple of years." According to Streit, if everyone in the building placed three pint flasks in his toilet tank, the Ontario could save 150,000 gallons of water a year—or, as he put it, *150,000* gallons of water a year. Mrs. Pappas urged residents who took up Streit's suggestion to submit their names for publication in order to encourage others. No one did; at least I assume no one did from the fact that Mrs. Pappas never again referred to the Flask Water Dollar Saver Plan. In the August *Bulletin*, however, the water meter was definitely fingered; it turned out to be not just out of order but thoroughly obsolete. A photograph of the new water meter appeared as an illustration.

If I have any complaint at all about the *Ontario Bulletin*, it is simply that its even-handed approach occasionally leaves something to be desired. Accurate reporting was simply not enough to convey the passions engendered by the paint selections of the 1976 Painting Project, nor was it adequate to describe the diabolical maneuverings of President Turpin and the Ontario board in the face of these passions. Residents who read the loving tribute in the August *Bulletin* to the Great Red Oak and the account of its mysterious incurable disease could hardly have been prepared for the stunning moment at the annual meeting in September when it was moved that no tree be cut down without a membership vote. Mrs. Pappas's low-key description of the restored iron grille entrance doors—"Unfortunately, the 'Ontario' inscription now faces the interior of the building since it could not be relocated from its solid iron casting to the outside"—does not quite do justice to the situation.

And I cannot imagine that *Bulletin* readers were in any position to judge the item in March, 1976, which announced Dr. Allan Angerio's resignation as House Maintenance Committee Chairman. "In protest of the Board's sanction of extensive remodeling in a neighboring apartment, Dr. Allan Angerio has resigned five months after his appointment. In a recently circulated letter to all residents Dr. Angerio states that during the extended period of renovation he was 'unable to use my apartment for either business or pleasure.' He also states that his letter has engendered a considerable response from the membership, many of whom have indicated interest in a proposed revision of the Bylaws and House Rules of the Corporation to preclude further extensive structural 'modernization' efforts in the Ontario." This is certainly a fair summary of what happened—but it is not enough. I know. I am married to the man who hired the contractor who accidentally drilled the hole into Dr. Angerio's bedroom wall.

In any case, mine are small complaints. The main function of a newspaper is to let its readers know what's going on; I doubt that there are many communities that are served as well by their local newspapers as this tiny community is by the *Ontario Bulletin*. And I would feel even more warmly toward the publication than I do but for the fear I have, each month, that I will pick it up to read: "The residents of 605 had a fight last Thursday night over the fact that one person in the apartment never closes her closet doors." I like neighborhoods, you see, but I worry about neighbors. Fortunately, my husband and I also have an apartment in New York. And

I was extremely pleased several weeks ago when we moved to new quarters there in an extremely unfriendly-looking brownstone on an extremely haughty block. In the course of the week's move, we carried some garbage out of the apartment and left it on the street for the garbage collectors. Ten minutes later—*ten minutes later*—a memo arrived from the 74th Street Block Association concerning the block rules on refuse. I'm not going to quote from it. All I want to say is that its author, Emma Preziosi, while not in the same league with Christine Turpin, definitely shows promise.

March, 1977

The Revitalization of Clay Filter:
Yet Another Passage

On the surface, Clay Filter would appear to have had everything he had ever wanted. (His name is fictitious.) The ginger-haired magazine editor might not have wanted the middle-age spread that occasionally caused his shirt buttons to pop off, but otherwise he had achieved his life's dream. He had *gained his authenticity.* He had spent most of his Deadline Decade dreaming of running his own magazine, and finally he had come to do so. He lived in a beautiful apartment with a double-height living room which, had it faced south, which it did not, would have reflected the city he had built a magazine to. He had spent ten years off and on with the same woman, in a relationship I would call an *Off-and-On Relationship*; he had served as her Mentor (see pp. 14, 27, 51–2, 54, 76–7, 85, 109, 128, 131–2, 189–90, 280, 293; see also Career Women and Mentors, pp. 128, 132–5, 225, 226, 227), and he had only two complaints about her: he worried she would write about him someday and disguise him as thinly as she disguised everyone else she wrote about; and he occasionally became irritated at her uncanny ability to predict every adult crisis that was to befall him and then say, "I told you so," as soon as it did. Sometimes she went even further by insisting he had had a crisis when he thought he had merely had a bad cabdriver, but when he accused her of a priori reasoning, she simply reminded him that he was a classic wunderkind (see pp. 189–98) and that all wunderkinder tend to deny they have mid-life crises. He dozed off as she rattled on about patterns of wunderkinder: "They were afraid to admit they were not all-knowing. Afraid to let anyone come too close. Afraid to stop filling their time with external challenges they could probably surmount, for fear of glimpsing that vast and treacherous interior which seems insurmountable. Afraid that the moment they let down their guard, someone might ridicule them, expose them, move in on their weaknesses and reduce them again to the powerlessness of a little boy. It is not their wives they are afraid of. It is themselves. That part of themselves I have called the Inner Custodian, which is derivative of parents and other figures from childhood." She paused. "Do you understand what I'm saying, darling?"

Clay Filter snapped awake and nodded comprehendingly. The truth, though, was that he could never figure out what she was talking about when she went on in this way. He knew it sold magazines, and books, and that someone must understand it, but he knew he didn't, and he wasn't sure what he could do about it if he did. He had pushed himself through the Trying Twenties and the Catch Thirties and the Switch Forties. He had fought the fight between his Merger Self and his Seeker Self, giving in to his Merger Self on only two or three occasions, if you counted living arrangements. He had survived the Seesaw Years and the Pulling Up Roots Years, and now here he was, and part of the problem was that he wasn't sure just where he was at. Years before, he had altered his birth date in *Who's Who*, and he now no longer knew for certain how old he was. Freud would call this *self-deception*, and Jung would call this *silliness*, and Erikson would call this *ridiculous vanity*, but I call it *The Refusal to Deal with the Age-Forty Crucible*. The catch was that he no longer knew whether he was at the tail end of the Switch Forties or on the verge of the Fractious Fifties, and while he didn't much care one way or the other about it, the woman he had been with for ten years in the *Off-and-On Relationship* cared deeply.

"The crisis will emerge . . . around fifty," she said. "And although its wallop will be greater, the jolt may be just what is needed to prod the resigned middle-ager toward seeking revitalization."

"I'm sick of all this talk about my crisis!" Clay Filter shouted. "I'm too old to have a crisis!"

"It's never too late to have a crisis," she said. "Anyway, darling, don't think of it as a crisis. Think of it as a *passage*. Does that help?"

"No, it doesn't help!" he shouted. "Crisis is a perfectly good word. Why coin another?"

At moments like this, she wondered whether he might not turn out to be an exception to all her theories. He had an explosive temper. Perhaps he would spend his crisis in little bursts, piggyback one mini-crisis atop another and avoid the big bang. Just the other night, unaccountably, he had blown up at her for using piggyback as a verb. Then, when she defended herself, he threatened to rip the italic bar from her typewriter. Outbursts like that were becoming more frequent. She realized it was more important than ever for her to be supportive in order to help him find his way up the developmental ladder.

"Each one of us has our own *step-style*," she said one day as he stared, preoccupied, at the rug, "the characteristic manner in which we attack the tasks of development and react to the efforts we make. Some of us take a series of cautious steps forward, then one or two back, then a long skip up to a higher level. There are those of us who thrive on setting up sink-or-swim situations. . . . Others, when face to face with each task, side step it for a time in a flurry of extraneous activity."

"Do you think I should buy *The Village Voice*?" he asked, looking up.

"This could be your long skip up to a higher level," she replied.

"I don't know anything about money," he said.

"On the other hand," she said, "this could be your flurry of extraneous activity."

"This isn't my flurry of extraneous activity," he said. "That comes later, when I recklessly fly off to the Bahamas."

"Then perhaps it's your sink-or-swim activity."

"I think I'll let Felix make the deal," said Clay Filter.

She made a note for a new syndrome. She would call it *You Can Turn Over the Closing to the Broker, But YOU Pay the Mortgage*. She would tell him about it at some point, but now he had fallen asleep.

Some months later, when he awoke, he discovered that Felix had got things backward. In the course of buying *The Village Voice* for Clay Filter's magazine, Felix had accidentally sold Filter's magazine to *The Village Voice*. This was an extremely confusing turn of

events. Confusing turns of events often precipitate crises. Just as often, they do not. It is possible that had
Clay Filter realized either of these points, he might
have been able to avert what was to happen. Instead,
he started a new magazine and began flying back and
forth across the country each week. He was spreading
himself too thin, except for the aforementioned part
of him that was simply spreading itself. One morning,
after he stepped off the Red Eye from Los Angeles, he
was forced to stand for two hours in the freezing cold
at Kennedy airport, and when he finally got a taxi,
the driver was surly and unpleasant and a reader of
Cue. This so infuriated Filter that he marched into a
board of directors meeting and demanded a raise, two
houses and a limousine. The board of directors, already
upset about the profit picture, turned Filter down in
an extremely acrimonious session and then went off to
plot ways to sell their stock.

"I think I'm having a crisis," he said to her that night.

"Don't be silly, darling," she replied. "You merely had
a bad cabdriver."

When the crisis finally began, he recklessly flew off to
the Bahamas. When he returned, he lost his temper and
alienated the principal stockholder, who decided to sell
out to an Australian. In the end, Clay Filter got one and
a half million dollars and the love and devotion of several
dozen employees who had previously been ambivalent
toward him. But he lost his magazine, and his magazine was his life. He had offers, and he had ideas, and he
would return, but there was a nagging part of himself—
the part of himself physiologists call the *Brain*—that
suspected that all of this could have been avoided. He
suggested this to her.

"Wrong, darling, wrong," she said. "All of it was necessary. And more than that, it was thrilling. It was so *predictable*. The wallop. The jolt. Just what is needed to prod the resigned middle-ager toward seeking revitalization." She smiled. "Oh, darling," she said. "I'm so happy for you."

April, 1977

Double-Crostics

It is one of the great surprises of my adult life that I am not particularly good at doing the Double-Crostic. When I was growing up, I thought that being able to do the Double-Crostic was an adult attribute, not unlike buying hard-cover books, and that eventually I would grow into it. My mother, who was indirectly responsible for this misapprehension, was a whiz at Double-Crostics and taught me how to do them. In those days, the Double-Crostic was available through three sources: every week in the *Saturday Review*, every other week in the *New York Times Magazine* and twice a year in a Simon and Schuster anthology containing fifty or so new puzzles. The first two puzzles in each anthology were geared to beginners—to idiots, to be more precise—and I could usually solve one of them in about a month, using an atlas, a dictionary, a thesaurus, a Bartlett's and an occasional tip from my mother, who would never have been caught dead using any source material at all. There are many things I will never forgive my mother for, but heading the list is the fact that she did the Double-Crostic in ink.

Back then, the Double-Crostic was called the Kingsley Double-Crostic after Elizabeth S. Kingsley, who invented the form and eventually passed the puzzle-making on to Doris Nash Wortman. I had a very clear idea of what Mesdames Kingsley and Wortman looked like: jolly fat gray-haired ladies with large bosoms and cameo brooches and voluminous silk dresses covered with little flowers. As it turns out, I was right. Mrs. Wortman was succeeded in 1967 by one Thomas H. Middleton, and until I began researching this column, I had always imagined that he was Mrs. Wortman's loyal disciple, a faithful fan who had spent years corresponding with her and sending in his own constructions to be printed in the fans section in Double-Crostic anthologies. Presumably he had been rewarded upon her death with the puzzles. As it turns out, I was wrong. He got the job by being Norman Cousins's brother-in-law.

I called up Thomas Middleton the other day to find out about his life. He told me that he lives in Brentwood, in Los Angeles, that he is an actor and can currently be seen in a Life Savers commercial, and that George C. Scott loves Double-Crostics. He said he constructs one hundred seventy-five puzzles a year himself and in addition writes a column on language for the *Saturday Review* in which he has twice tackled the subject of "hopefully." "My feeling is that 'hopefully' is here to stay," he said. In short, it wasn't much of a phone call, and I came away from it with the impression that Middleton regards the making of Double-Crostics as a job, not a passion. This made perfect sense—ever since he took them over, I have regarded the *solving* of Double-Crostics as a job, not a passion—but it hardly seemed fair. In any case, I got quite sentimental about Elizabeth Kingsley and Doris Nash Wortman, about whom I knew next to nothing, and set about learning a bit.

Elizabeth Seelman Kingsley was born in Brooklyn in about 1878 and grew up working scrambled-word puzzles in *St. Nicholas* magazine; after graduating from Wellesley in 1898, she became an English teacher until her marriage. During the national crossword-puzzle binge of the 1920s, she worked several crosswords and then remarked: "How futile! There is a certain fun in the thrill of the puzzle, to be sure, but what is the goal?" A few years later, at a Wellesley reunion, she became so disturbed at the undergraduates' enthusiasm for James Joyce and Gertrude Stein that she determined to do something about it. "Suddenly it dawned upon me," she said years later, "that a puzzle which stimulated the imagination and heightened an appreciation of fine literature by reviewing English and American poetry and prose masters would be a puzzle *with* a goal." Thus was born the first Double-Crostic, and in 1934 Mrs. Kingsley sold her first puzzle—and the rights to the name—to the *Saturday Review of Literature*.

It is not easy to describe a Double-Crostic, but basically it consists of a series of definitions to which one supplies answers. The letters of the answers are transferred into a diagram that eventually spells out a quotation from a work of literature. The initials of the correct answers spell out the author's name and the work from which the quote is taken, and if you have managed to follow this so far, you will no doubt have figured out that Mrs. Kingsley's puzzles relied heavily on the works of Shakespeare, Keats, Defoe and the like and utterly shunned Joyce, Stein and any other writer she thought of as less than a master.

Mrs. Kingsley, who was widowed, lived for many years in the Henry Hudson Hotel in Manhattan, where she worked out her puzzles using anagram blocks on a piece of felt. She earned about ten thousand dollars a year—not a great deal, even for a small-scale literary heroine, which in a way she was. She was often referred to as Queen Elizabeth, and various Double-Crostic fans fussed over her; Arthur Hays Sulzberger invited her to lunch at the *New York Times*, and Philip Hamburger profiled her in *The New Yorker.*

She told Hamburger that *h*'s were the bane of her existence, with *f*'s and *w*'s close behind; these letters were constantly left over and she was constantly forced to do something with them. "Powwow" was a favorite answer; "tow-row" set off a terrible fracas among her fans. Once, a reader wrote in to accuse her of an overwhelming affection for Vedic divinities. "Vedic divinities are not a spontaneous choice for definitions," Mrs. Kingsley replied. "They are a godsend after hours of juggling. If you were constructing a puzzle and had letters left over and they made a Vedic divinity, what would *you* do?" Mrs. Kingsley carried a notebook with her and was constantly jotting down words that might someday come in handy. She told Philip Hamburger: "Here's 'wow-wow.' A lovely thing! *Four w*'s. 'Hiwi hiwi.' What a word! Means a small marine fish in New Zealand. And 'chiffchaff'—just an English bird. All my people need do is look up 'chiffchaff' under 'willow wren.' Ah, yes! 'Dingdong.' *And* 'omoo,' a romance in the South Seas. Don't tell *me* people aren't better educated for knowing these things!"

In her later years, Mrs. Kingsley became a small-scale prima donna. According to Margaret Farrar, the grand old lady of the *New York Times* crossword puzzle, she talked of nothing but Double-Crostics. She dropped the names of her famous fans, who included Elmer Rice, Ogden Nash and Frank Sullivan. Helen Barrow, who designed the puzzle books for Simon and Schuster, saved several of Mrs. Kingsley's letters; in them she complains about her harried life: she was constructing some two hundred puzzles a year, and it wasn't getting any easier. Finally, in 1952, Queen Elizabeth retired—she died in 1957—and she was succeeded by Princess Doris.

Doris Nash Wortman, born in New Jersey in 1890, was a Smith graduate and past president of the National Puzzlers' League. She worshiped Mrs. Kingsley; she had been proofreading Double-Crostics for her since 1939, when she had submitted an extremely complicated construction—a valentine to her husband, Elbert—to a fans section. On the evidence, she appears to have been among the most good-natured women who ever lived. Her puzzles had a light-hearted quality Mrs. Kingsley would never have tolerated; she introduced modern writers and witty quotations and definitions. Her fans sections contained lovely tidbits about each of her correspondents; she was a gracious, chattering den mother to her troop. Her letters and book introductions are positively ebullient. "WOW! What an ad!!" she wrote Helen Barrow when the fiftieth Double-Crostic anthology was published. "Everyone thinks Series 50 *utter*, especially I!"

Mrs. Wortman lived in Jackson Heights, Queens, with Elbert, a sometime advertising man, and according to her daughter, DeNyse Pinkerton, she worked all the time. "She started at five a.m. and worked until eleven p.m.," said Mrs. Pinkerton. "It was ghastly. The worst part was my father. He had had one glorious failure after another. She really paid the rent, and he made her make him a three-course dinner every night." Mrs. Wortman earned about fifteen thousands dollars a year.

Doris Nash Wortman had only two problems. One was Elbert. The other was that she occasionally irritated her puzzlers by using made-up expressions in order to use up left-over letters. Once, for example, she printed a definition reading, "The corn is evidently higher than Hammerstein thought." The answer was "giraffe's eye." Also, Mrs. Wortman had an unfortunate tendency to let her politics seep into her puzzles. Laura Z. Hobson, the novelist and author of *Gentleman's Agreement*, was a Double-Crostic solver; one day, while having lunch with *Saturday Review* editor Norman Cousins, she brought up the subject of Mrs. Wortman's leanings.

As Mrs. Hobson recalls it: "I said, 'Say, Cuzz, doesn't anybody edit those things?' 'Why, L.H., what's wrong?' he said. I told him that that very week there was a clue that said, 'Describing some of the people in the South,' and the answer was 'blacks and tans.' He blanched. For the *Saturday Review* to talk about blacks and tans! I gave him other examples. One thing she frequently did was to have the definition indicate a noun though the answer was a participle. Once, for instance, she had used 'A gift for an institution,' and the answer was 'endowing' instead of 'endowment.' It was just sloppy. Cuzz was appalled and asked me to edit the puzzles, and I have done it ever since. Twice I asked her to kill puzzles completely. One of the quotes was anti-labor, and the other was a John Masefield poem on the death of President Kennedy. I don't think that's what you expect to come across in a puzzle. In my opinion she was nowhere near as good as Mrs. Kingsley."

After Mrs. Wortman's death, Elbert decided to carry on the puzzles—something even his wife had thought he was not equipped to do. He began lurking in the offices of the *Saturday Review* with sample puzzles. He claimed he had done all his wife's work. He threatened to sue. "It was somewhat sticky," says Norman Cousins. A few fans had submitted tryout puzzles; in addition, Cousins contacted his sister's husband and asked him to take a crack at it. Laura Hobson judged the entries, voted for Middleton, and that was that.

Mrs. Hobson thinks Tom Middleton does a bang-up job, and so does Margaret Farrar. I think he prints too many definitions that require looking up, too many arcane musical comedy references and too many quotes that are not as felicitous as he thinks. There is a glorious point in the working of a Double-Crostic when the puzzle falls together, you see what the quote is going to be about and you realize who the author is—and that moment is not so glorious when the quote is from *Phyllis Diller's Marriage Manual.*

I see that I am on the verge of blaming Thomas Middleton for my ineptitude at his puzzles, and I suppose that really isn't fair. I still like Double-Crostics. I sit with my dictionary and my atlas and eventually I solve them. In pencil. Erasing a lot. Still, I long for a giraffe's eye or two, and I remember the time Mrs. Wortman's definition said: "This really ought to be next to a church," and the answer was "laundry." That was nice. I miss it.

May, 1977

The Sperling Breakfast

No one in Washington quite knows how Godfrey Sperling's breakfast group got to be quite the thing it has become. Godfrey Sperling himself, who started holding his breakfasts eleven years ago, claims to have no idea whatsoever. "I didn't set up a group," he said recently. "I just had a breakfast. And it wasn't even a breakfast. It was a lunch. Chuck Percy was coming to Washington, and he didn't know anyone, so I called up Bob Novak and Alan Otten and Peter Lisagor and three or four other reporters, and before I knew it I had twelve people. And they came. It made a lot of ripples, so I had another. And another. The second year I did it people started saying, You've got something this city needs. I said, I can't imagine it. But I kept having them. Each time I'd say, This will be the last one. After a while, people started saying it was an institution. I couldn't believe it. I couldn't believe it."

There have now been nearly eight hundred Sperling breakfasts, and thirty-seven members of the print press are invited to attend; over the years, they have met with almost every major American political figure. The Sperling Breakfast is indeed an institution. Some of its members think it's a good institution, useful and convenient, and that it would have to be invented if it did not exist. Others think it's a bad institution, dangerous and silly, and that it ought to be taken out like an old horse and shot. I'd like to tell you who said the line about the horse, but he asked not to be quoted. He doesn't want to hurt Godfrey Sperling's feelings. Also, he doesn't want Godfrey Sperling to throw him out of the breakfast group.

I recently spent a week in Washington attending five Sperling breakfasts. I had a wonderful time, except for the eggs. On Monday, Governor Jay Rockefeller of West Virginia was the guest. On Tuesday, Governor James "Big Jim" Thompson of Illinois. On Wednesday, Treasury Secretary Michael Blumenthal. On Thursday, White House counsel Robert Lipshutz. On Friday, Budget Director Bert Lance. I also interviewed many of the members of the breakfast group. I had a wonderful time doing that too. Everyone I spoke to was helpful. Many of them said it was only a breakfast. Sometimes it produces stories, sometimes it doesn't. That's not why it's valuable, they said. It's valuable because it provides an opportunity for the press to see how politicians perform. And why is it dangerous? I asked. It's dangerous, they said, because it's pack journalism and it can become a substitute for real reporting. This interested me, because it seemed to me they had it backward. The Sperling Breakfast is *valuable* because it's pack journalism and it does substitute for real reporting. And it's *dangerous* because it provides an opportunity for the press to see how politicians perform. How a politician performs does not prove anything about him except for his ability to hornswoggle journalists and pay his respects to their egos. But I'm getting carried away.

• • •

The Sperling Breakfast is supposed to be an informal way for politicians to meet with journalists, but it is actually a formal, ritualized, on-the-record press conference that happens to take place over breakfast. Columnists Joseph Kraft, Carl Rowan, David Broder and Robert Novak attend regularly. So do most of the bureau chiefs of the major news organizations—Mel Elfin of *Newsweek*, Hugh Sidey of *Time*, Jack Nelson of the *Los Angeles Times*, Jim Wieghart of the New York *Daily News*, Hedrick Smith of the *New York Times*, among others—and when they don't feel like coming they send their staff members. (Women are allowed as substitutes, but there are only two female regulars; representatives of the wire services and of television are banned.) Breakfast costs six dollars per member.

The group meets with a guest two or three mornings a week at a long oval table in a banquet room of the Sheraton Carlton Hotel. Godfrey Sperling, bureau chief of the *Christian Science Monitor*, presides. At 8 a.m., he asks the first question. He also asks the second, third, fourth, fifth and sixth questions. Then he calls on other members of the group. They ask questions. Sperling asks more questions. The guest answers the questions. At three minutes to nine, Sperling calls for "one last question." Then he calls for "the final question." Then he calls for "the final final question." Just after 9 a.m., the breakfast ends. If something has happened at it, the reporters from the afternoon papers run for the phones. The rest walk back to their offices, comparing notes on what the story was, and complaining about the eggs.

Occasionally, major stories break at a Sperling Breakfast. You've seen them: the second sentence of the article says, "So-and-so made these remarks at a breakfast with reporters." Bobby Kennedy agonized over whether to run for President at a breakfast with reporters; Spiro Agnew called Hubert Humphrey "soft on Communism"; Earl Butz told a dirty joke about the Pope; John Rhodes suggested that Nixon might be impeached. The breakfast is also an ideal launching pad for trial balloons. In the last days of the Nixon administration, White House aide Patrick Buchanan used a breakfast to test the strategy of conceding the House of Representatives to pro-impeachment forces; by day's end, the story was in the papers, along with negative responses from congressional leaders; Buchanan realized the approach wouldn't work and junked it.

Most of the time, however, nothing happens at a Sperling Breakfast. This does not necessarily mean that no stories are written. For example, here is what happened the day Big Jim Thompson appeared:

Governor Thompson was asked what he thought of President Carter's performance thus far. He said it was too soon to tell. He was asked about the future of the Republican party. He said that what the Republican party really needed was candidates who could win in 1978 and 1980. He was asked if he had the Presidential bug. "Sure," he said, "there's nothing new in that." Toward the end of breakfast, Warren Weaver of the *New York Times* turned to Andrew Glass of the Cox newspapers. "This guy is very impressive," he said.

Later in the day, I went to see Richard Dudman, bureau chief of the *St. Louis Post-Dispatch.* "I got a story today," he said. "I wrote that Governor Thompson met with the national press today and despite his disclaimers left no doubt that he's already running for President."

"What disclaimers?" I asked. "He admitted it. He has always admitted it."

"I know it," said Dudman. "I even called Springfield and they told me there's nothing new in it. But it's a story when he says it to us."

"You have to understand something," Jack Nelson of the *L.A. Times* said. "The first time Jimmy Carter was ever taken seriously in Washington was at a Sperling Breakfast."

I think I understand: You cannot be taken seriously in Washington *until* you have done the Sperling Breakfast. The Sperling Breakfast is a screening committee. But I'm getting carried away.

On Wednesday, Treasury Secretary Blumenthal came to the breakfast. He spoke of inflation, budget underruns and the New York financial mess. After breakfast, everyone agreed that he had performed well, and the reporters for afternoon papers ran for the phones. There would be front-page stories that afternoon and next morning. I walked over to the Treasury Building with Blumenthal's press aide, Treasury Assistant Secretary Joseph Laitin. "The session served a useful purpose for Blumenthal," Laitin said. "He wanted to talk to a cross section of the press to get a few things out. I didn't feel we should have a press conference because television always dominates it. You also get everybody in town, and if you don't produce eight-column headlines it's a letdown. We had a standing invitation from the Sperling people, so I called up and said we'd like to accept. Now about what Blumenthal said— there wasn't anything really new, yet it was important for these guys to hear it. All the financial reporters knew about the underruns and they've written about them, but none of them has dramatized it. They will now. Why haven't they before? Too unimaginative. Too lazy. Don't have the time. It's been out, but until now it hasn't been packaged. That's the word I want. Packaging."

Bob Strauss loves doing the Sperling Breakfast. He did nine of them as Democratic national chairman, and he invited the entire group to his home for dinner the day the five hundredth breakfast was held. Then along came the six hundredth Sperling Breakfast, and Gerald Ford invited everyone to the White House. That seemed like only yesterday, and suddenly the seven hundredth breakfast rolled around, and the eight hundredth is coming up. The members are getting grouchy; the anniversaries are getting closer and closer together; there are more and more breakfasts. No one minds getting up for somebody interesting, but the other day the group was actually asked to turn up for Senator Alan Cranston. Alan Cranston, for God's sake. The group has gotten too big; the group is too elite; the questions are too general; the questions are too specific. (The eggs are the only subject on which there is total agreement.) Even when Godfrey Sperling leaves town, the Sperling Breakfast goes on. Roscoe Drummond plays host, or Richard Strout. "It started out," says one of the original members, "and practically every guest was somebody you really wanted to see. But somewhere along the line it all became a Godfrey Sperling Production. He felt an obligation to serve up two guests a week, three guests a week, four guests a week. You turn out a lot of crap that way. He was producing guys you could walk up to the Hill and call off the floor at any time."

But I was talking about Bob Strauss, who loves doing the Sperling Breakfast. "I've grown very attached to it," he says. "I'll tell you why. I go in there with something to say and I say it. I bring in my medicine and I give it out. Some of them think it's red medicine, and some of them think it's blue medicine. But it tastes just fine."

Whenever there is a Sperling Breakfast, an announcement appears on the Sheraton Carlton bulletin board. BREAKFAST WITH GODFREY, 8 A.M., it reads. This is extremely embarrassing to Godfrey Sperling—not the announcement, you must understand, but the reference to his first name. Godfrey Sperling is not known as Godfrey. He is known as Budge. "I have two older sisters," he explained, "and they didn't care for the name Godfrey, and they called me Brother. Don't ask me how, but it became Budgie. I shortened it to Budge in college. The nice thing about the name Budge is it's informal. I never have been Godfrey. The name's been in my family and I use it as a by-line. But in my mind I'm always Budge Sperling."

Sperling, sixty-one, is a pleasant, fussy man who looks like Elmer Fudd and indeed occasionally gives the impression of being thoroughly befuddled. Here, for example, is a question he asked Budget Director Lance at Friday's breakfast: "Isn't what you really mean is that you're going to spend this defense money more slowly? Isn't that what you mean? More slowly? Or is it less fastly? More slowly? You get me so doggone confused with all this. I'm just so doggone confused." Budge Sperling really enjoys his breakfasts. "It's a great help to me," he says. "The self-interest just oozes in every direction.

But I've been engulfed by the thing. I can't tell if I'm running it or it's running me. This week I didn't want five, but I must admit I can't say no, I can't say no. This is a sideline that occupies me, interests me, irritates me. Sometimes it takes me over. If anyone had said to me, the thing you'll be remembered for is your breakfast group, I would have gone into another career. A breakfast group?"

I asked Sperling if he thought he was at all powerful. "Powerful?" he said. "I don't know. That's not Budge Sperling. It might be Godfrey Sperling, but not Budge. I have always felt that the Godfrey is too formal. It's not me."

In the course of a week, I heard a lot of things about the Sperling Breakfast. I was told that the whole purpose of the group was to promote peer approval and a feeling of joint accomplishment. I was told that the only reason anyone goes is for protection on those infrequent occasions when something interesting happens. I was even told that Godfrey Sperling had become so powerful he was dangerous. Well, I don't buy it. I think no one gives the Sperling Breakfast the credit it deserves. It provides a way for our politicians to get out of bed and come to show their dependence on the press; the press responds graciously by passing on exactly what the politicians come in to say. It provides a way for our politicians to pay tribute to the role of the press in the electoral process; the press reciprocates by certifying the politicians as heavyweights and contenders. It provides a way for the out-of-power party to survive those long stretches between elections; right now, while the rest of us lie around playing Scrabble, the Sperling Breakfast is doing its damnedest to find Republican candidates for 1980. It even seems possible to say that the Sperling Breakfast is single-handedly saving the two-party system in America. But I'm getting carried away.

June, 1977

Enough

I started to write this column about the new special sections in the *New York Times*. I had a nice lead for it, and I had a funny story to tell, and I had a few points to make about the Cuisinarting of America. I went over to the *Times* and had an amazing interview with a *Times* business executive who talked about something called psychographics. "One of the biggest psychographics," he said, "is self-improvement and self. Self is very strong." I also had a problem with the piece. About a year ago, I wrote something about the influence of city magazines on journalism, about the you-are-what-you-buy syndrome, and I didn't want to repeat myself. Oh, well. It really doesn't matter, because I decided not to write that column after all.

When I started writing a media column a couple of years ago, my primary interest was not to become a media critic—and I hope I have managed to succeed at not becoming one—but simply to find some subject to write about in order to get back into the front of *Esquire* magazine. I like being in the front of this magazine. It's nice up here. The subject of media was suggested over a lunch, and it seemed like a good idea. I could write about newspapers and magazines and television, and occasionally go out and do some reporting, and it might work. The reporting was the easy part. Journalists are wonderful sources. They are wonderful sources on the record, and they are even more wonderful sources off the record.

Those of us who work in this profession are very lucky, and we know it. I have known it ever since the day in 1963 when I walked into the *New York Post* city room to start work as a reporter: This is what I have always wanted, and here I am, and it's wonderful. I think this all the time. I am giddy about working in this profession. Every so often I hear someone complaining about how movies like *The Front Page* have tended to romanticize journalism, and I don't understand what they're talking about. I grew up under the influence of a remake of *The Front Page—His Girl Friday*, in which Rosalind Russell played the Hildy Johnson part. I grew up wanting to be Hildy Johnson, and as it turns out, Hildy Johnson is someone worth wanting to grow up to be.

In recent years, however, there have been some changes. One of them has to do with celebrity. Journalists are now celebrities. Part of this has been caused by the ability and willingness of journalists to promote themselves. Part of this has been caused by television: the television reporter is often more famous than anyone he interviews. And part of this has been caused by the fact that the celebrity pool has expanded in order to provide names to fill the increasing number of column inches currently devoted to gossip; this is my own pet theory, and I use it to explain all sorts of things, one of whom is Halston.

The point, though, is that the extent to which a column like this contributes to this makes me extremely uncomfortable; what's more, this development of celebrity has been reinforced by a parallel change in journalism, a swing from highly impersonal "objective" reporting to highly personal "subjective" reporting. Last week, while preparing for the column on the *New York Times* I decided not to write, I reread the last few months of the "Weekend," "Living" and "Home" sections of the *Times*, and I began to overdose on the first person singular pronoun. I am tired of the first person singular pronoun. I am tired of reading about how this journalist serves her guests dinner on the bed and about how that journalist has a Shetland pony with a nervous tic. I am also tired of my own first person singular pronoun. "Self is very strong," said the *Times* business executive. Yes indeed. I figure if I stop writing a column for a while, it will reduce the number of first person singular pronouns in circulation by only a hair; still, it seems like the noblest thing I can think of to do this week.

David Eisenhower once said something that made me realize that he could not possibly be as silly as he seems. "Journalists," he said, "aren't nearly as interesting as they think they are." Actually, he's not quite right. Journalists *are* interesting. They just aren't as interesting as the things they cover. It is possible to lose sight of this.

I would like not to.

July, 1977

Acknowledgments

There is really no way for me to thank the many friends and colleagues who have helped me in the course of over two years of writing about the media. But there are a few friends who were consistently there: Barbara and Richard Cohen, Helen Dudar, Delia Ephron, Marty Nolan, Liz Smith, and, at *Esquire*, Geoffrey Norman, Don Erickson, Lee Eisenberg, Pat Thorpe, and Michaela Williams. To my agent Lynn Nesbit and my editor Bob Gottlieb, my gratitude and love.

ALSO BY NORA EPHRON

HEARTBURN

Seven months into her pregnancy, Rachel Samstat discovers that her husband, Mark, is in love with another woman. The fact that the other woman has "a neck as long as an arm and a nose as long as a thumb and you should see her legs" is no consolation. Food sometimes is, though, since Rachel writes cookbooks for a living. And in between trying to win Mark back and loudly wishing him dead, Ephron's irrepressible heroine offers some of her favorite recipes.

Fiction/Literature

I FEEL BAD ABOUT MY NECK

Ephron chronicles her life as an obsessed cook, passionate city dweller, and hapless parent. She hates her chaotic mess of a purse. She searches for the divinely flaky cabbage strudel of her youth and finds it twenty-three years later. She endures the daily tribulations of feminine maintenance: removing unwanted hair, moisturizing patches of skin the consistency of a loofah, and recovering from treadmill injuries. Utterly courageous, uproariously funny, and unexpectedly moving in its truth-telling, *I Feel Bad About My Neck* is a scrumptious, irresistible treat of a book, full of laugh-out-loud moments that will appeal to readers of all ages.

Humor/Essays

I REMEMBER NOTHING

In *I Remember Nothing*, Ephron takes a hilarious look at the past, present, and the future, bemoans the vicissitudes of modern life, and recalls with her signature clarity and wisdom everything she hasn't (yet) forgotten. Filled with insights and observations that instantly ring true—and could have come only from Nora Ephron—*I Remember Nothing* is pure joy.

Humor

IMAGINARY FRIENDS

Although Lillian Hellman and Mary McCarthy probably only met once in their lives, their names will be linked forever in the history of American literary feuds: they were legendary enemies, especially after McCarthy famously announced to the world that every word Hellman wrote was a lie, "including 'and' and 'the'." The public battle and the legal squabbling that ensued ended, unsatisfactorily for all, with Hellman's death. Ephron brilliantly resuscitates these two bigger-than-life woman to give them a post-mortem second act, and the chance to really air their differences.

Fiction/Literature

VINTAGE BOOKS
Available wherever books are sold.
visit www.randomhouse.com